Introduction to ART

Design, Context, and Meaning

Editor-in-Chief | **Pamela J. Sachant, Ph.D.**

Peggy Blood, Ph.D. | Jeffery LeMieux, M.F.A | Rita Tekippe, Ph.D.

UNG
UNIVERSITY *of*
NORTH GEORGIA™
UNIVERSITY PRESS
Dahlonega, GA

ISBN: 978-1-940771-29-8

Produced by:
University System of Georgia

Published by:
University of North Georgia Press
Dahlonega, Georgia

Cover Art:
The Burning of the Houses of Parliament (1834) by William Turner

Cover Design and Layout Design:
Corey Parson

For more information, please visit http://ung.edu/university-press
Or email ungpress@ung.edu

TABLE OF CONTENTS

1

What is Art?

Jeffrey LeMieux and Pamela J. Sachant

1.1 LEARNING OUTCOMES

After completing this chapter, you should be able to:

- Recognize various historical arguments about the definition of art and who is an artist.

- Engage arguments that distinguish between art and craft.

- Critically evaluate claims about whether an object is or is not art from multiple points of view.

- Engage questions about who is considered an artist and the role of the viewer.

- Productively speculate about various reasons why people have made and continue to make art.

- Recognize your intuitive understanding of art, and potentially build a broader, more comprehensive view of the nature and definition of visual art, one which incorporates historically and culturally diverse art objects and answers conceptual challenges.

1.2 INTRODUCTION

We live in a rapidly changing world in which images play an important, even central, role. With widespread use of personal electronics, we instantaneously deliver and receive sound, video, and text messages. Corporations and governments worldwide recognize the power of advertising. Art museums worldwide are putting large parts of their collections online. Today we are seeing theater-quality movies made with inexpensive equipment that was unavailable ten years ago. Selfies, personal video, and memes are everywhere. In 1968, artist Andy Warhol (1928-1967, USA) said, "In the future everyone will be world-famous for fifteen minutes." (*Self Portrait*, Andy Warhol: http://art.newcity.com/wp-content/uploads/2011/05/Warhol_SelfPortrait.jpg) We are seeing that prediction come true with the advent of personal electronics that rival the sophistication of the most advanced professional studios of only twenty years ago. We are surrounded by images, but, for all of our clever technical abilities, the fundamental dynamics of visual art remain the same.

Figure 1.1 | Blind Homer with Guide
Artist: Bouguereau
Author: User "Thebrid"
Source: Wikimedia Commons
License: Public Domain

Take a few minutes to look over the accompanying image, *Blind Homer and His Guide*. (Figure 1.1) It was painted in 1875 by a leading member of the French École des Beaux Arts, or School of Fine Arts, William-Adolphe Bouguereau (1825-1925, France), and serves as a good example of the kinds of paintings made in Europe during that time. We might wonder what a painting made more than 100 years ago in a foreign country could have to do with us today.

The French Academic artist Bouguereau's painting is more than a literal presentation of a forgotten moment in ancient history. The painting challenges viewers from every age to go deeper, to see the symbolism behind the history. Homer, who is thought to have lived around 1000 BCE, was the chief poet of the ancient Greeks. Ancient Greek ideas about social roles and the nature of virtue come to us in part from Homer's epic poems the *Illiad* and the *Odyssey*. In Bouguereau's painting, Homer symbolizes civilization and culture. Homer wanders blindly through a savage wilderness with only a youth to shelter him. In this way, Bouguereau implies that a wilderness can be not only physical but also cultural, and in that sense, all of us wander through a wilderness that threatens the human spirit found in culture. His painting asks the question, "How are cultural values carried forward?" In Bouguereau's work, the young man has taken responsibility for protecting Homer, who symbolizes the refined wisdom of the past and the foundation of western culture. This image is a call to the youth of Bouguereau's generation (and to ours) to bring precious culture forward safely through an ever-threatening wilderness.

Wherever we find human beings, we find visual art. Works of visual art raise questions not only about our ancestors, but also about the nature of visual art itself. What is art? Who is an artist? Why do artists make art? What is the role of the viewer? Does everything count as art? How have people defined art through time? How do we define art today?

In this chapter, we will examine these questions in more detail. The purpose of this examination is twofold: to increase your awareness of the mechanics of those images and, thus, more effectively understand the visual art that we encounter in our daily lives. Images are powerful. Images are used in our culture in many ways, not all of them benign. When we enhance our visual literacy, we raise our awareness of the powerful images that surround us.

1.3 WHAT IS VISUAL ART?

To explore a subject, we need first to define it. Defining art, however, proves elusive. You may have heard it said (or even said it yourself) that "it might be art, but it's not Art," which means, "I might not know how to define it, but I know it when I see it."

Everywhere we look, we see images designed to command our attention, including images of desire, images of power, religious images, images meant to recall memories, and images intended to manipulate our appetites. But are they art?

Some languages do not have a separate word for art. In those cultures, objects tend to be utilitarian in purpose but often include in their design the intent to delight, portray a special status, or commemorate an important event or ritual. Thus, while the objects are not considered art, they do have artistic functions.

1.3.1 Historic Development of the Idea of Art

The idea of art has developmentally progressed from human prehistory to the present day. Changes to the definition of art over time can be seen as attempts to resolve problems with earlier definitions. The ancient Greeks saw the goal of visual art as copying, or mimesis. Nineteenth-century art theorists promoted the idea that art is communication: it produces feelings in the viewer. In the early twentieth century, the idea of significant form, the quality shared by aesthetically pleasing objects, was proposed as a definition of art. Today, many artists and thinkers agree with the institutional theory of art, which shifts focus from the work of art itself to who has the power to decide what is and is not art. While this progression of definitions of art is not exhaustive, it is instructive.

1.3.1.1 Mimesis

The ancient Greek definition of art as **mimesis**, or imitation of the real world, appears in the myth of Zeuxis and Parhassios, rival painters from ancient Greece in the late fifth century BCE who competed for the title of greatest artist. (Figure 1.2) Zeuxis painted a bowl of grapes that was so lifelike that birds came down to peck at the image of fruit. Parhassios was unimpressed with this achievement. When viewing Parhassios's work, Zeuxis, on his part, asked that the curtain over the painting be drawn back so he could see his rival's work more

Figure 1.2 | Zeuxis conceding defeat: "I have deceived the birds, but Parhassios has deceived Zeuxis."
Artist: Joachim von Sandrart; engraving by Johann Jakob von Sandrart
Author: User "Fae"
Source: Wikimedia Commons
License: Public Domain

clearly. Parhassios declared himself the victor because the curtain *was* the painting, and while Zeuxis fooled the birds with his work, Parhassios fooled a thinking human being—a much more difficult feat.

The ancient Greeks felt that the visual artist's goal was to copy visual experience. This approach appears in the realism of ancient Greek sculpture and pottery. We must sadly note that, due to the action of time and weather, no paintings from ancient Greek artists exist today. We can only surmise their quality based on tales such as that of Zeuxis and Parhassios, the obvious skill in ancient Greek sculpture, and in drawings that survive on ancient Greek pottery.

This definition of art as copying reality has a problem, though. Jackson Pollock (1912-1956, USA), a leader in the New York School of the 1950's, intentionally did not copy existing objects in his art. (Figure 1.3) While painting these works, Pollock and his fellow artists would consciously avoid making marks or passages that resembled recognizable objects. They succeeded at making artwork that did not copy anything, thus demonstrating that the ancient Greek view of art as mimesis—simple copying—does not sufficiently define art.

Figure 1.3 | Left: *The She-Wolf*; Right: *Gothic*
Artist: Jackson Pollock
Author: Gorup de Besanez
Source: Wikimedia Commons
License: CC BY-SA 4.0

1.3.1.2 Communication

A later attempt at defining art comes from the nineteenth-century Russian author Leo Tolstoy. Tolstoy wrote on many subjects, and is the author of the great novel *War and Peace* (1869). He was also an art theorist. He proposed that art is the **communication of feeling**, stating, "Art is a human activity consisting in this, that one man consciously by means of certain external signs, hands on to others feelings he has lived through, and that others are infected by these feelings and also experience them."[1]

This definition does not succeed because it is impossible to confirm that the feelings of the artist have been successfully conveyed to another person. Further, suppose an artist created a work of art that no one else ever saw. Since no feeling had been communicated through it, would it still be a work of art? The work did not "hand on to others" anything at all because it was never seen. Therefore, it would fail as art according to Tolstoy's definition.

---

1   Leo Tolstoy, *What is Art? And Essays on Art*, trans. Aylmer Maude (London: Oxford University Press, 1932), 123.

1.3.1.3 Significant Form

To address these limitations of existing definitions of art, in 1913 English art critic Clive Bell proposed that art is **significant form,** or the "quality that brings us aesthetic pleasure." Bell stated, "to appreciate a work of art we need bring with us nothing but a sense of form and colour."[2] In Bell's view, the term "form" simply means line, shape, mass, as well as color. Significant form is the collection of those elements that rises to the level of your awareness and gives you noticeable pleasure in its beauty. Unfortunately, **aesthetics**, pleasure in the beauty and appreciation of art, are impossible to measure or reliably define. What brings aesthetic pleasure to one person may not affect another. Aesthetic pleasure exists only in the viewer, not in the object. Thus significant form is purely subjective. While Clive Bell did advance the debate about art by moving it away from requiring strict representation, his definition gets us no closer to understanding what does or does not qualify as an art object.

1.3.1.4 Artworld

One definition of art widely held today was first promoted in the 1960s by American philosophers George Dickie and Arthur Danto, and is called the **institutional theory** of art, or the "Artworld" theory. In the simplest version of this theory, art is an object or set of conditions that has been designated as art by a "person or persons acting on behalf of the artworld," and the artworld is a "complex field of forces" that determine what is and is not art.[3] Unfortunately, this definition gets us no further along because it is not about art at all! Instead, it is about who has the power to define art, which is a political issue, not an aesthetic one.

1.3.2 Definition of Art

We each perceive the world from our own position or perspective and from that perception we make a mental image of the world. Science is the process of turning perceptions into a coherent mental picture of the universe through testing and observation. (Figure 1.4) Science moves concepts from the world into the mind. Science is vitally important because it allows us to understand how the world works and to use that understanding to make good predictions. Art is the other side of

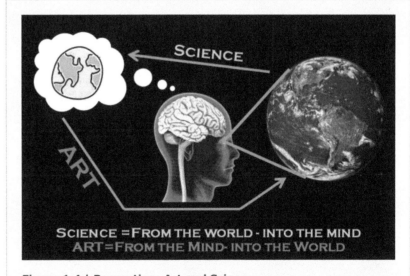

Figure 1.4 | Perception: Art and Science
Author: Jeffrey LeMieux
Source: Original Work
License: CC BY-SA 4.0

2   Clive Bell, "Art and Significant Form," in *Art* (New York: Frederick A. Stokes Company, 1913), 2
3   George Dickie, *Art and the Aesthetic: An Institutional Analysis* (Ithaca, NY: Cornell University Press, 1974), 464.

Figure 1.5 | Portrait of Percy Bysshe Shelley
Artist: Alfred Clint
Author: User "Dcoetzee"
Source: Wikimedia Commons
License: Public Domain

Figure 1.6 | Portrait of Jean-Jacques Rousseau
Artist: Maurice Quentin de La Tour
Author: User "Maarten van Vliet"
Source: Wikimedia Commons
License: Public Domain

our experience with the world. *Art moves ideas from the mind into the world.*

We need both art and science to exist in the world. From our earliest age, we both observe the world and do things to change it. We are all both scientists and artists. Every human activity has both a science (observation) and an art (expression) to it. Anyone who has participated in the discipline of Yoga, for example, can see that even something as simple as breathing has both an art and a science to it.

This definition of art covers the wide variety of objects that we see in museums, on social media, or even in our daily walk to work. But this definition of art is not enough. The bigger question is: what art is worthy of our attention, and how do we know when we have found it? Ultimately, each of us must answer that question for ourselves.

But we do have help if we want it. People who have made a disciplined study of art can offer ideas about what art is important and why. In the course of this text, we will examine some of those ideas about art. Due to the importance of respecting the individual, the decision about what art is best must belong to the individual. We ask only that the student understand the ideas as presented.

When challenged with a question or problem about what is best, we first ask, "What do I personally know about it?" When we realize our personal resources are limited, we might ask friends, neighbors, and relatives what they know. In addition to these important resources, the educated person can refer to a larger body of possible solutions drawn from a study of the history of literature, philosophy, and art: What did the English poet Percy Bysshe Shelley say about truth in his essay *Defense of Poetry* (1840)? (Figure 1.5) What did the French philosopher Jean-Jacques Rousseau claim about human nature in his treatise *Emile or On Education* (1762)? (Figure 1.6) What did Johannes Vermeer (1632-1675, Netherlands) show us about the quiet dignity of the domestic space in his painting *Woman Holding a Balance*? (Figure 1.7) Through experiencing these works of art and literature, our ideas about such things can be tested and validated or found wanting.

We will examine works of visual art from a diverse range of cultures and periods. The challenge for you as the reader is to increase your ability to interpret works of art through the use of context, visual dynamics, and introspection, and to integrate them into a coherent worldview. The best outcome of an encounter with art is an awakening of the mind and spirit to a new point of view. A mind stretched beyond itself never returns to its original dimension.

1.3.3 The Distinction of Fine Art

From our definition of art proposed above, it would seem that craft and fine art are indistinguishable as both come from the mind into the world. But the distinction between craft and art is real and important. This distinction is most commonly understood as one based on the use or end purpose of an object, or as an effect of the material used. Clay, textiles, glass, and jewelry were long considered the province of craft, not art. If an object's intended use was a part of daily living, then it was generally thought to be the product of craft, not fine art. But many objects originally intended to be functional, such as quilts, are now thought to qualify as fine art. (Figure 1.8)

So what could be the difference between art and craft? Anyone who has been exposed to training in a craft such as carpentry or plumbing recognizes that craft follows a formula, that is, a set of rules that govern not only how the work is to be conducted but also what the outcome of that work must be. The level of craft is judged by how closely the end product matches the pre-determined outcome. We want our houses to stand and water to flow when we turn on our faucets. Fine art, on the other hand, results from a free and open-ended exploration that does not depend on a pre-determined formula for its outcome or validity. Its outcome is surprising and original. Almost all fine art objects are a combination of some level both of craft and art. Art stands on craft, but goes beyond it.

Figure 1.7 | *Woman Holding a Balance*
Artist: Johannes Vermeer
Author: User "DcoetzeeBot"
Source: Wikimedia Commons
License: Public Domain

Figure 1.8 | Quilt
Artist: Lucy Mingo
Author: User "Billvolckening"
Source: Wikimedia Commons
License: CC BY-SA 4.0

1.3.4 Why Art Matters

American physicist J. Robert Oppenheimer is considered a "father of the atomic bomb" for the role he played in developing nuclear weapons as part of the Manhattan Project during World War II (1939-1945). (Figure 1.9) Upon completion of the project, quoting from the Hindu epic tale *Bhagavad Gita,* he stated, "Now I am become Death, the destroyer of worlds." Clearly, Oppenheimer had read more than physics texts in his education, which fit him well for his important role during World War II.

When we train in mathematics and the sciences, for example, we become very powerful. Power can be used well or badly. Where in our schools is the coursework on how to use power wisely? Today a liberal arts college education requires students to survey the arts and history of human cultures in order to examine a wide range of ideas about wisdom and to humanize the powerful. With that in mind, in every course taken in the university, it is hoped that you will recognize the

Figure 1.9 | J. Robert Oppenheimer
Author: Los Alamos National Laboratory
Source: Wikimedia Commons
License: Public Domain

need to couple your increasing intellectual power with a study of what is thought to be wisdom, and to view each educational experience in the humanities as part of the search for what is better in ourselves and our communities.

This text is not intended to determine what is or is not good art and why it matters. Rather, the point of this text is to equip you with intellectual tools that will enable you to analyze, decipher, and interpret works of art as bearers of meaning, to make *your own* decisions about the merit of those works, and then usefully to integrate those decisions into your daily lives.

1.4 WHO IS CONSIDERED AN ARTIST? WHAT DOES IT MEAN TO BE AN ARTIST?

In much of the world today, an artist is considered to be a person with the talent and the skills to conceptualize and make creative works. Such persons are singled out and prized for their artistic and original ideas. Their art works can take many forms and fit into numerous categories, such as architecture, ceramics, digital art, drawings, mixed media, paintings, photographs, prints, sculpture, and textiles. Of greater importance, artists are the individuals who have the desire and ability to envision, design, and fabricate the images, objects, and structures we all encounter, use, occupy, and enjoy every day of our lives.

Today, as has been the case throughout history and across cultures, there are different titles for those who make and build. An artisan or craftsperson, for example, may produce decorative or utilitarian arts, such as quilts or baskets. Often, an artisan or craftsperson is a skilled worker, but not the inventor of the original idea or form. An artisan or craftsperson can also be someone who creates their own designs, but does not work in art forms or with materials traditionally associated with the so-called Fine Arts, such as painting and sculpture. A craftsperson might instead fashion jewelry, forge iron, or blow glass into patterns and objects of their own devising. Such inventive and skilled pieces are often categorized today as Fine Craft or Craft Art.

In many cultures throughout much of history, those who produced, embellished, painted, and built were not considered to be artists as we think of them now. They were artisans and craftspeople, and their role was to make the objects and build the structures for which they were hired, according to the design (their own or another's) agreed upon with those for whom they were working. That is not to say they were untrained. In Medieval Europe, or the Middle Ages (fifth-fifteenth centuries), for example, an artisan generally began around the age of twelve as an apprentice, that is, a student who learned all aspects of a profession from a master who had their own workshop. Apprenticeships lasted five to nine years or more, and included learning trades ranging from painting to baking, and masonry to candle making. At the end of that period, an apprentice became a journeyman and was allowed to become a member of the craft guild that supervised training and standards for those working in that trade. To achieve full status in the guild, a journeyman had to complete their "masterpiece," demonstrating sufficient skill and craftsmanship to be named a master.

Figure 1.10 | Gudea
Source: Met Museum
License: OASC

We have little information about how artists trained in numerous other time periods and cultures, but we can gain some understanding of what it meant to be an artist by looking at examples of art work that were produced. *Seated Statue of Gudea* depicts the ruler of the state of Lagash in Southern Mesopotamia, today Iraq, during his reign, c. 2144-2124 BCE. (Figure 1.10)

Gudea is known for building temples, many in the kingdom's main city of Girsu (today Telloh, Iraq), with statues portraying himself in them. In these works, he is seated or standing with wide, staring eyes but otherwise a calm expression on his face and his hands folded in a gesture of prayer and greeting. Many of the statues, including the one pictured here, are carved from diorite, a very hard stone favored by rulers in ancient Egypt and the Near East for its rarity and the fine lines that can be cut into it. The ability to cut such precise lines allowed the craftsperson who carved this work to distinguish between and emphasize each finger in Gudea's clasped hands as well as the circular patterns on his stylized shepherd's hat, both of which indicate the leader's dedication to the well-being and safety of his people.

Although the sculpture of Gudea was clearly carved by a skilled artisan, we have no record of that person, or of the vast majority of the artisans and builders who worked in the ancient world. Who they worked for and what they created are the records of their lives and artistry. Artisans were not valued for taking an original approach and setting themselves apart when creating a statue of a ruler such as Gudea: their success was based on their ability to work within standards of how the human form was depicted and specifically how a leader should look within that culture at that time. The large, almond-shaped eyes and compact, block-like shape of the figure, for example, are typical of sculpture from that period. This sculpture is not intended to be an individual likeness of Gudea; rather, it is a depiction of the characteristic features, pose, and proportions found in all art of that time and place.

Objects made out of clay were far more common in the ancient world than those made of metal or stone, such as the *Seated Statue of Gudea*, which were far more costly, time-consuming, and difficult to make. Human figures modeled in clay dating back as far as 29,000-25,000 BCE have been found in Europe, and the earliest known pottery, found in Jiangxi Province, China, dates to c. 18,000 BCE. Vessels made of clay and baked in ovens were first made in the Near East c. 8,000 BCE, nearly 6,000 years before the *Seated Statue of Gudea* was carved. **Ceramic** (clay hardened by heat) pots were used for storage and numerous everyday needs. They were utilitarian objects made by anonymous artisans.

Figure 1.11 | Panathenaic Prize Amphora with Lid
Artist: Nikodemos
Source: The J. Paul Getty Museum
License: Open Content

Among the ancient Greeks, however, pottery rose to the level of an art form. But, the status of the individuals who created and painted the pots did not. Although their work may have been sought after, these potters and painters were still considered artisans. The origins of pottery that can be described as distinctively Greek dates to c. 1,000 BCE, in what is known as the Proto-geometric period. Over the next several hundred years, the shapes of the vessels and the types of decorative motifs and subjects painted on them became associated with the city where they were produced, and then specifically with the individuals who made and decorated the pots. The types of pots signed by the potter and the painter were generally large, elaborately decorated or otherwise specialized vessels that were used for ritual or ceremonial purposes.

That is the case with the *Panathenaic Prize Amphora*, 363-362 BCE, signed by Nikodemos, the potter, and attributed to the Painter of the Wedding Procession, whose name is not known but is identified through similarities to other painted pots. (Figure 1.11) The Panathenaia was a festival held every four years in honor of Athena, the patron goddess of Athens, Greece, who is depicted on the **amphora**, a tall, two-handled

Figure 1.12 | *Pear Blossoms*
Artist: Qian Xuan
Source: Met Museum
License: OASC

jar with a narrow neck. On the other side of the storage jar, Nike, the goddess of victory, crowns the winner of the boxing competition for which this pot—containing precious olive oil from Athena's sacred trees—was awarded by the city of Athens. Only the best potters and painters were hired to make pots that were part of such an important ceremony and holding such a significant prize. While the vast majority of artisans never identified themselves on their work, these noteworthy individuals were set apart and acknowledged by name. The makers' signatures demonstrated the city's desire to give an award of the highest quality; they acted as promotion for the potter and painter at that time, and they have immortalized them since. It must not be forgotten, however, that the prize inside the pot was considered far more important than the vessel or the skilled artisans who created it.

China was united and ruled by Mongols from the north, first under Kublai Kahn, in the period known as the Yuan Dynasty (1271-1368). The hand scroll painting *Pear Blossoms* was created with ink and colors on paper around 1280 by Qian Xuan (c. 1235-before 1307, China). (Figure 1.12) After the establishment of the Mongolian government, Qian Xuan abandoned his goal of obtaining a position as a scholar-official, as the highly educated bureaucrats who governed China were known, and turned to painting. He was part of a group of artists known as scholar-painters, or literati. The work of scholar-painters was desirable to many admirers of art because it was considered more personal, expressive, and spontaneous than the uniform and realistic paintings by professional, trained artists. The scholar-painters' sophisticated and deep knowledge of philosophy, culture, and the arts—including calligraphy—made them welcome among fellow scholars and at court. They were part of the elite class of leaders, who followed the long and noble traditions within Confucian teachings of expressing oneself with wisdom and grace, especially in the art of poetry.

Qian Xuan was one of the first scholar-painters to unite painting and poetry, as he does in *Pear Blossoms*:

> All alone by the veranda railing,
> teardrops drenching the branches,
> Although her face is unadorned,
> her old charms remain;
> Behind the locked gate, on a rainy night,
> how she is filled with sadness.
> How differently she looked bathed in golden waves
> of moonlight, before the darkness fell.

The poem is not meant to illustrate or describe his painting of the branch with its delicate, young foliage and flowers; rather, the swaying, irregular lines of the leaves and the gently unfurling curves of the blossoms are meant to suggest comparisons to how quickly time passes—delicate blooms will soon fade—and evoke memories of times past.

In thirteenth-century China, as has been the case throughout much of that country's history, the significance of a painting is closely associated with the identity of the artist, and with the scholars and collectors who owned the work over subsequent centuries. Their identities are known by the **seals**, or stamps in red acting as a signature, each added to the work of art. Specific subjects and how they were depicted were associated with the artist, and often referred back to in later works by other artists as a sign of respect and acknowledgment of the earlier master's skill and expertise. In *Pear Blossoms*, as was often the case, the poem, and the calligraphy in which the artist wrote it, were part of the original composition of the entire painted scroll. The seals appended and notes written by later scholars and collectors continued adding to the composition, and its beauty and meaning, over the next seven hundred years.

When James Abbott McNeill Whistler (1834-1903, USA, lived England) painted *Arrangement in Flesh Colour and Black, Portrait of Theodore Duret* in 1883, he was making references back to the makers' marks Chinese and Japanese potters used as signatures on their ceramics in the monogram he adopted for his work: a stylized design of a butterfly based on his initials. (Figure 1.13) Whistler began

Figure 1.13 | *Arrangement in Flesh Colour and Black: Portrait of Theodore Duret*
Artist: James Abbott McNeill Whistler
Source: Met Museum
License: OASC

Figure 1.14 | *Nocturne in Black and Gold: The Falling Rocket*
Artist: James Abbott McNeill Whistler
Source: Wikimedia Commons
License: Public Domain

signing his work with the recognizable but altered figure of a butterfly, which often appeared to be dancing, in the 1860s. He had begun collecting Japanese porcelain and prints, and was tremendously influenced by their colors, patterns, and compositions, which reflected Japanese principles of beauty in art, including elegant simplicity, tranquility, subtlety, naturalness, understated beauty, and asymmetry or irregularity.

Whistler was among numerous American and European artists in the second half of the nineteenth century who felt compelled to break away from what they believed were the inhibiting constraints in how and what art students were taught and in the system of traditional art exhibitions. For Whistler and others, such restrictions were intolerable; as artists, they must be allowed to freely follow their own creative voices and pursuits. In adopting Japanese principles of beauty in art, Whistler could pursue what he called "Art for art's sake." That is, he could create art that served no other purpose than to express what he, as the artist, found to be elevating, harmonious, and pleasing to the eye, the mind, and the soul:

Art should be independent of all claptrap—should stand alone, and appeal to the artistic sense of eye or ear, without confounding this with emotions entirely foreign to it, as devotion, pity, love, patriotism, and the like. All these have no kind of concern with it; and that is why I insist on calling my works "arrangements" and "harmonies."[4]

Setting the artist apart in this way, as someone with special qualifications and sensibilities at odds with the prevailing cultural and intellectual standards, was far from the role played by a scholar-painter such as Qian Xuan in thirteenth-century China. The work Qian Xuan created was in accord with prevailing standards, while Whistler often thought of himself and his art as conflicting with the conventions of his day. Continuing one notion or categorization of the artist that had been present in Europe since the sixteenth century (and, later, the United States), Whistler was the singular, creative genius, whose art was often misunderstood and not necessarily accepted.

That was indeed the case. In 1878, Whistler won a lawsuit for libel against the art critic John Ruskin, who described Whistler's 1875 painting, *Nocturne in Black and Gold: The Falling Rocket,* as "flinging a pot of paint in the public's face." (Figure 1.14) By around 1880, in the aftermath of that rancorous proceeding, Whistler often added a long stinger to his butterfly monogram, symbolizing both the gentle beauty of his art as well as the forceful, at times stinging, nature of his personality.

---

4   James Abbott McNeill Whistler, *The Gentle Art of Making Enemies* (New York: Frederick Stokes & Brother, 1908), www. gutenberg.org/files/24650/24650-h/24650-h.htm

1.5 THE ROLE OF THE VIEWER

An artist or craftsperson has an audience in mind when creating a work of art. Sometimes the audience *is* the artist. Most of the time, however, the audience—the viewer—is someone else. It may be an individual or a group of people the artist personally knows, or people the artist knows will be viewing the work in a specific context or with a certain purpose. The artist may also consider what meaning or impact the work of art will have for people who view it at an unknown time or place in the future, perhaps with little information about the artist or the work itself. Or, the artist may feel the need or desire to express an emotion and have no concern for how the viewer will react to the work, or even if the viewer will understand the work and why it was created.

As the viewer of a work of art, then, we are often aware that we do not have full knowledge of what the artist intended or, at times, even what the artist depicted. Not having that information, however, is not necessarily frustrating nor does it dampen our enjoyment of the piece. Instead, we may find the colors vibrant, or the subject intriguing, or the composition relaxing; in other words, we may simply enjoy looking at the work of art without feeling the need for particulars about it or the artist. But, there are other times when it is helpful to have some information about the artist or artwork for us to better understand and appreciate what we are looking at.

Sites exist around the world where images were painted or inscribed on cave walls during the Upper Paleolithic Period, c. 40,000-12,000 BCE. The majority of the images are of animals, but outlines of hands, human figures, instruments such as bows and arrows, and designs such as spoked wheels or parallel lines can also be found. They possess a number of notable features, including the fact that these images were painted over tens of thousands of years on every continent except Antarctica. Despite significant differences, the types of subjects depicted during all that time and in all those places are remarkably similar. But, as they were made during the pre-historic period, that is, before humans kept written records, all we know about them is what we can interpret by looking at the images themselves and by studying other objects we have found from the same places and time periods.

Scholars have put forth numerous ideas about why the images were made and what they could mean. The animals depicted include horses, bulls, bison, and deer, all of which were hunted during that span of approximately 30,000 years. For that reason,

Figure 1.15 | Replica of the Pech-Merle de Cabrerets Cave painting
Author: User "HTO"
Source: Wikimedia Commons
License: Public Domain

some scholars hypothesize the paintings acted as a form of **sympathetic magic**, expressing the hope or giving thanks for a successful hunt by depicting the animals hunted. If the images were associated with such activities, crucial for the survival of those who created them, then their makers, as scholars further speculate, were **shamans,** or spiritual leaders of the group. A shaman is an individual with the power to interact with the physical world and the otherworld of spirits in order to maintain harmony between the two, predict the future, cast spells, and cure the sick.

Figure 1.16 | Labyrinth at Chartres Cathedral
Author: User "Maksim"
Source: Wikimedia Commons
License: CC BY-SA 3.0

Venturing into a cave, where all light from the outside world quickly disappears, is akin to a journey into another realm of existence. The images painted, seen only by fire, would have flickered and danced on the walls as if they depicted visitors from another world. We do not know who saw the paintings other than those who created them, but in the *Panel of Spotted Horses* within the Chapel of Bison in the Pech-Merle de Cabrerets Cave, France, the handprints also present are evidence that there were others who viewed them. (Figure 1.15) The prints were made by placing a hand on the wall and blowing paint around it, perhaps through a hollow, reed-like object. Are they meant to identify or document those who were present, to indicate their hoped-for powers as hunters or their inclusion as part of a shamanistic experience? We do not know, but even with the little information we have as viewers today, we can nevertheless enjoy the painting's beauty and mystery.

A **labyrinth**, or maze, such as the one in the floor of the nave of Chartres Cathedral (1194-1250), France, is another example of an image or object found in a number of places, but about which we have little information. (Figure 1.16) A labyrinth is similar to a maze but generally has only one intricate and twisting path to the center. (Figure 1.17) There are labyrinths in the floors of numerous medieval Gothic cathedrals in Europe that were built in the twelfth to fifteenth centuries. The labyrinth at Chartres Cathedral was built in the thirteenth century and, at 42.3 feet in diameter, it fills the width of the

Figure 1.17 | Diagram of the Labyrinth of Chartres Cathedral
Author: User "Ssolbergj"
Source: Wikimedia Commons
License: CC BY-SA 3.0

nave, or central area of a church. While there is documentation that clergy performed dances during Easter celebrations upon labyrinths found in other cathedrals in France, no such records exist regarding Chartres. What it does seem to have in common with other labyrinths, however, is being used as a path to **circumambulate**, or walk, by visitors to the church who were on a **pilgrimage** or journey of faith. As was true of many Gothic churches, Chartres Cathedral held a **relic**, an object thought to have belonged to or been part of a holy person's body, in this case, a garment believed to be the tunic worn by the Virgin Mary when she gave birth. Pilgrims traveled to Chartres to venerate this relic as a demonstration of their religious devotion. While there, pilgrims and other visitors might follow the stones of the labyrinth while in prayer or a state of meditation; the inevitable outcome of the complex and turning path leading to the center mirrors the certainty that prayer will lead the believer to God. The repetitive and focused movement of walking while absorbed in prayer enhanced the devotional experience for the worshiper—who was also the viewer of the labyrinth—on both a physical and a spiritual level.

John Haberle (1856-1933, USA) was a painter who was born and spent most of his life in New Haven, Connecticut. He was well known for his ***trompe l'oeil*** works such as *A Bachelor's Drawer*: paintings that were so realistic they "fooled the eye." (Figure 1.18) Precisely rendering objects on a two-dimensional surface as if they were in three-dimensional space, he was able to create an illusion of reality that was meant to draw in his viewers, who were briefly unaware of the trick he was playing upon them. Quickly recognizing the painting was in truth an uncannily accurate semblance of actual objects, the viewer then became a participant in the artist's game of deception.

Figure 1.18 | *A Bachelor's Drawer*
Artist: John Haberle
Source: Met Museum
License: OASC

The various objects in *A Bachelor's Drawer*, including photographs, paper currency, theater ticket stubs, newspaper clippings, a thermometer, and a hair comb, that appear to be haphazardly fixed to a wooden drawer front are visually interesting because they are so life-like. Once the viewer shifts focus to look at these everyday and commonplace items—the sorts of things you take out of your pocket at the end of the day, often intending to throw them away—and think about what they are, we also wonder what they might mean. And, that is exactly what Haberle intended his viewers to do.

The artist even rewards his viewers for their close attention to the many details in his painting by placing some important ones in the center: several fragments of newspaper articles, including one stating, "A New Haven artist has plunged himself into trouble by making too perfect greenbacks in oil." Viewers who knew Haberle's work would probably have been aware the statement was true. Haberle frequently depicted paper currency in his paintings, in spite of having been warned to stop doing so by the U.S. Secret Service, which was formed in 1865 to stop the distribution of counterfeit money. Those who appreciated his work knew Haberle took pleasure in making it clear he was ignoring that demand.

A Bachelor's Drawer, painted 1890-1894, would turn out to be the artist's last *trompe l'oeil* painting of currency, though, as the exacting work had strained his eyes to the point that he could no longer paint such fine detail. Some of the other objects Haberle included, and the title of the work itself, seem to be referring to the end of an era. The pamphlet titled "How to Name the Baby," prominently displayed in the upper right, partially covers the postcard showing a finely-dressed dandy with his dashing moustache that is placed directly above a discreetly covered photograph of a nude woman. They all lead down to a small photograph that appears to be stuck in the bottom (painted) frame, which is a portrait of the artist. Was he the bachelor who once had the freedom to attend the theatre, but is now taking up the life of a young father? This trail of clues is typical of the dry humor in Haberle's work, here turned on himself, with an open invitation for his viewers to share the joke with him.

1.6 WHY DO WE MAKE ART?

Some of the earliest evidence of recognizable human activity includes not only practical things like stone tools and fire pits, but also decorative objects used for personal adornment. For example, these small beads made by piercing sea snail shells, found at the Blombos Cave on the southeastern coast of South Africa, are dated to the Middle Stone Age, 101,000-70,000 BCE. (Figure 1.19) We can only speculate about the intentions of our distant ancestors, but it is clear that their lives included the practice of conceiving and producing art objects. One thing we appear to share with those distant relatives is the urge to make art.

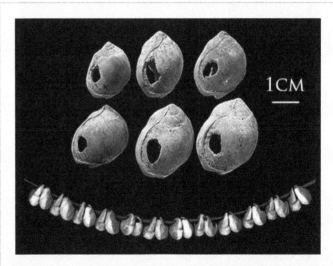

Figure 1.19 | Blombos Cave Nassarius kraussianus marine shell beads and reconstruction of bead stringing
Author: Marian Vanhaeren and Christopher S. Henshilwood
Source: Wikimedia Commons
License: CC BY-SA 3.0

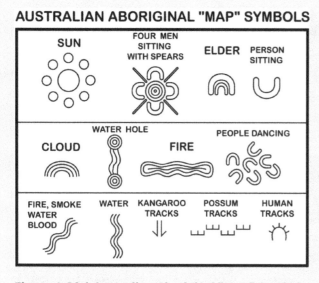

Figure 1.20 | Australian Aboriginal "Map" Symbols
Author: Jeffrey LeMieux
Source: Original Work
License: CC BY-SA 4.0

A culture can be defined as a group of people who agree about what is important. Today many different human cultures and sub-cultures co-exist; we can find in them a broad range of ideas about art and its place in daily living. One main goal of Australian Aboriginal artists, for example, is to "map" the world around them. (Figure 1.20) In this painting on bark, pictorial symbols tell the story of the great hunter snake in colors such as red for desert sand and yellow for the sun. (Figure 1.21) In a similar way, though with different materials, Buddhist sand paintings known as **mandalas** present a map of the cosmos. These circular diagrams also represent the relationship of the individual to the whole and levels of human awareness. (Figure 1.22)

The need to make art can be divided into two broad categories: the *personal need* to express ideas and feelings, and the *community's needs* to assert common values. In the following sections, we'll look at some of these motivations to more clearly understand and identify artist intent in the works of art that we encounter.

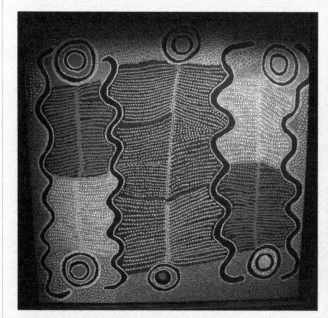

Figure 1.21 | Sand Painting
Author: Sailko
Source: Wikimedia Commons
License: CC BY-SA 3.0

Figure 1.22 | Wheel of Time Kalachakra Sand Mandala
Artist: Losang Samten
Author: Steve Osborne
Source: Wikimedia Commons
License: CC BY-SA 3.0

We should recognize that every person has lived a unique life, so every person knows something about the world that no one else has seen. It is the job of artists today to tell us about what they have come to know—individually or as part their community—using the art material or medium most suited to their abilities. While copying the works of others is good training, it is merely re-working what has already been revealed. Originality, however, is more highly valued in contemporary art. Georgia O'Keeffe (1887-1986, USA) explained her view on this matter when she wrote: (Figure 1.23)

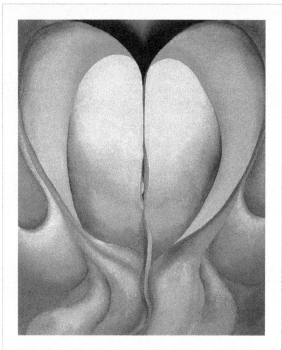

Figure 1.23 | *Series 1, No. 8*
Artist: Georgia O'Keeffe
Author: User "Prosfilaes"
Source: Wikimedia Commons
License: Public Domain

It was in the fall of 1915 that I first had the idea that what I had been taught was of little value to me except for the use of my materials as a language—charcoal, pencil, pen and ink, watercolor, pastel, and oil. I had become fluent with them when I was so young that they were simply another language that I handled easily. But what to say with them? I had been taught to work like others, and after careful thinking I decided that I wasn't going to spend my life doing what had already been done. . . . I decided I was a very stupid fool for not to at least paint as I wanted to and say what I wanted to when I painted.[5]

1.6.1 The Personal Need to Create

Many works of art come out of a personal decision to put a feeling, idea, or concept into visual form. Since feelings vary widely, the resulting art takes a wide range of forms. This approach to art comes from the individual's delight in the experience. Doodling comes to mind as one very basic example of such delight. Pollock's Abstract Expressionist works, also known as action paintings, are much more than doodles, though they may resemble such on the surface. (Autumn Rhythm-Number 30, Jackson Pollock: http://www.metmuseum.org/art/collection/search/488978?=&imgno=0&tabname=online-resources; *Number 10*, Jackson Pollock: http://www.wikiart.org/en/jackson-pollock/number-10-1949) They were the result of many levels of artistic thought but on a basic level were a combination of delight in the act of painting and in the personal discovery that act enabled.

Some art is intended to provide personal commentary. Artworks that illustrate a personal viewpoint or experience can fulfill this purpose. *Persepolis*, a graphic novel by Marjane Satrapi (b. 1969, Iran) published in 2000, recounts her experiences and thoughts during the 1979 Iranian revolution, and

---

5   O'Keeffe 1976, unpaginated.

is an example of such personal commentary. (*Keys to Paradise*: https://imaginedlandscapes. files.wordpress.com/2014/02/ pi-102.jpg) Satrapi is a leading proponent of the graphic novel, a new approach to art making. In an ironic critique of how different parts of Iranian society were affected by war, Satrapi compares the contorted figures of Iranian youth dying in a combat zone explosion with the dance movements at her high school celebration.

Artworks can be created thus as a means of exploring one's own experience, a way of bring-

Figure 1.24 | *The Raft of the Medusa*
Artist: Jean Louis Théodore Géricault
Source: Wikimedia Commons
License: Public Domain

ing hidden emotions to the surface so that they may be recognized and understood more clearly. The term for this process is **catharsis**.

Cathartic works of art can arise from perceptions of grief, good, evil, or injustice, as in *The Raft of the Medusa* by Théodore Géricault (1791-1824, France), which was an indictment of the French government of his day following the sinking of a ship. (Figure 1.24) When Whistler, on the other hand, became a proponent of "Art for art's sake," he was rejecting outside influences such as contemporary artistic and social standards in order to "purify" art of external corruption. (see Figure 1.18) The idea of removing influence from the creation of art is a modern one. Much of the art made before the nineteenth century was produced with the support and under the direction of religious, political, and cultural authorities in the larger community.

1.6.2 Communal Needs and Purposes

Across history and geography, we see religious and political communities that remain stable despite constant pressure from both internal and external sources. One way in which communities maintain stability is in the production of works of art that identify common values and experiences within that community and thus bring people together.

Architecture, monuments, murals, and icons are visible guides to community participation in the arts and often use image-making conventions. A **convention** is an agreed upon way of thinking, speaking, or acting in a social context. There are many kinds of conventions, including visual conventions. A good example in visual art would be a conventional sense of direction. In Western cultures, text is generally read left to right. Therefore, when they look at artwork, Western viewers tend to "enter" a picture on the upper left and proceed to the right. Objects that appear on the left side of an image are thought to be "first," while ones that appear on the right are thought to be "later." Since Asian texts follow a different convention, and tend to be read right to left, an Asian viewer would unconsciously assume the opposite.

Architecture, especially of public buildings, is an expression of a community's values. Courthouses, libraries, town halls, schools, banks, factories, and jails are all designed for community purposes, and their shapes become strongly associated with their function: the architectural shapes be-

Figure 1.25 | U.S. Supreme Court Building
Photographer: US Government Employee
Source: Architect of the Capital
License: Public Domain

come conventions. The use of older styles of architecture can be as references to the values of previous cultures. In the United States, for example, many government buildings are designed with imposing stone facades using classical Greek and Roman columns that symbolize strength and stability. Federal government buildings such as the United States Capitol and the Supreme Court (Figure 1.25) were designed so that the community would associate ancient Greek and Roman ideals of virtue and integrity with the activities inside those more modern buildings.

Figure 1.26 | The Bauhaus Building in Dessau, Germany
Author: User "Mewes"
Source: Wikimedia Commons
License: Public Domain

Many twentieth-century architects, however, have followed the guiding principle of American architect Louis Sullivan (1856-1924, USA), that "form follows function." In his design of the Bauhaus, Walter Gropius (1883-1969, Germany) rejected superfluous decoration and focused instead on the efficient and functional use of space and material. (Figure 1.26) The leading school of art, craft, and architecture in Germany from 1919-1933, the teachings of the Bauhaus, or "construction house," have strongly influenced domestic and industrial design internationally since that time.

Figure 1.27 | Colleoni on Horseback
Artist: Andrea del Verrocchio
Author: User "Waysider1925"
Source: Wikimedia Commons
License: CC BY-SA 3.0

Figure 1.28 | Burghers of Calais
Artist: Auguste Rodin
Author: User "Razimantv"
Source: Wikimedia Commons
License: CC BY 3.0

Communities can remind citizens of public virtues by commemorating the individuals who displayed those qualities in **monuments**. Since ancient times, they have commonly been statues of such individuals placed on pedestals, columns, or inside architecture. The *Equestrian Statue of Bartolomeo Colleoni* by Andrea del Verrocchio (1435-1488, Italy) is a good example of this type of monument. (Figure 1.27) Created for the city of Venice, Italy, during the Italian Renaissance, the sculpture of Colleoni on horseback shows him as the bold and victorious warrior he was. But *The Burghers of Calais* by Auguste Rodin (1840-1917, France) and *Vietnam War Memorial* by Maya Lin (b. 1959, USA) are monuments that violate that long-standing norm. Rodin placed the burghers, or leading citizens, on ground level to humanize the six men who offered themselves as sacrifices to save their city; he did so in order to bring their internal struggles down to the viewer's eye level. (Figure 1.28) Lin's memorial is below ground level, and displays the names of the approximately 58,000 Americans who died in the Vietnam War. (Figure 1.29) These choices reflect the belief that the Vietnam War was initially conducted "beneath the surface," that is, unknown to most Americans, and to remind visitors that its cost was paid by real individuals, not anonymous soldiers. These two works of art are unconventional and original in their conception and execution.

Since ancient times, **murals**, paintings on walls, have been created in both public and private places. Ancient Egyptians combined images with writing in wall paintings to commemorate past leaders. Some of these murals were intentionally erased when the leader fell out of favor. Roman murals were more often found inside homes and temples. The Roman mural located in a bedroom of the Villa of P. Fannius

Synistor was unearthed in Pompeii, Italy. (Figure 1.30) It depicts landscape and architectural views between a row of (painted) columns, as if viewed from inside the **villa**, or country house.

The Last Supper by Leonardo da Vinci (1452-1519, Italy, France) and the Sistine Chapel ceiling by Michelangelo (1475-1564, Italy) are murals from the Italian Renaissance. They were created for a wall in a refectory, or dining hall, of a monastery (Figure 1.31) and for the ceiling of the Pope's chapel. (Figure 1.32) Both depict crucial scenes in the teachings of the Catholic Church, the leading European religious and political organization of the time. Because many people at the time were illiterate, images played an important role in educating them about their religious history and doctrines.

Figure 1.29 | Vietnam Veterans Memorial Wall
Artist: Maya Lin
Author: User "Mariordo"
Source: Wikimedia Commons
License: CC BY-SA 3.0

Figure 1.30 | Cubiculum (bedroom) from the Villa of P. Fannius Synistor at Boscoreale
Author: Rogers Fund
Source: Met Museum
License: OASC

More modern examples of murals can be found around the world today. Diego Rivera (1886-1967, Mexico) was a world-renowned artist who executed large-scale murals in Mexico and the United States. His *Detroit Industry* murals consist of twenty-seven panels originally installed at the Detroit Institute of Arts. (Figure 1.33) The two largest panels depict workers manufacturing a V8 engine at the Ford Motor Company factory. Other smaller panels show advances in science, technology, and medicine involved in modern industrial culture, portraying Rivera's belief that conceptual thinking and physical labor are interdependent. These works are now considered a National Landmark. *The Great Wall of Los Angeles* designed by Judith Baca (b. 1946, USA) and executed

Figure 1.31 | *The Last Supper*
Artist: Leonardo da Vinci
Author: User "Thebrid"
Source: Wikimedia Commons
License: Public Domain

Figure 1.32| The Ceiling of the Sistine Chapel
Artist: Michelangelo
Author: Patrick Landy
Source: Wikipedia
License: CC BY 3.0

Figure 1.33 | Detroit Industry, North Wall
Artist: Diego Rivera
Author: User "Cactus.man"
Source: Wikipedia
License: Public Domain

by hundreds of community members is thirteen feet high and runs for more than one half mile through the city. (*The Great Wall of Los Angeles*, Judith Baca: http://sparcinla.org/wp-content/uploads/2012/12/great-wall_m.jpg) Its subject is the history of Southern California "as seen through the eyes of women and minorities."[6] The mural is part of a larger push in Los Angeles to adorn public spaces with murals that inform and educate the populace.

The term **icon** comes from the Greek word *eikon*, or "to be like," and refers to an image or likeness that is used as a guide to religious worship. The holy figures depicted in icons are thought by believers to have special powers of healing or other positive influence. An icon can also be a person or thing that symbolically represents a quality or virtue. A good example is the image of St. Sebastian. St. Sebastian was a captain of the Roman guard who converted to Chris-

6   Joyce Gregory Wyels, "Great Walls, Vibrant Voices," *Americas* 52, no. 1 (2000): 22.

tianity and was sentenced to death before a squad of archers. (Figure 1.34) He survived his wounds, and early Christians attributed this miracle to the power of their religion. (He was later stoned to death.) In the late Middle Ages during widespread plague in Europe, images of St. Sebastian were regularly commissioned for hospitals because of the legend of his miraculous healing and the hope that the images would be curative.

An example of a non-religious or **secular** icon might be the bronze bust of the famous football coach Knute Rockne at Notre Dame University in Indiana. (Figure 1.35) The nose of the bronze sculpture is bright gold because many consider it good luck to rub it, so it receives constant polishing by students before exams.

Figure 1.34 | The Martyrdom of St. Sebastian
Artist: Giacinto Diana
Source: Artstor.org
License: Public Domain

Figure 1.35 | Knute Rockne
Artist: Nison Tregor
Author: Matthew D. Britt
Source: Flickr
License: CC BY-SA-NC 3.0

We have touched only briefly on the questions of what art is, who an artist is, and why people make art. History shows us people have defined art and artists differently in various times and places, but that people everywhere make art for many different reasons. And, these art objects share a common purpose: they are all intended to express a feeling or idea that is valued either by the individual artist or by the larger community.

1.7 CONCEPTS EXPLORED IN LATER CHAPTERS

1.7.1 The Structure of Art: Form and Design

In order to read this you have spent considerable time and effort learning individual letters, combinations that form a word, the structure of a sentence, and the organization of multiple sentences to move from one idea to the next. You use all of those skills to make sense of and understand the written word. And from there, you can introduce your own ideas, knowledge, and experiences to expand upon and bring additional meanings to what you have read.

We follow a similar process in learning how to look at and understand art. In Chapter Two: The Structure of Art–Form and Design, we will first define forms of art and the materials and processes used in creating them. We will then examine the elements of art, such as line, color, and form, as well as the principles of design, or how those elements are combined to create a composition. With this new vocabulary we can better understand and talk about what we are looking at, enriching our experiences interacting with art and architecture in the world around us.

1.7.2 Significance of Materials Used in Art

One of the basic choices in creating any work of art is the material from which it will be made. The materials might make it more or less important, more or less valuable, or might bring a variety of associations not inherent in the actual form of the work. In Chapter Three: Significance of Materials Used in Art, we will examine both the monetary value and the cultural value of works of art based upon the media—the materials—employed, and some of the many sources from which those values are determined.

1.7.3 Describing Art: Formal Analysis, Types, and Styles

Taking the building blocks of the vocabulary we built in reading Chapter Two: The Structure of Art–Form and Design, in Chapter Four: Describing Art: Formal Analysis, Types, and Styles we will discuss how to critically analyze, or systematically describe, a work of art. We will examine the elements and principles of its design, the category in which it falls based on the relative representation of the natural world, and how we might group that work with others, or the work of other artists based on its appearance, or style.

These tools not only help us learn more about the work of art, they enhance our appreciation of art by providing us with a greater understanding of the individual work's components and its relationship with art in the same or other cultures and time periods.

1.7.4 Meaning in Art: Socio-Cultural Contexts, Symbolism, and Iconography

Studying the historical, social, personal, political, or scientific reasons a work of art was made provides us with further, and key, information in understanding its meaning and symbolism. A work of art is part of the culture in which it was made; all artists, even those who wish to rebel against some aspect of the time in which they live, are influenced (and perhaps constrained) by the world around them. In Chapter Five: Meaning in Art– Socio-Cultural Context, Symbolism, and Iconography, we will consider the many factors that influence the creation and our comprehension of works of art. And, we will explore meanings within a work, its symbolism, as a way of providing us with deeper understanding of what the work meant within the culture it was made.

1.7.5 Connecting Art to Our Lives

For art to have meaning, it must have some connection to us and our lives. Artists and those who hire them to create works of art have myriad reasons for doing so. In Chapter Six: Connecting Art to Our Lives, we will first look at aesthetics, the study of the principles and appreciation of beauty in art, from an historical perspective to gain an understanding of another way in which the value of art has traditionally been determined. We will also explore roles that art plays: it can be a means of expression, a symbol of inclusion or exclusion, a tool of communication, or a medium of education. When we find our connection to a work of art, we are engaged with and enriched by it.

1.7.6 Form in Architecture

Human beings have created a wide variety of architecture forms from pre-historic times to the present across the entire world. The continuous presence of architecture in human history indicates the vital and numerous roles structures play for both the individual and the society in which they are made. In Chapter Seven: Form in Architecture, we will examine purpose, function, and meaning in design and construction of sites and buildings within a variety of cultures. What can the history of constructed forms tell us about the needs, beliefs, and principles of our near and distant ancestors? Answering these questions sheds light on the role of architecture throughout history, as well as how it functions in our own time.

1.7.7 Art and Identity

Often today, when we think of art and identity, we are referring to the artist's identity, and what we mean is the artist's personal identity and what the artist is trying to communicate on a personal level. The notion of personal identity quickly expands, however, to include aspects that link the artist to others with similar characteristics, such as gender, ethnicity, spiritual beliefs, and nationality. From there, we can begin to talk about identity within a clan, culture, nation, and other groups that share like traits and properties.

In Chapter Eight: Art and Identity, we will look at how notions of identity influence artists and the art they create. Whether artists are attempting to express individual, private feelings, or capture the personality of a nation, they must first define what the characteristics are and determine how those chosen will be represented in the work of art. We will look at these visualizations of identity in a variety of forms, from small hand-held objects to large-scale works of architecture, to discuss the impact of materials, size, and audience. And, we will examine the circumstances surrounding the creation of these objects to investigate the role social, religious, and political forces play in defining and assigning identity in art.

1.7.8 Art and Power

Throughout history, art has been used as a means of communication by those in power. When rulers commission depictions of themselves, for example, they may or may not want them to be recognizable portraits, but the sculpture or painting will certainly communicate what the ruler wants those who see the work to know about the ruler's position, wealth, and attributes, that is, indications of the ruler's power. These signs of power can be used to reassure the ruler's own people or to warn potential adversaries of the forces at the ruler's disposal. Rulers and others in authority have the ability to enlarge a show of power beyond a bodily display of physical strength and dominance to more potent and permanent monuments such as murals, sculpture, and buildings.

The power of art extends far beyond uses by those in control. Art can be used to build influence, increase leverage, and give hope to those who possess little authority. It can be used as a form of protest against those in command. And, it can be used to induce change. In Chapter Nine: Art and Power, we will look at art as a tool to comment upon and garner power, and as a means of communicating power and power relations. We will identify common visual strategies, and note similarities and differences over time and in different cultures.

1.7.9 Art and Ritual Life: Symbolism of Space and Ritual Objects

Human beings possess the ability to project our thoughts forward to speculate about what will happen in our future. We can contemplate our own mortality and reflect on existence beyond our own lives. Doing so can plunge us into despair or elevate us to heights of exultation. In times of desperation, art can serve as a talisman, an object believed to have power to bring luck or offer protection, against those things or events we fear in hope the occurrence can be warded off. In the case of the inevitable, such as sickness and death, art is used to give comfort to the suffering and solace to the survivors. We also employ art to pay tribute to what we cherish and honor; with works made of the finest materials, crafted with ingenuity and the utmost skill we give expression not only to our fears, but also to our hopes.

In Chapter Ten: Art and Ritual Life–Symbolism of Space and Ritual Objects, we will look at how art helps us to understand ourselves as mortal creatures, and the role it plays in our spiritual lives as we strive to locate meaning and purpose in existence as a finite or infinite concept.

1.7.10 Art and Ethics

Art can introduce us to new ideas, and it can influence what we think about ourselves and others. Art informs us and it can change us. Does this potential for tremendous impact place an obligation upon the artist, the photojournalist, or the museum curator to act under certain guidelines of originality or truthfulness, for example? If so, how do we define what original art is, and whose truth are we telling?

Chapter Eleven: Art and Ethics introduces us to some of the issues facing artists and others in the world of art in how they present themselves and their art.

1.8 BEFORE YOU MOVE ON

Key Concepts

When studying a subject, it is important to have a working definition of that subject. Our subject is art. The four historical attempts at defining art surveyed here each had limitations. Ancient Greek mimesis excluded art that does not re-present objects. Tolstoy's communication theory is unverifiable and is spectator-dependent, Bell's significant form is circular reasoning, and Dickie's Artworld theory is about who has the power to decide what art is, not about art itself. The operating definition of art used in this text is "from the mind into the world." The images used in this survey are considered works of art. It is the task of the student to be able to recognize, analyze, and interpret works of art, and to integrate this understanding into a coherent worldview. The purpose of this effort at understanding is to practice recognizing value in new and diverse forms of visual art. One end result is to then have a greater appreciation of and to simply enjoy looking at art.

Art is found wherever we find human beings. Art fulfills a basic human need for expression. This need can be sub-divided into personal needs and needs of the community. Personal needs include art created for delight, decoration, for political and religious devotion, and for personal catharsis. Communal needs can include architecture, monuments, murals, and religious and secular icons.

Test Yourself

1. List and describe the four ways stated in the text in which people have defined art in the past.

2. Briefly re-state the operating definition of art for this text.

3. What is the significance of the ancient Greek myth of Zeuxis and Parhassios?

4. What do each of the four historical definitions of art reveal of how people thought about where truth is to be found?

5. Draw parallels between the sea snail shell necklace of c. 100,000 BCE and modern practices of personal decoration, for example, a pearl necklace.

6. Speculate about why images might be important in non-literate cultures? What might be one concern about images used in religious rituals? Can you identify an example of a non-religious icon other than the one noted in the text?

7. Speculate about why most early American federal buildings were built using classical Greek and Roman columns and imposing stone facades. Why were buildings in the twentieth century built with little reference to the architecture of classical antiquity? What ideas were lost and what ideas were gained with this shift in architecture?

8. Consider the change in the conventional presentation of public monuments by comparing how the monuments of Verrocchio and Rodin are presented, one on a high pedestal, the other at ground level. What does this change suggest about changing ideas about the heroic and monumental?

1.9 KEY TERMS

Architecture: the design and construction of buildings or other complex structures.

Artworld theory of art: an approach to defining art as whatever the artworld says it is.

Catharsis: the process of releasing pent up emotion resulting in personal change.

Circumambulate: to "walk around"—a ritual practice of circling a sacred site, following a set path either inside or outside of a structure.

Communication theory of art: an approach to defining art as a transfer of feeling from artist to spectator.

Convention: group consensus about the way something is usually done.

Icon: a person or thing regarded as representative of something, often religious.

Institutional theory of art: another name for the Artworld theory of art.

Labyrinth: similar to a maze, but generally has only one intricate and twisting path to the center.

Mimesis: an approach to defining art as a copy of perceived reality.

Monument: a statue or other structure meant to commemorate a famous person or event.

Mural: a work of art executed directly on a wall.

Relic: an object thought to have belonged to or been part of a holy person's body.

Secular: lacking in religious or spiritual content, not bound by religious rule.

Significant Form: an approach to defining art as what we notice.

Symbolism: the use of images to represent ideas or qualities.

Trompe l'oeil: art so realistic that it "fools the eye."

Zeuxis and Parhassios: an ancient Greek myth about two competing painters who vie for the title of greatest artist by copying reality most faithfully

2 The Structure of Art
Form and Design

Jeffrey LeMieux, Pamela J. Sachant, and Rita Tekippe

2.1 LEARNING OUTCOMES

After completing this chapter, you should be able to:

- Distinguish between various materials, processes, and methods in the production of art objects.

- Identify the characteristics of different art forms and distinguish one from another.

- Explain the roles of elements and principles of design in creating forms and compositions.

2.2 INTRODUCTION

When we look at the art objects that people have made over the centuries and around the world, we find they share some basic elements. They exist; they have substance; they are either flat or "in the round"; they use (or do not use) perspective, line, shape, mass, value, color, texture, and so on. Over time, both artists and art critics have developed a set of terms to describe art objects and their design. In this chapter, we will develop an art-specific vocabulary to use in identifying different types of art forms, discerning the materials and processes used to create them, understanding how the elements and principles of design are used by artists, and recognizing how they convey meaning in visual art.

The possible combinations in visual art are infinite, but the visual arts have traditionally been practiced and categorized in only a few broadly termed ways. The primary distinction in the visual arts is dimension. Two-dimensional art consists of **drawing, painting, and printmaking**; three-dimensional art consists of **sculpture, including installation, and kinetic art**. In addition to these traditional types of art, new technologies and new ideas about art have given us four-dimensional **or** time-based art, such as **video and performance**. Such art depends on the use of technology and the passage of time for its effect. Most recently, time-based art has grown to encompass a category known as new media art, which includes digital art, computer animation, interactive art, video games, virtual reality, robotics, and 3D printing.

Today the separate categories of space and time are becoming blurred as artists seek ways to combine disparate approaches into a single, encompassing, and rich art experience. An important lesson from the modern approach to visual art for both artists and viewers is to recognize that each formal element and each approach to design has unique expressive power.

2.3 ART SPECIFIC VOCABULARY

Every discipline has its "jargon," and the visual arts are no different. Visual artists use a variety of materials and processes to produce their work and art critics use specialized terms to describe that work. It is unavoidable that terms must be invented to serve the purposes of criticism and/or description. Many art terms are in common use and widely understood, some are less so. Some terms come from languages other than English. In the course of describing the different forms that visual art takes, this text will introduce terms by using a bold font, following them with explanations and definitions. As with any discipline, the goal in using specialized art terms here is to make things more clear and direct.

2.4 ART FORMS

Because of the limits of nature, art objects are limited to the dimensions of space—and time. For this reason, art objects fall into three categories: **two-dimensional art, three-dimensional art**, and **four-dimensional art**. Each category has divisions deriving primarily from differences between the materials and approaches used. Throughout history, art objects generally fit clearly into a discrete classification. In the nineteenth century, however, artists began exploring the limits of new materials as well as the boundaries of the categories into which they fell to see if they were real or arbitrary.

2.4.1 Two-Dimensional Art

Two-dimensional art occurs on flat surfaces, like paper, canvas, or even cave walls. This art can be further divided into three main categories: drawing, painting, and printmaking. All art that occurs on a flat surface is one or a combination of these three activities.

Figure 2.1 | Replication of Chauvet Cave Lion Wall
Author: User "HTO"
Source: Wikimedia Commons
License: Public Domain

2.4.1.1 Drawing

The term **drawing** describes both a visual object and an activity. At first glance, drawing appears to consist of making contrasting marks on a flat surface. The term implies something more, however. One can "draw" water from a well or be "drawn" to a charismatic person. There is something in the word "draw" that is related to extracting or delineating, the "pulling out" of an essence. To draw an object is to observe its appearance and transfer that observation to a set of marks. Ancient cave painters truly "drew" the animals they saw around them based on their deep familiarity with their essential nature. (Figure 2.1) So in this context, drawing is a combination of observation and mark making.

Drawing is usually—but not always—done with **monochromatic** media, that is, with dry materials of a single color such as **charcoal**, **conté crayon**, **metalpoint**, or graphite. Color can be introduced using pastels. In addition to these dry materials, free-flowing ink can also be used to make drawings. These materials have been highly refined over centuries to serve specific artistic purposes.

Charcoal is made from wood or other organic material that has been burned in the absence of oxygen. This process leaves a relatively pure black carbon powder. Artists compress this dry powder, or **pigment**, with a **binder**, a sticky substance like pine resin or glue made from the collagen of animal hides, to make hand-held charcoal blocks of various strengths and degrees of hardness. This compressed charcoal is used to make very dark marks, usually on paper. Compressed charcoal is challenging to erase.

Charcoal also comes in a form called **willow** or **vine charcoal**. This form of drawing charcoal leaves a very light mark as it is simply burned twigs. It is generally used for impermanent sketches because it does not readily stick to paper or canvas and is easily erased. Both compressed and vine charcoal drawings are easily smudged and should be protected by a fixative that adheres the charcoal to the drawing surface and creates a barrier resistant to smudging.

Conté crayon is a hand-held drawing material similar to compressed charcoal. Conté crayons are sticks of graphite or charcoal combined with wax or clay that come in a variety of colors, from white to sanguine (deep red) to black, as well as a range of hardness. Harder conté is used for details and softer varieties for broad areas. This portrait by Georges-Pierre Seurat (1859-1891, France) was drawn in black conté crayon on textured paper in order to break the image into discrete marks. (Figure 2.2)

Metalpoint is the use of malleable metals like silver, pewter, and gold to make drawing

Figure 2.2 | Edmond Aman-Jean
Artist: Georges-Pierre Seurat
Author: User "Pimbrils"
Source: Wikimedia Commons
License: Public Domain

Figure 2.3 | Head of a Girl
Artist: Leonardo da Vinci
Source: Wikiart
License: Public Domain

marks on prepared surfaces. (Figure 2.3) The surface must have a "tooth" or roughness to hold the marks. Any pure silver or gold object can be used for this, though artists today favor silver and gold wire held in mechanical pencils for the process.

Graphite is a crystalline form of carbon. In the sixteenth century, a large deposit of pure graphite was discovered in England, and it became the primary source for this drawing material. Because of its silvery color, it was originally thought to be a form of lead, though there is no actual lead in pencils. Today powdered graphite is mixed with clay to control hardness.

Pastels are similar to compressed charcoal but, instead of finely powdered carbon, finely ground colored pigment and a binder are used to create handheld colored blocks. (Figure 2.4) The powdery pigments smudge easily, so the image created must be displayed under glass or covered with a fixative. Edgar Degas (1834-1917, France) is famous for the subtle yet distinct layering of color he was able achieve in his pastel drawings. (Figure 2.5)

Figure 2.4 | Pastels
Author: User "Tau1012"
Source: Wikimedia Commons
License: Public Domain

Figure 2.5 | *Nach dem Bade sich abtrocknende Frau (After the Bath, Woman drying herself)*
Artist: Edgar Degas
Author: User "Crisco"
Source: Wikimedia Commons
License: Public Domain

Oil pastels are semi-solid sticks of high pigment oil paint that are used like crayons. They were originally invented to mark livestock, but artists quickly realized their aesthetic potential. Oil pastels are a convenient way to apply and blend heavily textured oil-based pigment onto any surface without using traditional brushes. The colors are vibrant, and the marks are gestural and immediate so oil pastel drawings can show the "hand" of the artist in a direct way, as can be seen here in *East Palatka Onions*, a 1983 oil pastel drawing by Mary Ann Currier (b. 1927, USA). (*East Palatka Onions*, Mary Ann Currier: https://ketorg.cdn.ket.org/wp-content/uploads/2016/07/currier-ep-onions1100px.jpg)

Ink is the combination of a colored pigment, usually black carbon or graphite, and a binder suspended in a liquid and applied with a pen or brush. A wide range of substances have been used over time to make ink, including lamp black or soot, burned animal bones, gallnuts, and iron oxide. The pigment must be finely ground and held together with a binder. There is a long tradition of fine art ink drawings. Although the example given dates to the fourteenth century, the oldest ink drawings come from China in the third century BCE and are done on silk and paper. (Figure 2.6)

Figure 2.6 | *Spring Dawn Over the Elixir Terrace*
Artist: Lu Guang
Source: Met Museum
License: OASC

2.4.1.2 Painting

Painting is a specialized form of drawing that refers to using **brushes** to apply colored liquids to a **support**, usually canvas or paper, but sometimes wooden panels, metal plates, and walls. For example, Leonardo da Vinci painted *Mona Lisa* on a wood panel. (Figure 2.7) Paint is composed of three main ingredients: pigments, binders, and solvents. The colored pigments are suspended in a sticky binder in order to apply them and make them adhere to the support. **Solvents** dissolve the binder in order to remove it but can also be used in smaller quantities to make paint more fluid.

As with drawing, different kinds of painting have mostly to do with the material that is being used. Oil, acrylic,

Figure 2.7 | Mona Lisa
Artist: Leonardo da Vinci
Author: User "Dcoetzee"
Source: Wikimedia Commons
License: Public Domain

watercolor, encaustic, fresco, and tempera are some of the different kinds of painting. For the most part, the pigments or coloring agents in paints remain the same. The thing that distinguishes one kind of painting from another is the binder.

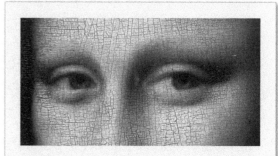

Figure 2.8 | Detail of the eyes of *Mona Lisa*
Artist: Leonardo da Vinci
Author: User "Cantus"
Source: Wikimedia Commons
License: Public Domain

Oil painting was discovered in the fifteenth century and uses vegetable oils, primarily linseed oil and walnut oil, as the binding agent. Linseed oil was chosen for its clear color and its ability to dry slowly and evenly. Turpentine is generally used as the solvent in oil painting. The medium has strict rules of application to avoid cracking or delamination (dividing into layers). Additionally, oil paint can oxidize and darken or yellow over time if not properly crafted. Some pigments have been found to be **fugitive**, meaning they lose their color over time, especially when exposed to direct sunlight. This can be seen in a detail of Leonardo's *Mona Lisa* where the figure's eyebrows and eye lashes are now "missing." (Figure 2.8)

Acrylic painting is relatively modern and uses water-soluble acrylic polymer as the binding agent. Water is the solvent. Acrylic dries very quickly and can be used to build up thick layers of paint in a short time. One problem with acrylic is that the colors can subtly change as it dries, making this medium less suitable for portraiture or other projects where accurate color is vital. Nevertheless, acrylic paint is preferred over oil paint by many artists today, in part due to its greater ease of use and clean up, and because its rapid drying time allows the artist to work at a faster pace.

Watercolor painting suspends colored pigments in water-soluble **gum arabic** distilled from the Acacia tree **as the binder**. Watercolor paints are mixed with water and brushed onto an absorbent surface, usually paper. Before the industrial era, watercolor was used as an outdoor sketching medium because it was more portable than oil paint, which had to be prepared for use and could not be preserved for long periods or easily transported. (Figure 2.9) Today, however, many artists use watercolor as their primary medium.

Figure 2.9 | *The Sponge Diver*
Artist: Winslow Homer
Author: User "Botaurus"
Source: Wikimedia Commons
License: Public Domain

Encaustic uses melted beeswax as the binder and must be applied to rigid supports like wood with heated brushes. The advantage of encaustic is that it remains fresh and vi-

Figure 2.10 | *Portrait of the Boy Eutyches*
Source: Met Museum
License: OASC

Figure 2.11 | *The Expulsion of Adam and Eve from Eden*
Artist: Masaccio
Source: Wikimedia Commons
License: Public Domain

brant over centuries. Encaustic paintings from ancient Egypt dating to the period of Roman occupation (late first century BCE-third century CE) are as brilliantly colored as when they were first painted. (Figure 2.10)

Fresco is the process of painting onto plaster; it is a long-lasting technique. There are two kinds of fresco: **buon fresco**, or "good" fresco, is painting on wet plaster, and **fresco secco**, or dry fresco, is done after the plaster has dried. Paintings made using the buon fresco technique become part of the wall because the wet plaster absorbs the pigment as it is applied. (Figure 2.11*)* The only way to correct a buon fresco painting is to chip it off the wall and start over. Buon fresco must be done in sections. Each section is called a **giornate**, which is Italian for "a day's work." Because it is done on dry plaster, fresco secco is more forgiving, but also less permanent as changes in moisture levels or damage to the wall can harm the painting. Due to the dry air and stable weather, there are fresco secco murals created as early as 3,000 BCE in ancient Egyptian tombs that remain largely intact. (Figure 2.12)

Tempera painting has been around for centuries. The most popular version of painting during the Middle Ages was **egg tempera**, in which dry colored pigments were mixed with egg yolk and applied quickly to a stable surface in layers of short brushstrokes. Egg tempera is a difficult medium to master because the egg yolk mixture dries very quickly, and mistakes cannot be corrected

Figure 2.12 | Nebamun Tomb Fresco Dancers and Musicians
Author: User "Fordmadoxfraud"
Source: Wikimedia Commons
License: Public Domain

without damaging the surface of the painting. *The Birth of Venus* by Sandro Botticelli (1445-1510, Italy) is an egg tempera painting. (Figure 2.13)

2.4.1.3 Printmaking

A **print** is an image made by transferring pigment from a **matrix** to a final surface, often but not always paper. Printing allows multiple copies of an artwork to be made. Multiple copies of an individual artwork are called an **edition**.

There are four main types of printmaking: relief, intaglio, planographic, and stencil. **Relief** prints are made by removing material from the

Figure 2.13 | The Birth of Venus
Artist: Sandro Botticelli
Author: User "Dcoetzee"
Source: Wikimedia Commons
License: Public Domain

matrix, the surface the image has been carved into, which is often wood, linoleum, or metal. (Figure 2.14) The remaining surface is covered with ink or pigment, and then paper is pressed onto the surface, picking up the ink. **Letterpress** is a relief printing process that transfers ink to paper but also indents an impression into the surface of the paper, creating a texture to the print that is often considered a sign of high quality.

Intaglio prints are made when a design is scratched into a matrix, usually a metal plate. Ink is wiped across the surface, and collects in the scratches. Excess ink is wiped off and paper is pressed onto the plate, picking up the ink from the scratches. Intaglio prints may also include texture.

Planographic prints are made by chemically altering a matrix to selectively accept or reject water. Originally, limestone was used for this process since it naturally repels water but can

Figure 2.14 | Relief Wood Carving
Author: User "Zephyris"
Source: Wikimedia Commons
License: CC BY-SA 3.0

Figure 2.15 | Stone used for lithography print
Author: User "AndreasPraefcke"
Source: Wikimedia Commons
License: Public Domain

be chemically changed to absorb it. In stone matrix **lithography**, black grease pencil drawings are made on a flat block of limestone, which is then treated with nitric acid. (Figure 2.15) The nitric acid does not dissolve the stone, but changes it chemically so that it absorbs water. The grease pencil is removed, and the stone wetted. Where the grease pencil protected the stone from the acid, the limestone repels water and remains dry. Next, oil-based ink is rolled over the stone. Where the stone is dry, the ink will stick, but where the stone is wet, the ink will not. The image is "brought up" to the desired darkness by passing an ink covered roller on it, then it is printed by pressing paper onto the surface to pick up the ink. Most commercial printing today is **lithographic printing**, using aluminum plates instead of limestone blocks, or offset printing, where the inked image is transferred from a metal plate to a rubber cylinder and then to paper. (Figure 2.16)

Figure 2.16 | Lithographic Press
Photographer: Clemens Pfeiffer
Author: User "Panoramafotors"
Source: Wikimedia Commons
License: Copyright - Permissions Granted

Stencil prints are made by passing inks through a porous fine mesh matrix. In **silkscreen printmaking**, for example, silk fabric is mounted tightly on a rigid frame. Areas of the fabric are blocked off to form an image. The fabric-lined frame is placed on top of paper, canvas, or cloth. Ink is then pulled across the frame with a rubber blade. Where the fabric is blocked off, the ink does not transfer. Where the fabric is clear, ink is pushed through onto the receiving surface.

It is important to be able to distinguish between original prints and reproductions. **Original prints** are handmade prints. Since each print is subtly different due to its handmade character, each print is considered an original work of art. (Figure 2.17) Editions of original prints can range from a few to dozens or hundreds of copies. **Reproductions** are mechanically produced. An original artwork is photographed; the photograph is then transferred to a print-

Figure 2.17 | Artist Preparing Linoleum Prints
Author: Kyle Van Horn
Source: Wikimedia Commons
License: CC BY 2.0

Figure 2.18 | Offset Press
Author: User "Rémih"
Source: Wikimedia Commons
License: CC BY-SA 3.0

ing plate on a mechanical press. Each print is nearly identical, and editions can run into the thousands or tens of thousands. (Figure 2.18)

The value of an individual print depends on a number of factors, including whether it is an original print or a reproduction and the number of prints in an edition. Recently a new kind of print has become popular, the **gicleé**. This is essentially a digital inkjet print. Those who buy gicleé prints should be careful that only acid-free paper and archival inks are used in its production. The fibers that make paper can come from many different sources, some of which contain acid that will turn the paper yellow with age. Over time, ink pigments can be fugitive, lose color intensity or even shift in hue. These effects will lower the value of the print. Acid-free paper and archival inks resist these defects and preserve the original appearance of the art object, thus maintaining its value.

2.4.2 Three-Dimensional Art

Three-dimensional art goes beyond the flat surface to encompass height, width, and depth. There are four main methods used in producing art in three dimensions. All three-dimensional art uses one or a combination of these four methods: carving, modeling, casting, or assembly. A form of three-dimensional art that emerged in the twentieth century is installation, a work in which the viewer is surrounded within a space or moves through a space that has been modified by the artist.

Sculpture can be either **freestanding**—"in the round"—or it can be **relief**—sculpture that projects from a background surface. There are two categories of relief sculpture: low relief and high relief. In **low relief**, the amount of projection from the background surface is limited. A good example of low relief sculpture would be coins, such as these ancient Roman types dating from c. 300 BCE to c. 400 CE. (Figure 2.19) Also, much Egyptian

Figure 2.19 | Common Roman Coins
Creator: Rasiel Suarez
Author: User "FSII"
Source: Wikimedia Commons
License: GFDL

wall art is low relief. (Figure 2.20) **High relief** sculpture is when more than half of the sculpted form projects from the background surface. This method generally creates an effect called **undercut**, in which some of the projected surface is separate from the background surface. Mythological scenes depicted on the Parthenon, an ancient Greek temple, (Figure 2.21) and the *Corporate Wars* series (*Corporate Wars*, Robert Longo: http://media.mutualart.com/Images/2 009_07/24/0205/582184/49777ffa-d61f-42aa-a3f1-9c47ed564b05_g.Jpeg) by Robert Longo (b. 1953, USA) are both examples of high relief using undercut.

Modeling is an **additive** process in which easily shaped materials like clay or plaster are built up to create a final form. Some modeled

Figure 2.21 | Lapith fighting a centaur
Author: User "Jastrow"
Source: Wikimedia Commons
License: Public Domain

Figure 2.20 | Egyptian Relief Carving
Author: User "GDK"
Source: Wikimedia Commons
License: Public Domain

Figure 2.22 | Bust of Maximilien Robespierre
Artist: Claude-André Deseine
Author: User "Rama"
Source: Wikimedia Commons
License: CC BY-SA 2.0

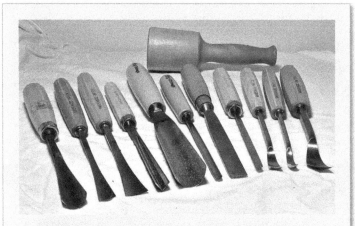

Figure 2.23 | A selection of woodcarving gouges, chisels, and a mallet
Author: User "Aerolin55"
Source: Wikimedia Commons
License: CC BY-SA 3.0

Figure 2.25 | Marble statue of Eirene (the personification of peace)
Artist: Kephisodotos
Source: Met Museum
License: OASC

forms begin with an **armature**, or rigid inner support often made of wire. An armature allows a soft or fluid material like wet clay, which would collapse under its own weight, to be built up. This method of sculpting includes most classical portrait sculpture in **terra cotta**, or baked clay. (Figure 2.22) Clay lends itself to modeling and is thus a popular medium for work of this kind, although clay may also be carved and cast.

Carving is the removal of material to form an art object. Carving is a **subtractive** process that usually begins with a block of material, most commonly stone. Tools—usually metal or metal tipped—are used to chip away the stone until the final form emerges. (Figure 2.23) The

Figure 2.24 | Sculptor Carving Stone
Author: Bain News Service
Source: Wikimedia Commons
License: Public Domain

Figure 2.26 | Naophorous Block Statue of a Governor of Sais, Psamtik
Source: Met Museum
License: OASC

Figure 2.27 | Jade ornament of flowers with grape design
Author: User "Mountain"
Source: Wikimedia Commons
License: CC BY-SA 3.0

main concern in carving, aside from achieving the correct form, is to be careful not to chip away too much material, as it cannot be replaced once it has been removed. (Figure 2.24) It is possible that the final shape of some carved stone sculptures result from not only the artist's intention, but also the subtle shifts caused by unpredictable variations in the stone causing the artist to "change course" when too much stone came away. This possibility is not to suggest that trained sculptors do not know the limits of their medium: artists often encounter surprises and innovative ones can sometimes work solutions that incorporate them.

Different kinds of stone vary in hardness as well as color and appearance. Not all stone is suitable for sculpting. Marble, a form of limestone, was preferred by the ancient Greeks and Romans for its softness and even color. (Figure 2.25) Diorite, schist (a form of slate), and Greywacke (a form of granite) were preferred by Egyptian and Mesopotamian cultures for their hardness and permanence. (Figure 2.26) The Chinese have traditionally used jade, a hard, brittle stone found in numerous shades, most commonly green, to indicate wisdom, power, and wealth. (Figure 2.27)

Wood is also often used as a carving material. Because of variations in grain size and texture, different species of wood have different sculptural qualities. In general, wood is prized for its flexibility and ease of forming, though it reacts to changes in humidity and lacks permanence. During the Heian era (794-1185 CE), the Japanese artist Jocho used joined wood to construct his sculpture of the *Seated Buddha*. (Figure 2.28)

Casting is a process that replaces, or **substitutes**, an initial sculptural material such as wax or clay with another, usually more permanent, material such as **bronze**, an **alloy**, or mixture of copper and tin. Casting is also a process that makes it possible to create multiple versions of the same object.

In the **lost wax process**, an original sculpture is modeled, often in clay, coated in wax, and then covered in plaster to create a **mold**. When the plaster dries, it is heated to melt the wax, which is poured out of the mold. Molten metal is then poured into the space within the mold between the (now lost) wax coating and the original sculpted form. When the metal has cooled and solidified, the plaster is broken away to reveal the cast metal object. (Figure 2.29) In order to create multiple versions of the object, the mold must be made in such a way that it can be removed without being destroyed. (Figure 2.30) This operation is generally achieved by separating a mold into several sections while the original is being cast. Sectional molds are also used to cast original objects that cannot be melted or otherwise removed from the mold. To cast the form, the original is removed, and the sections are then re-fastened together. In some cases, complex sculptures are cast in several pieces and the resulting metal sections are welded together.

Assembly, or assemblage, is a fairly recent type of sculpture. Before the modern period, carv-

Figure 2.28 | Seated Buddha
Artist: Jōchō
Author: User "Kosigrim"
Source: Wikimedia Commons
License: Public Domain

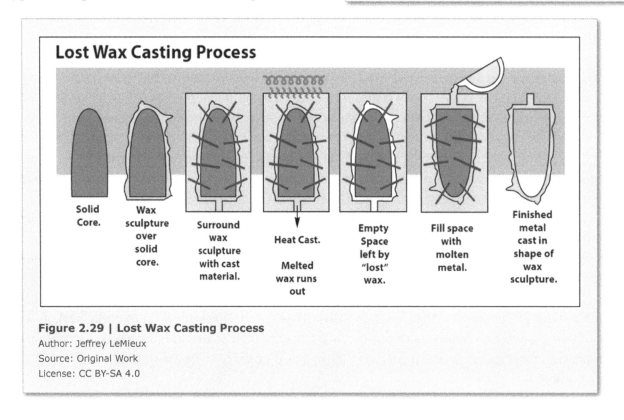

Figure 2.29 | Lost Wax Casting Process
Author: Jeffrey LeMieux
Source: Original Work
License: CC BY-SA 4.0

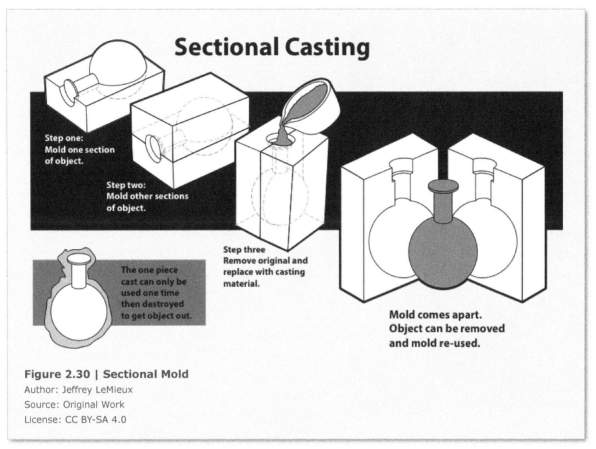

Figure 2.30 | Sectional Mold
Author: Jeffrey LeMieux
Source: Original Work
License: CC BY-SA 4.0

ing, casting, and modeling were the only accepted methods of making fine art sculpture. Recently, sculptors have enlarged their approach and turned to the process of **assembly**, manually attaching objects and materials together. Assemblies are often composed of **mixed media**, a process in which disparate objects and substances are used in order to achieve the desired effect.

Because she spent time near a cabinetry workshop, Louise Nevelson (1899-1988, Ukraine, lived USA) would retrieve wooden cut-offs and other discarded objects to use in her sculpture. Her art practice involved the use of **found objects**. Consider Nevelson's *Sky Cathedral*. (*Sky Cathedral*, Louise Nevelson: http://www.moma.org/collection/works/81006) She filled individual wooden boxes with found objects. She then arranged these boxes into large assemblies and painted them a single color, usually black or white. Each sub-unit box in the sculpture can be read as a separate point of view or separate world. The effect of the whole is to recognize that both unity and diversity are possible in a single artwork.

Installation is related to **assembly**, but the intent is to transform an interior or exterior space to create an experience that surrounds and involves the viewer in an unscripted interaction with the environment. The viewer is then immersed *in* the art, rather than experiencing the art from a distance. For example, Carsten Höller (b. 1961, Belgium, lives Sweden) installed *Test Site* in the Turbine Hall, a five-story open space, at the Tate Modern in London. (Figure 2.31) Part of a series of slides Höller created at museums worldwide, he wanted to encourage visitors

Figure 2.31 | *Test Site*
Artist: Carsten Höller
Author: User "The Lud"
Source: Wikimedia Commons
License: Public Domain

to use the practical, though unconventional, means of transport, and, while doing so, to experience the momentary loss of control and whatever emotional response each individual felt.

An installation that is intended for a particular location is called a **site-specific** installation. Good examples of site-specific installations would be *Tilted Arc* by Richard Serra (b. 1939, USA), (*Tilted Arc*, Richard Serra: https://en.wikipedia.org/wiki/File:Tilted_arc_en.jpg); *Lightning Field* by De Maria (1935-2013, USA), (*Lightning Field*, Walter de Maria: http://sculpture1.wikispaces.com/file/view/Walter_de_Maria_Lightning_Field_1977.jpg/310921734/800x686/Walter_de_Maria_Lightning_Field_1977.jpg); *Spiral Jetty* by Robert Smithson (1938-1973, USA), (Figure 2.32); and *Cadillac Ranch* by the art group known as Ant Farm. (Figure 2.33) In part because of the large scale of many of these works, installation is an increasingly popular form of public artwork.

Kinetic art is art that moves or appears to move. Generally this art is sculptural. Good examples of kinetic artworks are the suspended, freely moving **mobiles** of Alexander Calder (1898-1976, USA) that are meant to change shape as part of their design. (*Nénuphars Rouges*, Alexander Calder: http://www.wikiart.org/en/alexander-calder/red-lily-pads-n-nuphars-rouges-1956?utm_source=returned&utm_medium=referral&utm_campaign=referral) *Homage to New York* was a work of kinetic art Jean Tinguely (1925-1991, Switzerland) intended to self-destruct, although it never completed its purpose because a local

Figure 2.32 | *Spiral Jetty*
Artist: Robert Smithson
Author: User "Yonidebest"
Source: Wikimedia Commons
License: CC BY-SA 2.0

fire department stepped in and stopped the process. (*Homage to New York*, Jean Tinguely: http://www.wikiart.org/en/jean-tinguely/homage-to-new-york-1960) Reuben Margolin (USA) is a contemporary artist who uses intersecting waves to create beautifully undulating sculptures. Click the following link to view a video of Margolin's *Square Wave*: https://www.youtube.com/watch?v=4UQtDbybSWc. Beginning with simple materials like paper towel tubes, fishing swivels, and fishing line, and then moving to larger, more complex

Figure 2.33 | *Cadillac Ranch, Amarillo*
Artist: Ant Farm
Author: Richie Diesterheft
Source: Wikimedia Commons
License: CC BY 2.0

sculptures using more permanent materials like wood, metal, and wire, Margolin has made a career of creating meditatively flowing sculptures.

2.4.3 Four-Dimensional Art

Four-dimensional art, or **time-based art** is a relatively new mode of art practice that includes video, projection mapping, performance, and new media art.

Video art uses the relatively new technology of projected moving images. These images can be displayed on electronic monitors or projected onto walls or even buildings; they use light as a medium. The early video constructions of Nam June Paik (1932-2006, South Korea, lived USA) are a good example. In *TV Cello*, video monitors are assembled in the shape of a cello. (*TV Cello*, Nam June Paik: http://a141.idata.over-blog.com/356x499/1/96/04/42/s-rie-F/Paik-N.-J.-TV-Cello.jpg) When a bow was drawn across this object, images of a woman playing a cello appeared on the screens.

Projection mapping is another use of video projection. One or more two- or three-dimensional objects (often buildings) are spatially mapped into a virtual program that then allows the image to conform to the surface of the object upon which it is projected. (Figure 2.34) Evan Roth (b. 1978, USA, lives France) creates graffiti as a video projection and then photographs the results; thus, the work is temporary. This method of spatially augmented reality has been used by numerous artists (and advertisers) to "tag" everything from public spaces to the human face, without leaving permanent marks.

Performance art is art in which the artist's medium is an action. Performance artworks are generally documented by photography, but the artwork is in the act itself. *Cut Piece* is a performance work Yoko Ono (b. 1933, Japan, lives USA) originally created in 1964 in which audience members were given scissors to cut off pieces of her clothing while the artist sat on a stage.

(*Cut Piece*, Yoko Ono: https://en.wikipedia.org/wiki/File:CutPieceOno.jpeg) As the artist passively allowed her garments to fall away, the participants and viewers were in control of her transformation from whole to segmented.

New media art usually refers to interactive works such as digital art, computer animation, video games, robotics, and 3D printing, where artists explore the expressive potential of these new creative technologies. The international connectivity of the Internet has ushered in a globalization of information exchange which includes the arts. One example of the use of new media in art would be *10,000 Moving Cities* by Marc Lee (b. 1969, Switzerland). In this work, a viewer wears a video projection headset in which images from a chosen city are projected onto a digital urban architecture. The viewer can move within the new space through head motion. Real time social-media images and text from the chosen city are also captured and projected.

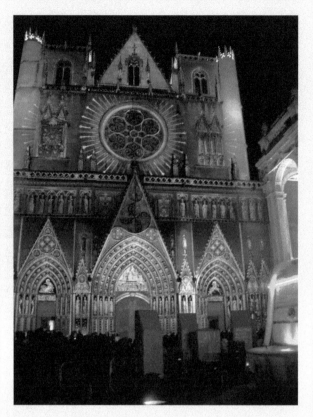

Figure 2.34 | *Cathédrale St Jean illuminée*
Author: User "Gonedelyon"
Source: Wikimedia Commons
License: User "Gonedelyon"

2.5 FORM AND COMPOSITION

When looking at art, many people today take a holistic or **gestalt** approach to understanding it. In this approach, the work of art is experienced as a single unified whole and an intuitive conclusion is drawn. This approach to art is a good place to start, but it can also be useful to examine the individual parts of an artwork and the relationships those parts have to the whole. When we examine an artwork by taking it apart, we are looking at its design. Design is divided into two broad categories: the elements of design and the principles of design. The **elements of design** are the physical parts of the artwork, or the **form**. The **principles of design** are the ways in which those parts are arranged or used, or the **composition**.

2.5.1 Elements of Design

A **design** is a governing plan or approach by which various parts of an artwork are created and assembled. It is rare to find a work of art that is entirely accidental or has come wholly out of the unconscious intuition of an artist. Further, looking at the way in which various parts of a work of art are arranged—even an intuitive or accidental work—can reveal clues to the goals and beliefs of the artist, the community in which the artist has worked, and the problems the work of art was meant to address.

There are six basic elements of design: line, shape, mass/volume, perspective, texture, and color. One way to think of these elements of design is to "walk up the ladder" of dimension. Our perceived world has three dimensions of space and one of time. Mathematically, a point has zero dimensions. A line has one dimension, length. A shape has two dimensions, length and height. A form with mass or volume has three dimensions, length, height, and width. In moving from points to volumes, we have "walked up the ladder" of dimension from zero to three. In addition to the three dimensions of physical space, there are two more things artists can incorporate into a given work. They can introduce texture, and they can introduce color.

Here is a brief explanation of the definition and dynamics of each element of design.

2.5.1.1 Line

Line is the first order element of design. A **line** is an infinite series of points that are arranged in a direction. The direction of a line may be straight (unchanging) or curved (changing). All kinds of objects are **linear**, or predominantly formed by using lines. **Calligraphy**, or "beautiful writing," is one popular use of line. The character of line in writing has two main functions. First, the linear figure or shape of a written symbol denotes its meaning. Second, the manner in which the figure is created can be seen as expressive in itself. A **tughra**, or the calligraphic signature of a sultan, and the refined text of Arabic calligraphy are renowned for their expressive beauty, as are many works of Asian script. In many writing cultures, the beauty of the script is as important as the message the script contains. (Figure 2.35)

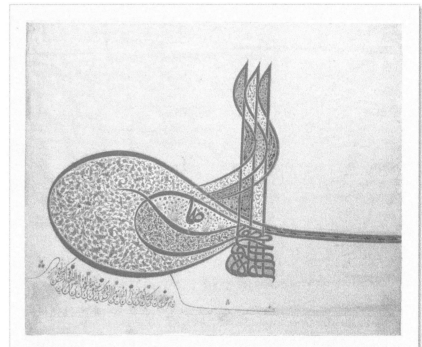

Figure 2.35 | Tughra (Official Signature) of Sultan Süleiman the Magnificent
Source: Met Museum
License: OASC

One quality of line is gesture. **Gesture** is the line produced by the movement of the artist's hand, arm, or body, of a kind of dance with the material, as can be seen in this photograph of Jackson Pollock in the midst of painting. (Jackson Pollock: https://upload.wikimedia.org/wikipedia/en/b/b7/Jackson-Pollock.jpg) For example, short, uneven staccato lines may be read as impatient, or lacking in confidence or grace. Evenly drawn horizontal lines express calm. Straight lines can represent rigidity, which is neither good nor bad, but depends on context. A rigid bridge is a good thing for those who depend on it not to give way. A rigid tree in a windstorm will sometimes be uprooted.

Contour is the line where differing areas meet and form edges. Human visual perception includes an enhanced ability to detect edges in nature. Contour lines follow the shapes of objects where they stand out from backgrounds. In mapmaking, contour lines indicate the shape of the landscape in regular increments of vertical height. On contour maps, lines that appear close together indicate a rapid change in height. Lines that are far apart indicate more gentle slopes. (GroundTruth Contours: http://wiki.openstreetmap.org/w/images/thumb/b/b5/GroundTruthContours_Detail.png/300px-GroundTruthContours_Detail.png)

Crosshatching is the use of uniformly spaced intersecting lines that create the perception of value

Figure 2.36 | Nude Male Figure with a Sword
Artist: Alexandre Cabanel
Source: Met Museum
License: OASC

or light and dark. These crosshatching lines generally follow the shape of an object. (Figures 2.4 and 2.36)

Some lines are not drawn at all. Instead, they are **implied** or suggested by an intentional alignment of shapes. The image of the square inside the circle is an example of implied line. (Figure 2.37) Lines that converge beyond the edge of an artwork are another because they imply a distant intersection. A third example of a line that is not actually there is **psychic** line. Two people looking at one another in an artwork create a psychic line between them.

Line has **expressive** content. By its nature, a line compels the viewer to follow

Figure 2.37 | Square inside a circle, demonstration of implied lines
Author: Jeffrey LeMieux
Source: Original Work
License: CC BY-SA 4.0

along its path. The character of the line can control the direction, speed, and attention of the viewer. The movement of a line can be curved or angular. It can progress smoothly or with a staccato rhythm. A line can be thick or thin, pale or bold. These qualities are "read" rationally and emotionally; thus, line can have an expressive and emotional content that can often be found by viewer introspection.

Line is not just a two-dimensional design element. For example, wire is a linear medium that can be extended into three dimensions. Alexander Calder's wire sculptures and portraits are fine examples of the expressive power of line in three dimensions. (*Acrobats*, Alexander Calder: http://www.calder.org/system/post_images/images/000/001/082/medium/A00504. jpg?1352222725) Another example is Pablo Picasso drawing in space with light for photographer Gjon Mili (1904-1984, Albania, lived USA) for *Life* magazine in 1949. (Light Drawings, Pablo Picasso: http://www.designboom.com/art/pablo-picassos-light-drawings-from-1949/)

2.5.1.2 Shape

The design element of shape is the next element in the walk up the ladder of dimension. **Shape** has two dimensions, length and width. Shapes can be regular or irregular, simple or complex. Shapes can have hard or soft edges. **Hard-edged** shapes have clearly defined boundaries, while **soft-edged** shapes slowly fade into their backgrounds. There are two broad categories of shape: geometric and organic. **Geometric shapes** are regular and ordered shapes using straight lines and curves. **Organic shapes** are generally irregular and often chaotic. Hans Arp (1886-1966, France, lived Switzerland), in his work *Untitled*, used torn paper and cut shapes to create an abstract composition. While squares are geometric objects, Arp's torn and irregular edges transform them into organic shapes. The orientation of

Figure 2.38 | Untitled (Collage with Squares Arranged according to the Laws of Chance)
Artist: Jean Hans Arp
Source: MoMA
License: Public Domain

those shapes roughly approximates a grid structure, but again, their deviation from a regular order implies a chaotic and accidental arrangement. In this work, Arp is dancing on the "edge of order." (Figure 2.38)

In two-dimensional artworks, shapes are figures placed on a two-dimensional surface that is known as a **ground**. This creates a relationship between foreground and background known as the **figure/ground relation**. The **figure** is the object that appears to be in front of the ground. In some artworks this relationship is intentionally unclear. In this case, an effect known as figure/ground reversal can occur. In **figure/ground reversal**, what was seen as the positive shape of the figure can also be seen as the negative space of the ground. This effect disrupts the sense of space in an artwork and disorients the viewer. (*Escher Woodcut II Strip 3*, Maurits Cornelis Escher: http://www.tau.ac.il/~tsurxx/FigureGround/Escher2.GIF)

2.5.1.3 Mass/Volume

The next and final step up the dimensional ladder is volume **or** mass. **Volume** has three dimensions: length, width, and height. Volumes may have interior or exterior contours, and they may be closed or open in form. **Mass** is the quantity of matter, often meaning its weight. A **closed form** is a volume that is not pierced or perforated. One goal of ancient Egyptian sculpture was to last for eternity. Therefore, they used closed sculptural forms, which are more structurally robust and more resistant to wear or breakage. (Figures 2.26 and 2.39) Empty space surrounds a closed form but does not move through it. Conversely,

Figure 2.39 | Sphinx of Hatshepsut
Source: Met Museum
License: OASC

empty space surrounds but also moves through an **open form**. Open form sculptures are closer in shape to the figures they represent and thus are more lifelike or "true" to the original reference.

Modern sculptors such as Henry Moore (1898-1986, England) have explored the abstract use of closed and open forms, as well as negative and positive space. (*Reclining Figure 1969-70*, Henry Moore: https://upload.wikimedia.org/wikipedia/commons/0/08/PikiWiki_Israel_12097_reclining_figure_by_henry_moore_in_tel_aviv.jpg) In three-dimensional art, **positive space** is the space occupied by a given volume, while **negative space** is the empty space within that volume. Notice how the figure twists around an imaginary boundary. The "saddle" in the middle suggests an invisible weight pressing down on the form there. This sculpture depends as much on the empty space around it as it does on the volume occupied by the bronze. In addition, its mass is lessened by the openness of its form, especially when compared to ancient Egyptian sculpture, an entirely closed form.

To convey the three dimensionality, mass and volume, of forms on a flat surface, artists use *chiaroscuro* (Italian: "clear-dark") or varying shades of light and dark. As a form turns toward a light source it appears brighter, and as it turns away from the light source it appears darker; the shift in light and shadow creates the illusion of volume in space. The face and hands of Leonardo's *Mona Lisa* are considered masterpieces of chiaroscuro. (Figure 2.7)

2.5.1.4 Perspective

Perspective in art is the illusion of space on a flat surface. Before the discovery of the geometric system of linear perspective in fifteenth-century Italy, the illusion of space was created by using three main visual cues to the recession of space. These three cues are height, scale, and overlap. Objects that are higher on the drawing surface, objects that are smaller in scale, and objects that are partially obscured by other objects all appear further away in space. (Figure 2.40)

Linear perspective is based on the regular geometric recession of space. Linear perspective uses a vanishing point and horizon line. The **vanishing point** is the spot where all receding lines seem to converge on the horizon line. The **horizon line** is the set of all possible eye-level vanishing points. (Figure 2.41) **Orthogonal lines** are the lines that appear to meet at the vanishing point and imply the regular recession of space. Horizon lines and vanishing points can provide clues to the artist's intent. In Leonardo's *Last Supper*, for example, the artist has located the vanishing point directly behind the head of Jesus. (see Figure 1.25) Because the vanishing point is the viewer's vision extended infinitely in one direction, Leonardo's placement of the vanishing point behind the head of Jesus associates Him with the infinity of the Christian God.

Before linear perspective was formulated as a coherent geometric system, painters used intuitive perspective to portray receding space. **Intuitive perspective** acknowledges that receding lines converge, but does not recognize that they converge at a single horizon line and vanishing point. Nonetheless, even

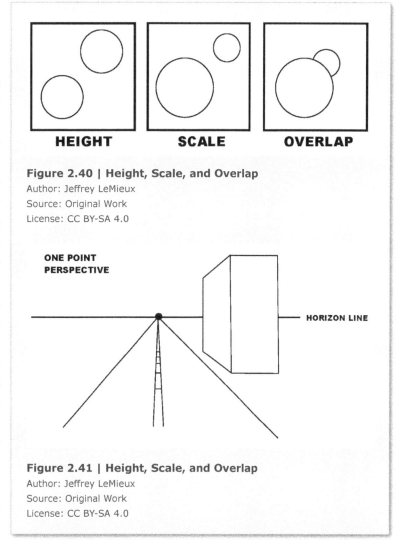

Figure 2.40 | Height, Scale, and Overlap
Author: Jeffrey LeMieux
Source: Original Work
License: CC BY-SA 4.0

Figure 2.41 | Height, Scale, and Overlap
Author: Jeffrey LeMieux
Source: Original Work
License: CC BY-SA 4.0

when paintings lack a rigorously coherent geometric system of linear perspective, determining where the horizon would be can inform us about how the artist views the subject. Compare two paintings of the same name, *Madonna Enthroned*, one by Cimabue (1240-1302, Italy) and the other by Giotto (1266/7-1337, Italy). (Figures 2.42 and 2.43) Both paintings use intuitive perspective. In Cimabue's painting of 1285, the implied horizon is low and the viewer sits at the foot of the throne, while Giotto's image, painted in 1310, has the horizon higher, and thus the viewer is on the same level as the Madonna. This difference of viewpoint signifies changing ideas about the Madonna's relation to the individual. Cimabue's painting places the viewer in subservient homage, while Giotto's painting may be seen as more approachable, indicative of a tiny but significant shift in European thought that eventually blossomed into the Italian Renaissance.

There are different types of linear perspective. The main types are one-, two-, and three-point perspective. The distinction is in the number of vanishing points used. **One-point perspective** uses a horizon line and one main vanishing point and is normally used when simple views are

Figure 2.42 | Santa Trinita Madonna
Artist: Cimabue
Author: User "Eugene"
Source: Wikimedia Commons
License: Public Domain

Figure 2.43 | The Ognissanti Madonna
Artist: Giotto
Author: User "Shizhao"
Source: Wikimedia Commons
License: Public Domain

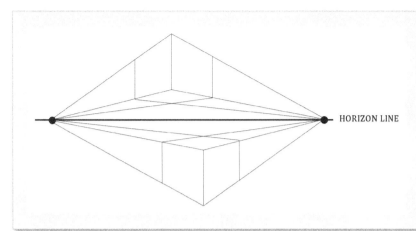

Figure 2.44 | Two-Point Perspective
Author: Jeffrey LeMieux
Source: Original Work
License: CC BY-SA 4.0

HORIZON LINE

depicted, such as a railway track disappearing into the distance directly in front of the spectator. **Two-point perspective** uses a horizon line and two separated vanishing points to present the illusion of a space that recedes in two directions. (Figure 2.44) **Three-point perspective** incorporates the recession of space in a third, vertical direction above or below the horizon line as well as the two horizontal directions in two-point perspective. As tall buildings recede upward from street level, they also diminish in apparent size in the same way railroad tracks appear to converge in the distance toward the horizon. (Figure 2.45)

Many people make the mistake of thinking that linear perspective gives a completely accurate picture of the world. It does not. Linear perspective is a limited tool for representing how the world looks. It is considered sufficiently "accurate" only within a limited "cone of perception" of about 60 degrees. So while linear perspective is an excellent tool to represent our experience of space, it has limitations that should be recognized.

Atmospheric perspective is the way in which the illusion of distance is created on a flat surface through the use of color and focus. In a landscape that extends into the distance, the haze of the intervening air alters the colors and clarity of objects. The further away an object is from the viewer, the more it approaches the color of air, which is a light blue-gray tone. Dark objects become lighter and more blue as they recede from the viewer. Additionally, the contrast between light and dark colored objects and the perception of detail decrease with increasing distance. Albert Bierstadt (1830-1902, Germany, lived USA) used this effect in his painting *The Rocky*

Figure 2.45 | *New York Daily News Building*
Artist: Hugh Ferriss
Author: Dover Publications
Source: Wikimedia Commons
License: OASC

Mountains, Lander's Peak to give a sense of monumental space. (Figure 2.46)

2.5.1.5 Texture

The term **texture** describes the surface quality of an artwork. Texture is an important element of design because it engages the sense of touch as well as vision. Objects can be rough or smooth, wet or dry, sticky or slick, hard or soft, brittle or flexible. The two main approaches to texture are *actual* texture and *implied* or simulated texture. **Actual texture** is primarily—though not exclusively—sculptural, while **implied texture** is primarily used in two-dimensional works of art.

Figure 2.46 | *The Rocky Mountains, Lander's Peak*
Artist: Albert Bierstadt
Source: Met Museum
License: OASC

The painters of the Northern Renaissance and the Dutch Golden Age, the fifteenth to the seventeenth centuries, were very interested in the simulation of a wide variety of textures. One main goal of artists from those periods was to excel at telling the truth about the material world. They worked to capture the full visual range of the sense of touch. Rembrandt van Rijn (1606-1669, Netherlands) is well known for his use of **impasto**, or very thick application of paint, in order to heighten the sense of reality in many of his paintings by adding actual texture. This can be seen in his handling of flesh on some of his self-portraits, as well as his rendering of metal and jewelry in his painting of *Belshazzar's Feast*. (Figure 2.47)

2.5.1.6 Color

Color is the most prominent element of design and is one of the most powerful and yet subjective elements in art. The nineteenth-century American transcendentalist Ralph Waldo Emerson noted this subjective quality of color when he wrote, "nature always wears the colors of the spirit."[1] Ideas about color

Figure 2.47 | *Belshazzar's Feast*
Artist: Rembrandt van Rijn
Source: Wikiart
License: Public Domain

1   C. A. Bartol, *Ralph Waldo Emerson: A Discourse in West Church* (Boston, Mass: A. Williams & Co., 1882), 14.

can be grouped into three broad categories: the history of color, physics of color, and perception of color.

The earliest use of color was limited to what kinds of pigments or coloring agents could be found in the local environment: ochres (yellow-browns) from various colors of earth, blacks and grays from ashes and burned wood or charcoal, reds and yellows from minerals, plants, and insects. Paleolithic cave painters used these materials for their murals. In addition to natural pigments, ancient Egyptians formulated synthetic pigments such as powdered glass to create Egyptian blue, a distinctive hue used on statues, walls, and monuments. In the Roman Empire, a rare form of purple was extracted from a particular kind of snail and, because of its rarity, was used primarily for royal garments. During the Renaissance, a deep blue was made from a finely ground gemstone, lapis lazuli.

Egyptians associated colors with the gods; the god Amon had blue skin, and Osiris had green. The ancient Greeks took a more scientific approach to color. The ancient Greek philosopher Empedocles thought that color fell into four categories: white/light, dark/black, yellow, and red. The ancient Chinese associated color with the five elements taught in traditional physics: water (black), metal (white), wood (green), earth (yellow), and fire (red). In a number of Asian traditions, black is the color of heaven and white is the color of death or mourning. In western culture the opposite is the case.

Figure 2.48 | Prism
Author: User "D-Kuru"
Source: Wikimedia Commons
License: CC BY-SA 3.0

Modern ideas about color were greatly refined beginning in the fifteenth century by architect and art theorist Leon Battista Alberti (1404-1472, Italy). In his treatise *Della pittura* (*On Painting*), published in 1435, Alberti stated:

> Through the mixing of colors infinite other hues are born, but there are only four true colors from which more and more other kinds of colors may be thus created. Red is the color of fire, blue of the air, green of the water, and grey of the earth . . . white and black are not true colors but are alterations of other colors.[2]

From this early framework, others made further discoveries.

The term "color" describes the sensation caused by variations in the wavelength and intensity of light as it interacts with the human eye. **Visible light** is the small portion of the **electromagnetic spectrum** that can be seen by humans. When the white light of the sun is passed through a prism, it is **refracted** into the colors of the rainbow from red through orange, yellow, green, and blue to violet. (Figure 2.48)

---

2   Leon Battista Alberti, *On Painting*, trans. John R. Spencer (New Haven, Connecticut: Yale University Press, 1956), 49-50.

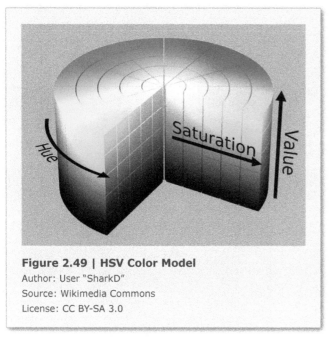

Figure 2.49 | HSV Color Model
Author: User "SharkD"
Source: Wikimedia Commons
License: CC BY-SA 3.0

Color as perceived by humans can be broken into three discrete parts: hue, saturation, and brightness. (Figure 2.49) **Hue** is the wavelength of a given color. Longer wavelength colors appear on the red end of the spectrum, while shorter wavelength colors are on the violet end. Hue is the color "name," e.g., red, yellow, blue, green, etc. Color can be either subtractive or additive. **Saturation** is the purity of a color and ranges from a neutral gray to the pure color while holding brightness as a constant. **Brightness** is the lightness or darkness of a color and ranges from fully illuminated (the pure hue) to fully darkened (black). Each pure hue also has a relative brightness, for example, pure yellow has a greater brightness than pure blue.

Subtractive color, or reflective color, occurs when white light is reflected off a surface, and all the colors of the spectrum are absorbed by that surface except for the color that is reflected back to the viewer. Subtractive color mixing starts with the **primary colors** of red, yellow, and blue. When these colors are mixed, the **secondary colors** of green, orange, and purple, are created. Mixing yellow and blue makes green, mixing red and yellow makes orange, and mixing red and blue makes purple.

The English mathematician and physicist Sir Isaac Newton demonstrated in the seventeenth century that white light, when refracted through a prism, could be separated into the visible spectrum. In the nineteenth century, writer and statesmen Johann Wolfgang von Goethe and chemist Michel Eugène Chevruel separately published research that concluded that red, yellow, and blue were primary colors and that all other colors could be mixed from them. At the beginning of the twentieth century, industrial chemists further refined the understanding of printing inks and derived the CMYK (cyan, magenta, yellow, and black) subtractive color model: beginning with white, as one adds color, the mixture moves toward black. (Figure 2.50)

With the advent of television, computers and digital imaging, the additive model of RGB (red, green, blue) in which colors are added together and the HSB (hue, saturation,

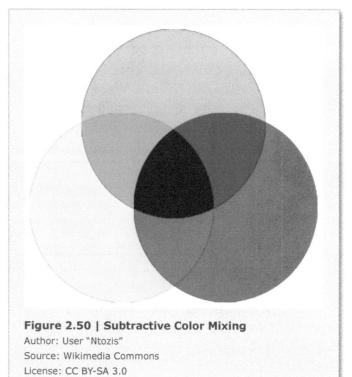

Figure 2.50 | Subtractive Color Mixing
Author: User "Ntozis"
Source: Wikimedia Commons
License: CC BY-SA 3.0

and brightness) color system, based on human perception, have become industry standards. **Additive color**, or transmission color, occurs when light of different colors is projected. The primary hues of additive color are red, green, and blue. This is the RGB color model. (Figure 2.51) When red and green lights overlap, yellow is seen. When red and blue lights overlap, magenta is seen, and when green and blue lights overlap, cyan appears. These are the secondary hues of additive color. When red, green, and blue lights all overlap, white light is seen. Television screens are actually tiny dots, or pixels, of red, green, and blue glowing lights. The colors we see coming off those screens are additive.

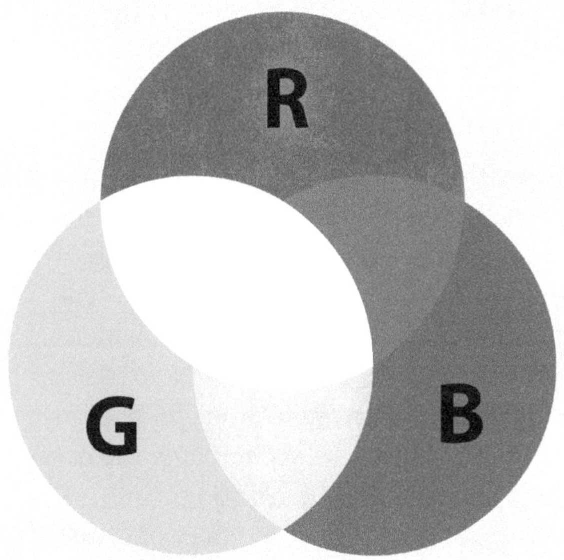

Our RGB model of additive color is directly dependent on how human eyes function. The human retina is a sheet of neurons that coats the inside of the eye. Within this sheet of neu-

Figure 2.51 | Additive Color
Author: User "SharkD"
Source: Wikimedia Commons
License: CC BY-SA 3.0

rons, there are specialized neurons called rods and cones. Rods are neurons that are sensitive to changes in light intensity, and cones are sensitive to red, green, or blue light. The reason we have RGB computer monitors is because we have RGB eyes.

Artists sometimes intentionally exploit the physiology of human vision. Because human vision is limited by unique biology, certain effects become possible. Neurons store chemical neurotransmitters to send signals. If a neuron must continually "fire" because it is being continuously stimulated, it can deplete its supply of neurotransmitter. There is a slight delay between the depletion and restoration

Figure 2.52 | U.S. Flag with Inverted Color
Author: User "Mike"
Source: Wikimedia Commons
License: Public Domain

of this chemical supply within the neuron. In the interim, an **after-image** occurs. Look at the green, orange, and black flag for 10 seconds, then look at a blank wall or empty white space. (Figure 2.52) For a few moments, you will see the **complement**, or opposite, of green (red), the complement of orange (blue), and the complement of black (white) in their correct place on the American flag. The fading of this image indicates that the neurotransmitters in the retina have been replenished.

This effect was regularly used by artists during the Impressionist movement (c. 1870-1886). Consider *Impression Sunrise* by Claude Monet (1840-1926, France), one of the first Impressionist paintings. (Figure 2.53) Looking for more than a moment at the expanse of blue in the painting "exhausts" the sensation of blue and creates a complementary afterimage response, which is orange. Then when we look at the orange of the rising sun, we see not only the orange pigment on the painting itself, we also have the additional effect of "tired blue" in our retina. For this reason, the orange paint of the sun looks brighter than it would if we saw that color by itself. Many Impressionist artists intentionally used this effect, and this is one reason why Impressionist paintings tend to look so vibrantly colored.

Figure 2.53 | *Impression Sunrise*
Artist: Claude Monet
Author: User "Paris 16"
Source: Wikimedia Commons
License: Public Domain

In his *Homage to the Square* series of paintings that he began in 1949, the Bauhaus artist Josef Albers (1888-1967, Germany, lived USA) experimented with the relative perception of color. (*Homage to the Square*, Josef Albers: https://upload.wikimedia.org/wikipedia/en/2/20/Josef_Albers's_painting_'Homage_to_the_Square'%2C_1965.jpg) His main interest was to demonstrate how a color can be affected by other colors that surround it. His book, Interaction of Color (1963), showed that perception of a single color can change depending on context. To demonstrate this, look at the accompanying image. (Figure 2.54) The band of gray in the center is one single color, but it appears to shift when placed on a contrasting background.

Contemporary artists employ specific terms for different uses of color. Natural, or **local color**, describes the body color of a given object. **Observed color**, on the other hand, is how the percep-

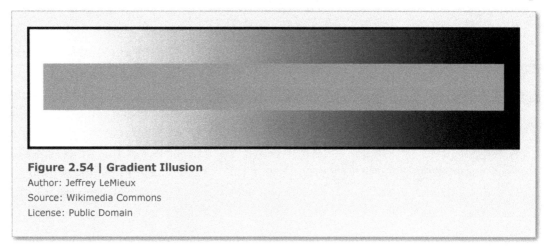

Figure 2.54 | Gradient Illusion
Author: Jeffrey LeMieux
Source: Wikimedia Commons
License: Public Domain

tion of that local color changes as light shifts on an object. In Monet's series of paintings of the Rouen Cathedral, his depictions of different lighting conditions are a good example of the difference between local color and observed color. The color of the stone of the Cathedral is a medium gray. But at different times of day, such as the waning light of sunset, it will reflect the oranges and blues of the lingering sun and the growing shadows. (Figure 2.55)

The Fauves were a group of artists in the early twentieth century who used **intuitive color** as the basis of their approach to making art. They were more interested in the expressive power of color than robotically reporting the local or observed color of their subjects. Consider this portrait by Henri Matisse (1869-1954, France) of his wife, Amélie Matisse. (Figure 2.56) Clearly she did not in reality have a green stripe running down the center of her face. The colors chosen by the artist were meant to express something other than simple visual observation.

Another aspect of color used by artists is **color temperature**. Colors can be either warm or cool. The **warm** end of the spectrum includes red, orange, and yellow. The **cool** end of the visible spectrum contains green, blue, and purple. That said, even yellow can be cool, and even blue can be warm. Warm and cool colors interact in different ways and artists are trained to notice and use this difference; for example, warm colors seem to "advance" while cool colors "recede" in space and consequently shapes represented in those colors appear to be at different depths.

In organizing ideas about color, artists and art theorists have evolved a series of color schemes, or ordered relations between different colors. A **monochromatic** color scheme uses a single color. *The Old Guitarist* by Picasso is a good example of a monochromatic color scheme. (Figure 2.57) The pose of the figure, the texture of the ragged clothing and hair, and the dominating use of blue work together to create a unified emotional response of weariness and loneliness to the image.

A **complementary** color scheme uses colors opposite to each other on the color wheel. As mentioned ear-

Figure 2.55 | *Rouen Cathedral, Facade (Sunset)*
Artist: Claude Monet
Author: User "Ribberlin"
Source: Wikimedia Commons
License: Public Domain

Figure 2.56 | *Portrait of Madame Matisse (The green line)*
Artist: Henri Matisse
Author: User "Sparkit"
Source: Wikimedia Commons
License: Public Domain

Figure 2.57 | *The Old Guitarist*
Artist: Pablo Picasso
Author: User "Chimino"
Source: Wikimedia Commons
License: Public Domain

Figure 2.58 | *Starry Night*
Artist: Vincent van Gogh
Author: User "Dcoetzee"
Source: Wikimedia Commons
License: Public Domain

lier, Impressionist painters exploited the effect of complementary color schemes to heighten the brilliance of their color palettes. While not an Impressionist, in his painting *The Starry Night*, Van Gogh (1853-1890, Netherlands, lived France) uses the blue of the night sky to charge the orange of his crescent moon. (Figure 2.58)

An **analogous** color scheme uses only one area of the color wheel. If the color green is chosen as the anchor color for the scheme, for example, the artist will use colors that occur between the yellow and blue points on the wheel. *Still Life with a Glass and Oysters* by Jan Davidsz. de Heem (1606-1684, Netherlands, lived Belgium) is a good example of an orange/yellow/green analogous scheme. (Figure 2.59) There are many other color schemes that are used for various applications, but these three suffice to illustrate the idea.

2.5.2 Principles of Design

The elements of design are the visual components that artists use to make artworks. The principles of design are

Figure 2.59 | *Still Life with a Glass and Oysters*
Artist: Jan Davidszoon de Heem
Source: Met Museum
License: OASC

the various ways in which those elements or components are arranged to produce a desired effect. There are as many ways to approach the arrangement of the elements of art as there are artists. Each work of art is unique in its conception, design, and execution. Recent developments in the visual arts have introduced accidental and irrational approaches to artmaking. In these approaches, the outcome of the work of art is not planned. While these works of art may be said to lack conscious design, sometimes they are successful. It is often possible to attribute the success of irrationally or accidentally produced works of art to one or more operating principles of organization. Becoming aware of the principles of design in a work of art allows the viewer to add depth to the analysis of those works. What follows are five principles of design. The list is not exhaustive but is a good place to start.

2.5.2.1 Unity/Variety

Unity is found in similarity, while variety is found in difference. A design that shows **unity** is one in which the elements of the work or relations between the elements are similar or identical. Leonardo's *Mona Lisa* (see Figure 2.7) is considered a breakthrough in Italian Renaissance art because the soft edges of the figure are similar in approach to the soft tones of the muted background, thus unifying the image. A design that shows **variety** is one in which the elements of the work are varied in size, color, shape, or some other attribute. One concern with the overuse of unity in design is visual monotony. Visual unity may occur on a **conceptual** level as well as a physical one. Elements that are chosen based on a theme can display conceptual unity and yet display a variety of form. A work of art that lacks variety may be monotonous and lack interest. Many artists introduce variety into their compositions by making sure that no two intervals are the same. An **interval** is the space between elements, figures, or objects in a work of art.

2.5.2.2 Scale/Proportion

The design principle of **scale** and **proportion** is the issue of size of elements both individually and in relation to other elements. A famous example of the subtle use of scale is the relative size of the figures in Michelangelo's *Pietà*. (Figure 2.60) The sculpture is a depiction of Mary holding the body of her son Jesus after His crucifixion. If we measure the bodies of Jesus and Mary from heel to knee, knee to hip, and so on, and then compare them, we find that Mary is larger than Jesus. In addition, the fig-

Figure 2.60 | *Pietà*
Artist: Michelangelo
Author: User "Juan M Romero"
Source: Wikimedia Commons
License: CC BY-SA 4.0

ure of Mary is out of proportion, that is, the sizes of the parts of her body are not in alignment. This unusual use of scale and proportion serves to infantilize Jesus in order to subtly emphasize the mother/child relationship. Another use of scale and proportion is the use of forced perspective. (Figure 2.61) **Forced perspective** is the arrangement of figure and ground that distorts the scale of objects, making small objects appear large or large objects appear small by juxtaposing them with opposites. Forced perspective is most convincing when done photographically.

2.5.2.3 Balance

The design principle of **balance** is the issue of visual "weight." Design elements like lines and shapes can attract our attention in a number of ways. For example, they can be brightly colored, they can be large in relation to other similar shapes, or they can be textured in unusual ways. Compositional balance is achieved when these competing visual weights are roughly equivalent. There are two kinds of compositional balance: symmetrical and asymmetrical.

Figure 2.61 | The Leaning Tower of Pisa: Forced Perspective
Author: User "Vin7474"
Source: Wikimedia Commons
License: Public Domain

Figure 2.62 | *The Great Wave off Kanagawa*
Artist: Katsushika Hokusai
Author: User "Durova"
Source: Wikimedia Commons
License: Public Domain

The lines and shapes in a composition that uses the principle of **symmetrical** balance are usually equally arranged around an **axis**, or central line. In *The Sacrament of the Last Supper* by Salvador Dali (1904-1989, Spain), notice the balance of like forms to the left and right of the central figure of Jesus. (*The Sacrament of the Last Supper*, Salvador Dali: https://upload. wikimedia.org/wikipedia/en/f/f1/ Dali_-_The_Sacrament_of_the_Last_ Supper_-_lowres.jpg) Vertical and horizontal axes are generally reserved for very stable compositions, and this strategy is often used in a religious context to imply unchanging truth.

Asymmetrical balance is achieved when visual weights do not correspond to one another in shape, size, or placement; they are not distributed equally in a composition. The woodblock print *The Great Wave off Kanagawa* by Katsushika Hokusai (1760-1849, Japan) and *Still Life with Apples and a Pot of Primroses* by Paul Cézanne (1839-1906, France) are good examples of asymmetrical compositions. The large space to the right of the Hokusai's Great Wave "offsets" the approaching wave in the left half of the composition. (Figure 2.62) In

a similar way, the large gray wall to the left in Cézanne's *Still Life with Apples* serves to offset the visually complex flowerpot on the right. (Figure 2.63) In each work, nearly one-third of the composition (the sky and the wall) is unoccupied, so to speak; there are no objects in those areas. Within the two-dimensional space of the work, however, we "read" each blank area as having a visual weight that counterbalances the forms in the remainder of the compositional space.

It is not always necessary for an artwork to be balanced. An obvious imbalance can produce the effect of unsteadiness, disorientation or distress, which can become a useful part of the larger idea

Figure 2.63 | *Still Life with Apples and a Pot of Primroses*
Artist: Paul Cézanne
Source: Met Museum
License: OASC

within the work of art. The large empty spaces in the painting by Odd Nerdrum (b. 1944, Norway) carry substantial visual weight and imply both physical and psychological isolation. (*Man and Abandoned Landscape*, Odd Nerdrum: https://s-media-cache-ak0.pinimg.com/736x/27/a3/3b/27a33b6c5d3c9e087d20f7cb3c34296a.jpg)

2.5.2.4 Emphasis/Movement

The design principle of emphasis or movement is the intentional use of directional forces to move the viewer's attention through a work of art. When we see a color shift within a shape, this implies movement. And, when we see a line in a work of art, we are compelled to follow it. For example, arrows of any shape will signify direction and are widely used in advertising to attract and direct the attention of potential customers.

There are more subtle means of moving a viewer's attention through a work of art. *Descent from the Cross* by Rogier van der Weyden (1404-1464, Belgium) uses the positions of the figures' arms, legs, and heads to trace the infinity symbol, which resembles the number 8 laying on its side. (Figure 2.64) This subtle reminder of Christ's everlasting life is meant to reassure and give hope to the faithful gazing upon this scene of death and grieving.

2.5.2.5 Rhythm/Repetition

The design principle of **rhythm** is the repetition of visual elements to establish a pattern. This pattern can then be used to provide a stage for a special object, or the pattern can be interrupted to direct attention to the change. In his commentary of mass consumer culture, Andy Warhol's use of repetition compels us to notice the small differences between the apparently identical elements of his installation of paintings, *32 Campbell's Soup Cans.* (Figure 2.65)

Figure 2.64 | *Descent from the Cross (Deposition)*
Artist: Rogier van der Weyden
Author: User "Argento"
Source: Wikimedia Commons
License: Public Domain

Figure 2.65 | *Campbell's Soup Cans*
Artist: Andy Warhol
Author: User "Gorup de Besanez"
Source: Wikimedia Commons
License: CC BY-SA 4.0

2.6 BEFORE YOU MOVE ON

Key Concepts

Visual art can be divided into dimensional categories: two-dimensional, three-dimensional, and four-dimensional art. Each category has unique and specific approaches and materials. Two-dimensional art consists of drawing, painting, and printmaking. Three-dimensional art consists of sculpture, including installation, and kinetic art. Four-dimensional or time-based art includes video and performance and depends on the use of technology and the passage of time for its effect. Time-based art has grown today to encompass digital art, computer animation, interactive art, video games, virtual reality, robotics, and 3D printing.

The elements and principles of design are the components and their organization within visual art. Line, shape, mass/volume, perspective, texture, and color are the primary elements of design. Time is a recently recognized additional element of design. Principles of design include unity and variety, scale and proportion, balance, emphasis and movement, and rhythm and repetition.

In this chapter we have also outlined many of the materials and processes used in creating art. In Chapter 3 Significance of Material Used in Art, we will examine the impact and meaning of substances employed to create works of art. In Chapter 4 Describing Art: Formal Analysis, Types and Styles of Art, we will utilize our understanding of materials and processes, and elements and principles of design to describe and explore meaning in art.

Test Yourself

1. Historically, the term fine art was limited to mean painting, architecture, and sculpture. Today, other approaches to the production of art objects have been discovered and exploited. This process of evolution has had both drawbacks and advantages. Discuss.

2. "_____-dimensional art occurs on flat surfaces, like paper, canvas, or even cave walls."

3. Art can be broken down into Form and _____

4. "To _____ an object is to observe its appearance and transfer that observation to a set of marks."

5. "For the most part, the pigments or coloring agents in paints remain the same. The thing that distinguishes one kind of painting from another is the _____."

6. The difference between open and closed sculptural forms is that closed forms are surrounded by _____, while open forms are penetrated by it.

7. Calligraphy is defined as "_____ writing."

8. Perspective in art is the _____ of space on a flat surface.

9. The three main cues to the illusion of space on a flat surface are:

10. The five elements of design mentioned in the text are:

   a. _____

   b. _____

   c. _____

   d. _____

   e. _____

11. The text mentions several principles of design. List and Describe three of them.

            Principle of Design: Description:

   a. _____   _____

   b. _____   _____

   c. _____   _____

12. The unique property of Kinetic sculpture is: _____

13. "The Fauves were a group of artists in the early twentieth century who used _____ **color**."

14. Suggest one potential reason for the use of a monochromatic color scheme, a complementary color scheme, and an analogous color scheme.

   a. Monochromatic   _____

   b. Complementary   _____

   c. Analagous   _____

2.7 KEY TERMS

2-Dimensional Art: art that is executed on a two dimensional surface that has length and width; a flat (or nearly flat) surface. These include, but are not limited to, paintings, drawings, and prints.

3-Dimensional Art: art that is executed in the three dimensions of length, width, and height. These include, but are not limited to, sculpture, architecture, ceramics, glass, textiles, assembly, and installation.

4-Dimensional Art: art that is executed in, and depends upon, both space and time, which is considered the "fourth dimension." Examples include but are not limited to performance art and video art.

Abstract Expressionism: or ABEX; this art historical term is specific to a group of painters working in New York after the Second World War. This group includes Jackson Pollock, Willem de Kooning, Lee Krasner, and Helen Frankenthaler. Their primary approach to painting was gestural, and "all over," a condition in which no single part of the work is visually predominant.

Acrylic: a fast drying water-soluble petroleum based painting medium.

Actual Texture: the condition in which texture is created, not represented. Actual texture is the opposite of simulated texture or the illusion of texture. Examples include brushstrokes, impasto, collage, and inclusion.

Additive Color: color based on projected light.

Additive: a sculptural process in which material is added.

Afterimage: the optical sensation that occurs after a visual stimulus is removed. The afterimage is a quickly fading complement of the original stimulus.

Analogous Color: a color scheme that uses colors adjacent to an initial point on the color wheel. For example, if an artist chose red for the initial color, then an analogous color scheme would employ the color range that occurs between orange, red, and purple.

Armature: a wire or wood substructure used to support a clay sculpture while it is being worked.

Assembly: a sculptural process in which disparate materials are combined to form the final artwork.

Asymmetric: lacking symmetry.

Atmospheric Perspective: the use of color to simulate the illusion of space.

Axis: an imaginary line around which objects are arranged.

Balance: the property of equality in visual weight.

Binder: a transparent fluid used to suspend colored pigment and attach it to a support.

Brush: tools used to apply paint to a support, usually hair or fiber attached to a wooden or plastic handle.

Buon Fresco: literally, "good fresco." A mural process in which pigment is painted on and absorbed into wet plaster.

Calligraphy: beautiful writing.

Carving: a sculptural process in which material is removed to reveal the final artwork.

Casting: a sculptural process in which material is substituted to form the final artwork.

Charcoal: an art medium made from burned wood used to make dark black marks usually on paper.

Closed Form: sculptural forms that are not penetrated by exterior space.

Color Scheme: an organized or formulaic approach to the selection of color. For example, Monochromatic (one color), Complementary (opposite colors), and Analogous (adjacent colors) color schemes.

Color Temperature: in visual art, the sensation of "warm" or "cool" relative to a given color. Warm colors tend toward red/orange, while cool colors tend toward blue/white. Every color, when compared to another can be seen to be either more warm or more cool.

Color: the sensation caused by differing qualities of light.

Complementary Color: colors that when blended together create a neutral gray. On a color wheel, complementary colors appear opposite to one another. Examples of a complementary color pair would be blue and orange or red and green.

Composition: the arrangement of visual elements.

Conte Crayons: in drawing, square sticks of compressed charcoal or pigment and wax or clay.

Conte: a mixture of pigment and clay used to make colored marks, usually on paper. Traditionally manufactured in black, white, and sanguine (red) colors.

Contour: the exterior boundary of a form.

Contrast: areas with a high difference in value, color, texture, or other scale.

Cool Color: a color that tends toward blue/white in hue. A cool color can be any color that tends toward blue/white when compared to another color. For example, alizarin crimson is a cool red when compared to cadmium red medium.

Crosshatching: intersecting marks that create value on a form.

Description: the process of enumerating the various elements of an artwork.

Design: a plan for the arrangement of visual elements.

Drawing: the process of making marks on a support, often but not always representative of an idea or object.

Edge: exterior boundary of a shape.

Edition: a series of prints made from a single matrix.

Electromagnetic Spectrum: continuous range of radioactive energy by wavelength.

Elements of Design: the physical components of visual art.

Emphasis: the strategy of directing attention with the use of high contrast.

Encaustic: a painting process which uses wax as the binder.

Figure/Ground Relation: the figure in front of the ground. Used to specify which objects qualify as figures.

Figure/Ground Reversal: ambiguous figure ground relation in which figures can be alternately seen as grounds and vice versa.

Figure: a shape that appears in front of a background.

Forced Perspective: use of perspective to create a distorted or unnatural scale relation.

Form: the physical components of visual art.

Found Objects: material incorporated into artwork that is not normally considered an artistic medium. Found objects serve the same purpose in sculpture that magazine cutouts serve in collage.

Freestanding: sculpture that can be viewed from all angles.

Fresco Secco: the process of painting on dry plaster.

Fresco: the process of painting on wet or dry plaster.

Fugitive: pigments that change color or become transparent with time or weathering.

Geometric: a shape with mathematically regular contours.

Gestalt: intuitive perception of an artwork as a single whole experience.

Gesture: direction interpreted as movement.

Gicleé: an Ink-Jet print, usually on acid free paper with archival inks.

Graphite: a carbon-based mineral mixed with clay to make pencil leads of varying hardness.

Ground: the stage on which a figure resides.

Gum Arabic: a water-soluble resin from the Gum tree used as a binder in watercolor.

Hard-Edged: a shape with clearly defined boundaries.

Height: vertical distance or measurement.

High Relief: sculpture that remains attached to a base, but uses undercut. Opposite of low relief.

Horizon Line: the visual limit of space where sky and land or water meet. In linear perspective, the vanishing point rotated 360 degrees.

Hue: the quality of wavelength in color; the color name.

Impasto: thick application of paint.

Implied Line: invisible line perceived by alignment of unrelated shapes.

Impressionism: a nineteenth century art movement, originating in Paris, in which changing variations of light become a principal subject. Examples include the work of Claude Monet, Edgar Degas, and Mary Cassatt.

Ink: a liquid pigment traditionally used with pens of various manufacture.

Installation: an art practice that surrounds the viewer in an environment.

Intaglio: a printing process in which a metal plate is scratched with a steel point to produce printed images.

Interactive: artwork in which the viewer is expected to participate.

Interval: the space between elements of an artwork.

Intuitive Color: an approach to the selection of color that relies on intuition or other internal state rather than observation of an external condition.

Kinetic Art: art that incorporates motion into its design.

Line: an infinite series of points with limited length.

Linear Perspective: geometrically constructed illusion of the recession of space.

Linear: of or pertaining to the quality of line.

Lithograph: a printing process that relies on the repulsion between oil-based ink and water. A stone (or aluminum plate) is drawn on and etched. Where the stone is etched will absorb water. Where the stone is not etched (protected by the drawing or image) the stone will remain dry. Water is applied to the stone. Ink is then rolled over the stone. Where the stone is wet, ink is repelled. Where the stone is dry, ink adheres. Paper is then pressed onto the inked stone resulting in a print.

Local Color: the color of an object under even illumination.

Lost Wax: a casting process in which a wax original is molded, then wax is melted out and replaced with metal.

Low Relief: sculpture that remains attached to a base and does not use undercut. Opposite of high relief.

Mass: the quality of possessing three dimensions.

Matrix: in printmaking, any material used to produce an image. For example, in relief printing, the matrix is usually a carved linoleum or wood block.

Metalpoint: drawing using ductile metal such as silver, gold, or pewter as the pigment. Usually on paper or gessoed panel.

Mixed Media: the use of unconventional or unusual combinations of materials in a single artwork.

Mobile: in sculpture, a kinetic artwork moved by wind or gravity.

Modeling: a sculptural process in which material is added to form the final artwork.

Mold: a hollow form used to shape a fluid or plastic substance.

Monochromatic: of or using a single color.

Motion: movement or change in position over time.

Negative Space: the absence of mass in space.

Non-Objective Art: art that does not have direct pictorial reference to objects seen.

Observed Color: the perception of color on an object illuminated by a directional light source. The perceived color of such an object varies as it tends toward highlight or shadow.

Oil Pastels: paper covered sticks of solid pigment and oil-based binder originally used to mark livestock.

Oil: in painting, a solvent soluble binder that dries slowly, usually linseed oil.

One-point perspective: a mathematical drawing system with the intention of making three dimensional objects and space look realistic in appearance as they converge on a single vanishing point.

Open Form: sculptural forms that are penetrated by exterior space.

Organic: shapes or forms that are loose or undefined.

Original Print: a handmade print.

Orthogonal: in perspective, lines that recede to the vanishing point.

Overlap: a shape or object which obscures or lies over something else.

Painting: the process of applying liquid pigment to a surface, or an art object resulting from this process.

Pastel: solid sticks of pigment.

Performance Art: an approach to art in which the object is an action by participants.

Performance: artworks consisting of actions, usually documented photographically.

Perspective: in art a system that portrays three dimensions on a flat surface.

Pigment: in art, the substance with gives color to a medium.

Pigment: the coloring agent in paints, pastels, inks, and other art media.

Planographic: a printing process which occurs on a flat surface, originally limestone.

Point: in perspective, an object with zero dimension.

Positive Space: the area occupied by a solid or filled object.

Primary Colors: in art the three basic colors by which all other colors are mixed, i.e., red, yellow, and blue.

Principles of Design: the strategies by which the elements of art are arranged to create a desired visual effect.

Print: an artwork produced by transferring pigment from a matrix to a support, usually paper. Most often done in a series of identical impressions. See "edition."

Printmaking: the process of producing multiple identical or nearly identical images from a single print matrix or set of matrices.

Psychic Line: in art, line that is understood without being seen by the eye.

Refracted Light: light that has been separated into distinct colors after having been passed through a prism.

Relief: the physical projection of an artwork beyond the support or base.

Reproduction: a mechanically produced print.

Rhythm: in art, a pattern formed by repeated objects.

Scale: the size of an object.

Sculpture: the production of artwork that exists in three dimensions. Examples are carving, casting, modelling, or assembly.

Secondary Colors: in art, the three colors formed by mixing two primary colors, i.e., green, orange, and purple.

Shape: an area of two dimensional space.

Simulated Texture: a visual representation of a tactile experience.

Site Specific: installations which use their location as part of the intended effect.

Soft-Edged: lacking a definite boundary.

Solvents: substances usually liquid, which dissolve a given paint binder.

Stencil: a printing process in which pigment passes through a mask onto a support.

Substitutes: in sculpture, replacing one substance with another. In casting, hot liquid metal is substituted for melted wax.

Subtractive Color: sensation of color created by reflection of light off of a surface.

Subtractive: a sculptural process in which material is removed.

Support: the surface on which an artwork is created.

Symmetric: shapes reflected equally about an axis.

Technological Change: notable shifts in available technology and science that play a part in the shift of culture and determine the availability of new artistic media.

Texture: the tactile quality of a surface.

Three-Point Perspective: a system of perspective that uses a third point above or below the horizon line to indicate the recession of space above the viewer.

Time Arts: the use of change as an element in art, usually performance art, kinetic art, or video.

Tughra: Islamic calligraphic device designating a high status individual.

Two-Point Perspective: a system of perspective that uses two points on the horizon to indicate the recession of space on either side of the viewer.

Undercut: in sculpture, an overhang created by removing material from underneath an object without detaching it from the base or support.

Value: in visual art, the characteristic of lightness or darkness of a color, ranging from near-white to black.

Vanishing Point: the point on the horizon where orthogonals meet, representing the viewer's vision extended infinitely in one direction.

Vector: the characteristic of having direction.

Video: moving images recorded and projected or displayed on a monitor.

Visible Light: the portion of the electromagnetic spectrum that can be seen by the human eye.

Volume: a bounded three dimensional area.

Warm Color: a color that tends toward red/orange in hue. A warm color can be any color that tends toward red/orange when compared to another color. For example, ultramarine is a warm blue when compared to cobalt blue.

Watercolor: a water soluble painting medium that uses gum arabic as binder.

Willow/Vine Charcoal: a drawing medium made from burned willow twigs, and used primarily for initial layout of paintings as it does not adhere well to drawing surfaces.

3 Significance of Materials Used in Art

Rita Tekippe and Pamela J. Sachant

3.1 LEARNING OUTCOMES

After completing this chapter, you should be able to:
- Describe the differences among valuation of art materials, especially with regard to intrinsic qualities of raw material versus produced objects
- Discuss the differences between monetary and cultural values for works of art
- Discuss the idea of "borrowed" significance that comes with the re-use of components from previous artworks
- Describe the significance of value added to objects by complex artistic processes or by changing tastes in different eras

3.2 INTRODUCTION

Among the aspects of an artwork that evoke response, aid understanding, and contribute meaning will be the material(s) used in its creation. These materials might make it more or less important, more or less valuable, or might bring a variety of associations that are not inherent in the essential form. For example, you might recognize a vase not merely as a vase, but as a Louis Comfort Tiffany (1848-1933, USA) Favrile glass vase. (Figure 3.1) Knowing the creator, material, and special processes involved in the artwork's creation would add to and might change your perception and appreciation in several important respects. For example, you could

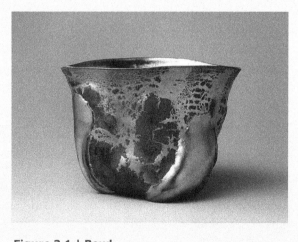

Figure 3.1 | Bowl
Artist: Louis Comfort Tiffany
Source: Met Museum
License: Public Domain

link it to an important artist, an innovative artistic technique, a significant period in American décor and manufacturing and marketing, a valuation based on its collectability, and numerous other interesting details about its creation and use.

The most apparent choices in this regard are for three-dimensional forms such as sculpture and architecture, where it is more likely that costly and precious materials such as gold, silver, gems, marble, or bronze are used in its creation. The distinction among material choices for drawing and paintings will also have certain effects for their meanings. For example, if a painter applied **gold leaf**, 22K gold pounded into extremely thin sheets, to a painting's surface, the monetary and cultural value of the work increases. (Figure 3.2) The **monetary value** refers to the amount a buyer is willing to pay, which in this case includes the cost of the materials the artist factors into the price of the artwork. The **cultural value** is the perceived quality or merit of the work: what it is worth according to that culture's standards of artistic importance or excellence. If a work of art has high monetary or cultural value, the owner's reputation and status are, in turn, elevated.

Without considering each and every possibility in this regard, we should look at a few pointed examples that will help us know what to consider when we examine artworks with a view to the

Figure 3.2 | *Annunciation to the Shepherds*, illumination from the *Book of Pericopes* (Lectionary) of Henry II, fol. 8v, 1002-1012 CE.
Source: Artstor.org
License: Public Domain

choices of materials that the artist (or patron) must have made. The techniques for many of these is discussed in greater detail in other parts of the text, so our primary focus here will be on the intrinsic materials, although the ways they are worked, used, and combined are inextricably significant in some of these cases.

3.3 UTILITY AND VALUE OF MATERIALS

The earliest drawings, paintings, vessels, and sculptures were made with whatever the artists could find and turn to their use for creating images and objects; such readily-available material includes mud, clay, twigs, straw, minerals, and plants that they could use directly or with slight alteration, such as grinding and mixing minerals with water to apply to cave walls. (Figure 3.3) Experimentation was surely part of the process and, just as surely, much of it is lost to us now, although we have some examples of works, materials, and tools to give us insight into the artistic processes and material choices.

Figure 3.3 | Reproduction of a bison of the cave of Altamira
Author: User "Rameessos"
Source: Wikimedia Commons
License: Public Domain

Figure 3.4 | Korean neolithic pot, found in Busan
Author: User "Good friend100"
Source: Wikimedia Commons
License: Public Domain

For example, in works such as this **earthenware**, or baked clay, vessel, the artist had explored sufficiently to discover that mixing a certain type of earth in certain proportions with water would yield a flexible substance. The resulting clay could be **handbuilt**, generally by wrapping and smoothing coils, into a vessel shaped with a conical bottom that would sit nicely in a coal fire for heating its contents. (Figure 3.4) A twig or string might be used to incise marks in the surface, not only to decorate it, but also to make it easier to hold onto than if it were completely smooth. Dating to c. 3,500 BCE, pots such as this from the late Neolithic era in Korea are known as Jeulmun pottery, meaning "comb-patterned." The clay could be found in different colors, textures, density, potential for adherence, etc. It could be manipulated by hand to make containers to store, transport, cook, or serve all sorts of goods.

The invention of the potter's wheel allowed artists to "throw" the clay on a rotating platform the artist operated by hand or powered with a kicking motion. When and where the potter's wheel first appeared is much debated, but it was widely used in Mesopotamia, Egypt, and Southeast Asia before 3,000 BCE. Using a potter's wheel allowed the artist to turn vessels with thinner walls, a greater variety of and more uniform shapes and sizes, and a larger array of painted and incised decorative elements for additional aesthetic appeal. They could, as well, make molds for serial production of commonly used types of pots.

By the time of the Ming Dynasty in China (1368-1644), vases such as this from the Xuande period (1426-1435) painted in imperial (cobalt) blue and white display both the technical innovations and the remarkable degree of refinement achieved. (Figure 3.5) The development of such

Figure 3.5 | A Ming dynasty Xuande mark and period (1426-1435) imperial blue and white vase
Author: User "Meliere"
Source: Wikimedia Commons
License: CC BY-SA 4.0

mineral resources as kaolin and petuntse allowed ceramicists to create porcelain, one of the most refined and hardest types of pottery, which became known as "china" because of the origins of the materials and processes; chinaware was soon emulated the world over for its beauty and utility as tableware and décor.

Traders from Portugal returned from China with chinaware (porcelain vessels) in the sixteenth century. The semi-translucent material, elegant shapes, and glass-like, intricately decorated surfaces of the pots were unlike anything produced in Europe at that time. The demand for such wares quickly spread throughout Europe, and ceramicists on that continent spent the next two centuries trying to unlock the secret of how to create such smooth, white, and hard pottery. Ehrenfried Walther von Tschirnhaus and Johann Friedrich Böttger, both employed for that purpose by Augustus II the Strong, Elector of Saxony (today Germany) and King of Poland (r. 1694-1733), are credited with producing the first European porcelain in 1708. It would become known as Meissen ware because it was produced at the factory set up in the town by Augustus II for that purpose to safeguard the formula and maintain his exclusive control over the creation and sale of European porcelain. (Figure 3.6)

The monopoly held by Augustus II was short-lived, however, as the secret was sold and a competing factory opened in

Figure 3.6 | Teapot
Artist: Königliche Porzellan Manufaktur
Author: Walters Art Museum
Source: Wikimedia Commons
License: CC BY-SA 3.0

Figure 3.7 | Pitcher
Artist: American Porcelain Manufacturing Company
Source: Met Museum
License: OASC

Figure 3.8 | Egyptian tomb wall painting
Author: British Library
Source: Wikimedia Commons
License: CC0 1.0

Vienna, Austria, by 1717. From there, variations of the formula and the production of porcelain spread throughout Europe as demand increased from the privilege of royalty, to the rich and titled, and eventually to all who could afford the status-giving ware. For example, this nineteenth-century commemorative pitcher made by the American Porcelain Manufacturing Company would have been presented to specially mark an occasion. (Figure 3.7) Although it is a distant relative of Chinese imperial porcelain ware and the royal courts of Europe, the techniques and materials used in its creation were still associated with tradition, wealth, and high social standing, elevating the cultural value of this mass-produced vessel to the level of a keepsake or even a family heirloom. Objects such as this are valued beyond their monetary worth or utilitarian purposes, both due to the tactile and aesthetic qualities that come from the physical substance and techniques used and to historical and social associations they hold.

Similarly, drawing and painting, apparently first confined to the rock walls of nature, were areas of exploration for artists who later applied color to the built walls of architecture, and then to portable objects of various types. Ceramic ware was decorated with images from nature, pictorial and narrative motifs, and messages of myth, power, and even everyday life. The same is true of tomb walls of Egypt (Figure 3.8), palace walls in ancient Iraq, (Ashurnasirpal II with Attendants and Soldier: http://www.museumsyndicate.com/item.php?item=36470) and Greek vessels used for practical or ritual purposes (Figure 3.9).

Figure 3.9 | Terracotta krater
Source: Met Museum
License: OASC

Eventually such vessels, as well as books and other objects, bore written information and pictorial explications of textual content: illustrations. Early textual works were often inscribed on stone tablets to ensure their durability or on relatively fragile materials like papyrus that required laborious preparation to make it suitable for conveying information. In either case, the materials used added to the work's significance. By the time of the development of the **codex** (probably in the Roman era), or manuscript with bound pages, the most common form of modern physical books, the choice material was animal skin, as seen in manuscripts throughout Late Antiquity and the Middle Ages, roughly the beginning of the fourth to the fifteenth centuries, in the Western and the Middle Eastern regions of the world. (Figures 3.10 and 3.11) Sheepskin, or parchment, the most commonly used support for written works, was obtained by laborious preparation of the pelts, through scraping and buffing the surface to make it suitable for use by scribes and illustrators who added the words and pictures. The most refined book arts

Figure 3.10 | Historiated Letter L, with illustration of the *Tree of Jesse, Capuchin's Bible*, f. 7v, c. 1180. BNF
Author: User "Soefrm"
Source: Wikimedia Commons
License: Public Domain

were often presented on **vellum**, or calfskin, prized for its smoother and finer surface. When used for especially important works or those made for royal purposes, it was often dyed purple or dark blue, with script applied in gold or silver ink and illustrations that included areas of gold or silver. (see Figure 3.2) These lustrous images were known as **illuminations**, that is, given light. The viewer would at once recognize the special and distinctive treatment implied by the use of such precious materials and know that the patron had paid well for an elegant and important book.

3.4 PRECIOUS MATERIALS, SPOLIA, AND BORROWED GLORY

Objects made for sacred or royal use were often wrought of such lavish and treasured components as vellum, silk, linen, wool, ivory, gold, silver, gems, and rare stones and minerals. Frequently crafted for further refinement, such works

Figure 3.11 | *Kitab al-Bulhan: Middle Eastern House and Lifting Machine*, Arab scientific manuscript leaf. 1. 14th century
Author: User "Peacay"
Source: Wikimedia Commons
License: Public Domain

show their precious properties to advantage. In ancient Rome/Byzantium, there were quarries for **porphyry,** a rich purple marble stone (the basis for the association of the color purple with royalty). Because it was restricted to royal purposes, its very appearance carried connotations of the imperial significance of any work made from it. It was often used for columns and other architectural components that thereby accentuated important structures or parts of them. Once the imperially controlled mines were abandoned in the fifth century CE, new items could not be made of porphyry, so older monuments were sometimes pillaged and re-used, with the royal significance transferred to the plunderers, implying not only the replacement of the old order by the new, but also the superiority of the conquerors.

Porphyry burial containers were especially prized in antiquity and the Middle Ages. Constantina was the eldest daughter of Emperor Constantine the Great (r. 306-337 CE), the Roman ruler who in 313 CE decreed early Christians could practice their faith without persecution and confiscated land should be returned to the Church. Although Constantine considered himself a Christian, he did not abandon the Roman gods and religious rituals. For example, in 321 CE he stated that Christians and pagans alike should observe the day of the sun (later named Sunday); the cult of the sun god had been popularly observed in Roman culture for centuries, and associations of the sun as the source of light, warmth, and life had been adopted by those of the Christian faith. Constantine, according to legend, was baptized a Christian on his deathbed in 337 CE.

When his daughter Constantina died in 354 CE, she was entombed in a porphyry **sarcophagus**, or stone coffin, that was richly carved with motifs from both the pagan Roman and Christian faiths. (Figure 3.12) There are small, winged cupids gathering grapes among garlands of grape vines with peacocks and a ram below on the front and back of the coffin, and cupids treading on grapes on both ends. In Roman mythology, such scenes were associated with Bacchus (known to the Greeks as Dionysus), the god of the wine harvest and wine making who as a baby was reborn after having been slaughtered by the Titans. Interpreted as Christian motifs, the cupids, who became known as **putti** or small, winged angels, are seen as preparing the grapes for the **Eucharist**, the sacrament commemorating the Last Supper by consecration of the bread and wine as the Body and Blood of Jesus Christ. Such re-imaging and re-purposing of motifs and their meanings were frequently seen at this time of transition from paganism to Christianity; further,

Figure 3.12 | Sarcophagus of Constantina
Author: User "Jean-Pol GRANDMONT"
Source: Wikimedia Commons
License: CC BY-SA 3.0

having been adopted by Constantine and his family, they were associated with imperial power and carried connotations of the Christian conquest of paganism.

Later, in the eighth and ninth centuries CE, Charlemagne (r. 768-814 CE) used pillaged porphyry columns inside arches on the upper level of his imperial chapel, a building intended for his own entombment. (Figure 3.13) The Palatine Chapel (c. 796-798 CE, consecrated 805 CE) was part of the palace complex Charlemagne had built at Aachen, in what is now Germany. The interior of the chapel is an octagon topped by a dome supported by heavy piers with arches on the second level, where the imperial throne is located, with a view to the high **altar** (the ta-

Figure 3.13 | Aachen, Palace Chapel of Charlemagne. c. 800
Author: User "Velvet"
Source: Wikimedia Commons
License: CC BY-SA 3.0

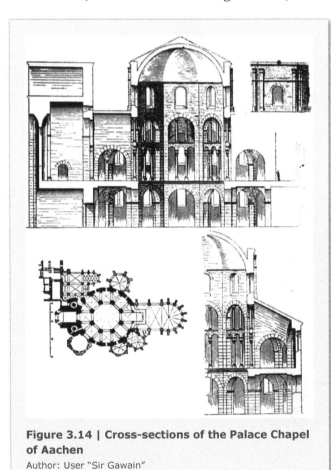

Figure 3.14 | Cross-sections of the Palace Chapel of Aachen
Author: User "Sir Gawain"
Source: Wikimedia Commons
License: Public Domain

ble or other surface where religious rituals are carried out) located across the church on the first floor below. (Figure 3.14) The design of the building is modeled on **mausolea**, or buildings containing tombs, and churches from the late Roman, early Christian, and early Byzantine periods (fourth-seventh centuries), such as San Vitale (526-647 CE) in Ravenna, Italy. (Figure 3.15) Charlemagne, who was not only King of the Franks and King of the Lombards but was also crowned as the first Holy Roman Emperor in 800 CE, used that design and the plundered columns to signify the revival and replacement of the old Roman Empire with his own reign as a Christian world ruler.

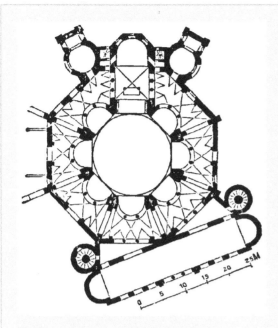

Figure 3.15 | San Vitale, Ravenna
Author: User "Väsk"
Source: Wikimedia Commons
License: Public Domain

Among others, Holy Roman Emperor Henry (or Heinrich) II (r. 973-1024) similarly borrowed and supplanted Charlemagne's glory by adopting his palace complex at Aachen and adding to its structure and furnishings with his own statements of imperial power. Henry II commissioned a lavish pulpit for the chapel that was completed in 1014. (Figure 3.16) The semi-circular pulpit has a smaller semi-circle to either side, a shape known as a **trefoil**. The center is made up of nine rectangular panels covered with **chased** gilt copper that has been formed by hammering into low relief images of the Four Evangelists. The panels are adorned with gemstones and embellished with **enamel**, powdered glass fused to the surface by heat, and **filigree**, beads or threads of gold or silver arranged in designs on a metal surface. The three ivory panels on each of the smaller semi-circles depict pagan mythological figures; the panels were made in Egypt in the sixth century CE. Re-used parts such as the porphyry columns, gemstones, and ivory panels are known as **spolia**, remnants that had been taken from older art and architecture and incorporated into new art objects and places with the implications of conquest, superiority, and heritage for the new patrons.

Figure 3.16 | Ambon (11th-century) of Henry II, Holy Roman Emperor. Aachen Cathedral, Germany.
Author: User "HOWI"
Source: Wikimedia Commons
License: CC BY-SA 3.0

Figure 3.17 | The Barbarossa chandelier
Author: User "Lokilech"
Source: Wikimedia Commons
License: CC BY-SA 3.0

Figure 3.18 | Shrine of Charlemagne, Interior of palatine chapel in Aachen Cathedral, Germany.
Author: User "ACBahn"
Source: Wikimedia Commons
License: CC BY-SA 3.0

Figure 3.19 | Shrine of Charlemagne
Author: User "HOWI"
Source: Wikimedia Commons
License: CC BY-SA 3.0

Figure 3.20 | Cross of Lothair
Author: CEphoto, Uwe Aranas
Source: Wikimedia Commons
License: CC BY-SA 3.0

Another, later Holy Roman Emperor, Frederick I (r. 1155-1190), and his wife, Beatrice, commissioned a chandelier to hang below the octagonal dome in the chapel. (Figure 3.17) This was called the Barbarossa chandelier, reflecting the emperor's nickname after his red beard; it was installed between 1165 and 1170 in honor of the Virgin Mary and as a tribute to Charlemagne. The chandelier's forty-eight candles cast a tremendous spread of light in an age when artificial illumination was costly, emphasizing its association with earthly wealth and heavenly light.

As a continuation of the work undertaken by his grandfather Frederick I, which also included exhuming Charlemagne's bones, Frederick II (r. 1220-1250), following the plans Barbarossa had made, completed the creation of a lavish, new jeweled and gilded shrine for the remains of Charlemagne, seeking to elevate him to the rank of sainthood. These statements in rich material forms, imply the surpassing glory of their imperial predecessor, shared by those who followed in his lineage. Moreover, the associations of royalty and honor for earthly rulers was often intertwined in very pointed ways to artwork associated with the Christian God and saints. Notable in this regard

Figure 3.21 | Augustus cameo
Author: User "Absalypson2"
Source: Wikimedia Commons
License: CC BY-SA 3.0

is the shrine for Charlemagne—clearly a statement of imperial power—made of rich materials that reflect popular Christian notions of the Heavenly Jerusalem, where these saintly rulers were thought to act as intercessors for the believer. (Figures 3.18 and 3.19) Often such imperial works actually featured objects or significant decorative details from imperial Roman works, such as the antique cameo of the Roman Emperor Augustus that was applied to the *Cross of the Emperor Lothair II.* (Figures 3.20 and 3.21) The gilded cross, dated to c. 1000, is covered with 102 gemstones and thirty-two pearls and has a rock crystal seal near its base bearing a portrait of Lothair II (r. 835-869). Including the portraits of earlier emperors further emphasized the wealth and power of the ruler who had it made, believed to be Otto III (r. 983-1002). In addition, gemstones on such devotional works were selected for their qualities associated with healing, good fortune, the ability to ward off evil, and their mystical translucence, that fostered spiritual illumination.

3.5 LIQUIDATION OF TREASURES

Figure 3.23 | The mid-12th-century silver altar piece surrounding the shrine of Saint Remaclus
Author: User "Kleon3"
Source: Wikimedia Commons
License: Public Domain

Figure 3.22 | *Screen of Charlemagne*
Artist: Piersac
Source: www.medart.pitt.edu
License: Public Domain

Works such as these often implied the storing of riches as heavenly treasure and also represented a means of storing material wealth that could be used for mundane purposes in time of need. We have records of a number of extravagant shrines and **liturgical** (relating to worship) furnishings that have not survived because they were taken apart and sold to feed a famine-stricken community or to provide for a new building project or an updated expression of devotion. Such works as the sumptuous Screen of Charlemagne (Figure 3.22) and the enormous Stavelot Altarpiece (Figure 3.23) are known to us only from drawings and small fragments that remain from the original objects. The disappearances of such works indicate that their rich material components, while once intrinsic to their great spiritual implications, at some point came to be seen as an important source of wealth that could be put to other use.

3.6 WOOD, INLAY, AND LACQUER

Sculptures, objects, and architectural components of wood were also fashioned with a view to their monetary and cultural value. Some varieties of wood are more rare, others have qualities that make them easier to work in certain types of process, and there have been waves of "fashion" in wood choices at many eras. For example, lindenwood and limewood are associated with the Middle Ages, mahogany with eighteenth-century England and Scotland, oak with the Arts and Crafts work of the mid-nineteenth to early twentieth centuries, and delicately lacquered wooden goods with Yuan Dynasty China.

Wooden sculpture was a far more predominant art form than painting in northern Europe during the Romanesque (c. 1000-1200) and Gothic periods (c. 1200-1500) in that region. The material favored was lindenwood or limewood due to the fineness of the wood's grain, which allowed the sculptor to carve intricate detail. Generally, the sculpture was then **polychromed**, or painted, to increase the lifelike quality of the figure. Suggesting that spark of life was important in works such as *The Throne of Wisdom* because Mary, the compassionate and merciful Mother of God and Queen of Heaven, was believed to have the power to intercede with her Son, the infant Christ, on behalf of the faithful. (Figure 3.24)

Figure 3.24 | Throne of Wisdom
Author: User "Okapi07"
Source: Wikimedia Commons
License: CC BY-SA 3.0

Mahogany was discovered as a marketable wood by European explorers and traders in the Caribbean islands, Central America, and South America by the seventeenth century. The naturally reddish-brown wood was prized for its beauty and strength and, throughout the 1700s, was frequently used in England and Scotland to create fine furniture for the market there and in the American colonies. A table such as this was a status symbol indicating the owner's wealth and taste, which was further enhanced by its use: this was not a utilitarian piece but a display table for chinaware. (Figure 3.25)

The Arts and Crafts movement began in England in the middle of the nineteenth century, but quickly spread throughout Europe and to the United States. In a time of growing industrialization, with an ever greater number of people moving to urban areas, working in factories, and consuming machine-made goods, some felt the need to reclaim the handmade. With romantic associations of simpler times, greater authenticity, and individual labor, furniture and decorative objects made as part of the Arts and Crafts movement were prized for their workmanship, design based on forms from nature, and respect for the natural materials used. For example, this cabinet is thought to have been made by Daniel Pabst (1826-1910, Germany, lived United States), one of the leading furniture makers of his day. It features elaborately carved surfaces and **inlay**, where one material is cut and fit into another in complex patterns. (Figures 3.26 and 3.27) Although the types of wood used—walnut, maple, and white pine—are not exotic or rare, the mastery with which they have

Figure 3.25 | China table
Source: Met Museum
License: OASC

been painstakingly cut and applied conveys a sense of preciousness. Inlay techniques were often used to provide visual contrast and to emphasize both the distinctive and diverse qualities among the materials brought together and the refined craftsmanship involved. A piece of furniture made with such skill was prized for its singularity and for the intricacy of the craft involved in its creation.

Figure 3.26 | Cabinet
Artist: Daniel Pabst
Source: Met Museum
License: OASC

Figure 3.27 | Detail of Cabinet
Artist: Daniel Pabst
Source: Met Museum
License: OASC

Lacquer has been used in art throughout Asia since Neolithic times, but carved lacquer is created in China only. **Lacquer** is resin from trees found in continental Asia that hardens to a natural plastic when exposed to the air; it is resistant to water and durable. The base of a lacquered object is wood, to which the liquid resin is applied in up to 200 layers. This tray was made in the fourteenth century, during the Yuan Dynasty, when lacquer was most often tinted red by adding cinnabar, powdered mercury sulfide. (Figure 3.28) Once hardened, the lacquer was carved away to create detailed scenes of court life, such as we see here, floral motifs, nature scenes, dragons or abstracted patterns. While the resin itself is of little monetary value, the laborious process and high level of skill required for such delicate carving meant the completed objects had, and still have, significant cultural value.

3.7 INTRINSIC VALUES AND ENHANCED WORTH OF METALS

Some of the materials prized by artists and patrons become more valuable because of these artistic uses; others are valuable for their intrinsic worth as raw substance. From the earliest times, metals such as gold, silver, iron, and copper were used and traded in their natural states, as they came from the earth. They were mixed with other materials to create alloys, used for minting coins and forming sculptural objects. Among the most prominent metal materials first used for art were iron and bronze; forging and casting them were among the earliest complex artistic processes devised. Brass (copper alloyed with tin, lead, and/or other metals) and the harder, more durable bronze have been widely used for grand public monuments that have fine detail, weather well, and can be hollow cast to reduce the amount of metal used. (Figures 3.29 and 3.30). Because forging and casting are complex and highly skilled processes, a viewer should know that an object made of this material was a significant statement for the artist or patron to make, one involving considerable planning and staging to accomplish the work.

3.8 RARE MATERIALS AND PROHIBITED USES

The economic and ecological factors involved in some materials have sometimes moved consideration of their use far beyond the discussion of artistic

Figure 3.28 | Tray with women and boys on a garden terrace
Source: Met Museum
License: OASC

Figure 3.29 | Bronze statue of Buddha
Author: User "Dirk Beyer"
Source: Wikimedia Commons
License: CC BY-SA 3.0

production. An example is work in ivory, especially that obtained from elephants, although it was also taken to use for sculpture from their kin, the extinct mammoth, as well as from walruses and other mammals. Its rarity and workability led to its valuation for finely carved works, often for aristocratic patrons and very special purposes, such as the devotional objects (*The Virgin and Child*, Unknown: http://collections.vam.ac.uk/item/O166591/the-virgin-and-child-polyptych-unknown/) and personal toilet articles (*Attack on the Castle of Love*, Unknown: http://collections.vam.ac.uk/item/O88416/attack-on-the-castle-of-mirror-back-unknown/) that were popular among the court ladies of the late Middle Ages. Its exploitation has led to scarcity and, ultimately, now threatens the very existence of elephants, since they have been savagely hunted and their herds decimated in the interest of profit. Consequently, both the sale and purchase of ivory objects, even

Figure 3.30 | The Minute Man
Artist: Daniel Chester French
Author: User "Flying Jazz"
Source: Wikimedia Commons
License: Public Domain

those considered antiques and historical treasures, are now widely boycotted in the interest of preservation of the species.

3.9 MATERIAL CONNOTATIONS OF CLASS OR STATION

Other more mundane materials and appropriated components might also have strong political connotations that intensify the meaning of the artwork. Korean artist Do Ho Su chose and assembled military dog tags to create a larger-than-life figural impression of an imperialistic robe with a hollow core. It carries connotations of the political strength of his native land being built upon such things as the dehumanizing mandatory military service he had performed, and the relationships between individuals and the collectives they form. (*Some/One*, Do Ho Suh: https://2yhr3j6imaw4e4zzg38k38ar-wpengine.netdna-ssl.com/wp-content/uploads/2016/10/suh-inst-002.jpg; *Some/One* detail, Do Ho Suh: https://2yhr3j6imaw4e4zzg38k38ar-wpengine.netdna-ssl.com/wp-content/uploads/2016/10/suh-inst-001.540.jpg)

3.10 BEFORE YOU MOVE ON

Key Concepts

One of the basic artistic choices for any creation is the material from which it will be made and so should be an area for careful attention in our analysis of any artwork. Deliberate choices can also involve the pointed spurning of rich resources in favor of humbler stuff, as in the robe created by Do Ho Su, and less refined surfaces, such as cardboard or burlap for paintings; things that are only more recently available than those traditionally used, like plastics for sculpture, titanium for architecture; and the technologically evolved media that move into the realms of the physically immaterial. Choices and implications have expanded exponentially, and our examination of them should be broad, deep, and careful.

Test Yourself

1. Discuss the differences between materials that are intrinsically precious, and those that are made more valuable by the processes or creative ideas in works of art, by considering specific examples.

2. Consider the use of *spolia* in at least three specific examples and discuss how they changed the significance of the art work to which they were applied.

3. Review and describe a specific process for creating artwork that involved procedures for combining diverse materials into the product.

4. Considering such common materials as clay or wood, discuss the ways in which an artist might use it for making an object of much greater value than the inherent worth, and what factors, other than the creation process, might lead people to value it highly.

3.11 KEY TERMS

Codex: the book form in which pages (or leaves) of material such as parchment, vellum, or paper, are gathered into bundles and bound together—initially by sewing, now usually by glueing—and then provided with a cover to protect the sheets. Its ancestor was the scroll, in which the sheets were joined into a long continuous roll that was opened out from one side, rolled up at the other, for viewing the contents.

Cultural value: the perceived quality or merit of the work: what it is worth according to that culture's standards of artistic importance or excellence.

Earthenware, or objects made from clay: such as vessels that are formed for specific uses and hardened either by drying in the air or by baking in high heat. Often, earthenware goods are distinguished from more refined clay-based objects that are creating with additional processing of the material or different/more complex firing methods. See **porcelain**

Gold leaf: 22K gold pounded into extremely thin sheets, to be applied selectively to areas of 2-d or 3-d objects.

Handbuilt: clay objects that are shaped by hand, often by wrapping and smoothing coils of clay into the desired form. These are distinguished from **wheel-thrown** or mold-made goods.

Illumination: literally, given light, specifically through the use of gold or silver for letting of illustrative touches in a manuscript. The term is also sometime used to describe manuscripts that have images added to them, as opposed to simply including lettered text

Manuscript: literally, hand-written presentation of script and/or images. The form was supplanted by books produced with a printing press, although the term is still used for a singular copy of a written work.

Mausolea, plural of **mausoleum**: a building designed to house one or more tombs, usually for an important person. These were most often centrally-planned, with a design that pivoted around the burial site. In Christian usage, these were sometimes attached to a larger, congregational structure, but sometimes stood alone. They might house more than one tomb.

Monetary value: the worth of materials or objects, in terms of "market value." This might be determined by the value of the materials use or of the finished art object, considered differently from the cost of the materials.

Parchment: sheepskin, prepared for use in manuscripts—less refined than **vellum**, used for finer and more expensive works.

Polychrome: painted in several colors.

Porcelain: highly refined ceramic ware, initially produced in China, with select materials like petuntse and kaolin, to create semi-translucent material, with elegant shapes, and glass-like, intricately decorated surfaces, and high-temp fired for hardened finishes.

Potter's wheel, wheel-thrown: pottery made with the use of a potter's wheel, a device for turning the clay body on a rotating platform for a more uniform shape. These were first turned by hand, knee, or pedal motion, later electrified.

Putti plural of *putto*: a small winged baby angel, a cherub.

Spolia: bounty taken from and original context, as in the "spoils of war." Often, items of spolia were re-used in later works to imply the conquest (and superiority) of the new owner over the original.

Vellum: calfskin, prepared for use in luxury manuscripts, more highly prized than the rougher, less expensive **parchment.**

4 Describing Art
Formal Analysis, Types, and Styles of Art

Jeffrey LeMieux, Rita Tekippe, and Pamela J. Sachant

4.1 LEARNING OUTCOMES

- Employ a vocabulary of art specific terms and critical approaches to conduct a formal analysis of works of art.

- Identify different types of art based on the degree of representation or non-representation a work displays.

- Distinguish between variations of representational qualities within a work of art.

- Identify characteristics that relate an individual or group of works to a cultural style, stylistic movement or period, or an individual artist's style.

4.2 INTRODUCTION

Developing the ability to examine and understand works of art makes sense for many good reasons. For one, art is powerful. In subtle but real ways, we are influenced by the visual culture that surrounds us.

In Chapter Two: The Structure of Art—Form and Design, we identified, defined, and discussed the elements and principles of design. Now, we will focus on the analysis of art. **Formal** or **critical analysis** is an examination of the elements and principles of design present in an artwork and the process of deriving meaning from how those elements and principles are used by visual artists to communicate a concept, idea, or emotion.

How and what is communicated in a work of art is linked to the type or category in which it falls: representational or non-representational. Within the broad category of **representation**, that is, a visual reference to the experiential world, we can further characterize the work of art using terms such as naturalistic, idealized, or abstract. Art that does not attempt to present an aspect of the recognizable world is **non-objective** or **non-representational**. In such work meaning is communicated through shapes, colors, and textures.

Style can refer to the general appearance of a work or a group of works that were created in accordance with a specific set of principles about form or appearance. Style can refer to the art as a whole that was made during a particular era and within a certain culture. More specifically, we can consider whether the artwork belongs to a stylistic movement such as the Italian Renaissance, Realism, or Abstract Expressionism. Style can also refer to how elements and principles of design are employed by an individual artist: the visual characteristics of that artist's work.

4.3 FORMAL OR CRITICAL ANALYSIS

While restricting our attention only to a description of the formal elements of an artwork may at first seem limited or even tedious, a careful and methodical examination of the physical components of an artwork is an important first step in "decoding" its meaning. It is useful, therefore, to begin at the beginning. There are four aspects of a formal analysis: **description, analysis, interpretation,** and **evaluation**. In addition to defining these terms, we will look at examples.

4.3.1 Description

What can we notice at first glance about a work of art? Is it two-dimensional or three-dimensional? What is the medium? What kinds of actions were required in its production? How big is the work? What are the elements of design used within it?

Starting with line: is it soft or hard, jagged or straight, expressive or mechanical? How is line being used to describe space?

Considering shape: are the shapes large or small, hard-edged or soft? What is the relationship between shapes? Do they compete with one another for prominence? What shapes are in front? Which ones fade into the background?

Indicating mass and volume: if two-dimensional, what means if any are used to give the illusion that the presented forms have weight and occupy space? If three-dimensional, what space is occupied or filled by the work? What is the mass of the work?

Organizing space: does the artist use perspective? If so, what kind? If the work uses linear perspective, where are the horizon line and vanishing point(s) located?

On texture: how is texture being used? Is it actual or implied texture?

In terms of color: what kinds of colors are used? Is there a color scheme? Is the image overall light, medium, or dark?

4.3.2 Analysis

Once the elements of the artwork have been identified, next come questions of how these elements are related. How are the elements arranged? In other words, how have principles of design been employed?

What elements in the work were used to create unity and provide variety? How have the elements been used to do so?

What is the scale of the work? Is it larger or smaller than what it represents (if it does depict someone or something)? Are the elements within the work in proportion to one another?

Is the work symmetrically or asymmetrically balanced?

What is used within the artwork to create emphasis? Where are the areas of emphasis? How has movement been conveyed in the work, for example, through line or placement of figures?

Are there any elements within the work that create rhythm? Are any shapes or colors repeated?

4.3.3 Interpretation

Interpretation comes as much from the individual viewer as it does from the artwork. It derives from the intersection of what an object symbolizes to the artist and what it means to the viewer. It also often records how the meaning of objects has been changed by time and culture. Interpretation, then, is a process of unfolding. A work that may seem to mean one thing on first inspection may come to mean something more when studied further. Just as when re-reading a favorite book or re-watching a favorite movie, we often notice things not seen on the first viewing; interpretations of art objects can also reveal themselves slowly. Claims about meaning can be made but are better when they are backed up with supporting evidence. Interpretations can also change and some interpretations are better than others.

4.3.4 Evaluation

All this work of description, analysis, and interpretation, is done with one goal in mind: to make an evaluation about a work of art. Just as interpretations vary, so do evaluations. Your evaluation includes what you have discovered about the work during your examination as well as what you have learned, about the work, yourself, and others in the process. Your reaction to the artwork is an important component of your evaluation: what do you feel when you look at it? And, do you like the work? How and why do you find it visually pleasing, in some way disturbing, emotionally engaging?

Evaluating and judging contemporary works of art is more difficult than works that are hundreds or thousands of years old because the verdict of history has not yet been passed on them. Museums are full of paintings by contemporary artists who were considered the next Michelangelo but who have since faded from the cultural forefront.

The best art of a culture and period is that work which exemplifies the thought of the age from which it derives. What we think about our own culture is probably not what will be thought of it a century from now. The art that we believe best embodies our time may or may not last. As time moves on, our evaluations and judgments of our own time may not prove to be the most accurate ones. We live in a world full of art, and it is almost impossible to avoid making evaluations—possibly mistaken—about its value. Nonetheless, informed evaluations are still possible and useful even in the short term.

4.3.5 Examples of Formal Analysis

Snow Storm—Steam-Boat off a Harbour's Mouth by J. M. W. Turner

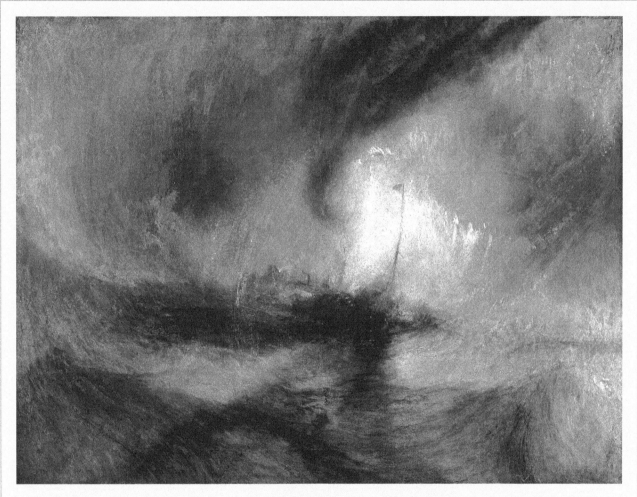

Figure 4.1 | *Snow Storm: Steam-Boat off a Harbour's Mouth*
Artist: J. M. W. Turner
Source: Wikimedia Commons
License: Public Domain

Snow Storm—Steam-Boat off a Harbour's Mouth by Joseph Mallord William Turner (1775-1851, England) is a chaotic, atmospheric oil on canvas painting. (Figure 4.1) First, on the level of description, the dark structure of the foundering steamboat is hinted at in the center of the work, while heavy smoke from the vessel, pitching waves, and swirling snow surround it. The brown and gray curving lines are created with long strokes of heavily applied paint that expand to the edges of the composition. Second, on the level of analysis, we note that the paint application, heavy, with long strokes, adds dramatic movement to the image. We see that the design principle of scale and proportion is being used in the small size of the steamboat in relation to the overall canvas. Now let us interpret these elements and their relation: The artist has emphasized the maelstrom of sea, snow, and wind. A glimpse of blue sky through the smoke and snow above the vessel is the only indication of space beyond this gripping scene of danger, and provides the only place for the viewer's eyes to rest from the tumult. This scene is of humanity's struggle for survival against powerful forces of nature. And finally, we are ready to evaluate this work. Is it powerfully effective in reminding us of the transitory nature of our own limited existence, a memento morii, perhaps? Or is it a wise caution of the limits of our human power to control our destiny? Does the work have sufficient power and value to be accepted by us as significant? The verdict of history tells us it is. J.M.W. Turner is considered a significant artist of his time, and this work is one that is thought to support that verdict. In the end, however, each of us can accept or reject this historical verdict for our own reasons. We may fear the sea. We may reject the use of technology as valiantly heroic. We may see the British colonial period as one of oppression and tyranny and this work as an illustration of the hubris of that time. Whatever we conclude, this work of art stands as a catalyst for this important dialogue.

Another example of formal analysis. Consider *Lady at the Tea Table* by Mary Cassatt

Lady at the Tea Table by Mary Cassatt

Figure 4.2 | *Lady at the Tea Table*
Artist: Mary Cassatt
Source: Met Museum
License: OASC

Mary Cassatt (1844-1925, USA, lived France) is best known for her paintings, drawings, and prints of mothers and children. In those works, she focused on the bond between them as well as the strength and dignity of women within the predominantly domestic and maternal roles they played in the nineteenth century.

Lady at the Tea Table is a depiction of a woman in a later period of her life, and captures the sense of calm power a matriarch held within the home. (Figure 4.2) First, a description of the elements being used in this work: The white of the wall behind the woman and the tablecloth before her provide a strong contrast to the black of her clothing and the blue of the tea set. The gold frame of the artwork on the wall, the gold rings on her fingers, and the gold bands on the china link those three main elements of the painting. Analysis shows the organizing principle of variety is employed in the rectangles behind the woman's head and the multiple circles and arcs of the individual pieces of the tea set. The composition is a stable triangle formed by the woman's head and body, and extending to the pieces of china that span the foreground from one edge of the composition to the other. Let us interpret these observations. There is little evidence of movement in the work other than the suggestion that the woman's hand, resting on the handle of the teapot, may soon move. Her gaze, directed away from the viewer and out of the picture frame, implies she is in the midst of pouring tea, but her stillness suggests she is lost in thought. How to evaluate this work? The artist expresses a restrained but powerful strength of character in her treatment of this subject. Is the lack of obvious movement in the work a comment on the emergence of women's roles in society, a hope or a demand for change? Or is it a monument to the quiet dignity of the domestic life of Victorian era Paris? The gold of the frame, the rings, and the china dishes appear to unify three disparate objects into one statement of value. Do they symbolize art, fidelity, and service? Is this a comment on the restrictions of French domestic society, or a claim to its strength? One indication of the quality of a work of art is its power to evoke multiple interpretations. This open and poetic richness is one reason why the work of Mary Cassatt is considered to be important. The above examples are only one of many ways in which we can interpret and evaluate works of art. We will examine a few more approaches to analysis and critique. The point of this exercise is to equip the interested student with tools to become more fully aware of the dynamics and content of works of art, not only in museums and textbooks, but in the world of images that continually surrounds us today.

4.4 TYPES OF ART

4.4.1 Representation and Abstraction

The most basic point of style, perhaps, is type or category, whether a work is **representational** or **abstract**. In the broadest terms, if the work has visual reference to the phenomenal world, we consider it to be representational. That definition suffers from over generality, though, since any physical or visual expression that has some reference to the physical world includes some aspect that we see as reflecting the physical world. And, to some extent, all works are also

abstract, in that they might remind us of what we see in the phenomenal world by only reflecting some physical feature(s) rather than detailing the object, place, or person itself. Having said that, we can proceed to see art in terms of its relative representation or relative abstraction of the original form.

It may help to start here by examining a number of works; each is based on the artist's observations of cows but is distinctive in what the artist elected to convey in their artwork about cows on the continuum from representation to abstraction. The first of these works is by Rosa Bonheur (1822-1899, France), who depicted a variety of animals in great detail with regard to their anatomy and physiognomy, and took great care to render her illustrations with fidelity to the appearance to the actual animals she had observed. (Figure 4.3) Artistically gifted and thoroughly trained, she went on to deepen her own knowledge and to hone her skills by visiting farms, veterinarian dissections, and slaughterhouses in order to develop extensive knowledge of her preferred subject matter, with which she created imagery of animals and other features of rural farm life. Her cows would be correctly described as very **naturalistic** in appearance—their forms are quite similar in appearance to actual cows.

Figure 4.3 | *Ploughing the Nevers*
Artist: Rosa Bonheur
Source: Wikimedia Commons
License: Public Domain

In comparison, if we examine the renditions by folk artist Edward Hicks (1780-1849, USA), we see cows that are much less rigorous in their resemblance, most likely the result of his not having had exacting training and practice in precise replication. (Figure 4.4) A Quaker minister,

Hicks treated his painting at first as a supplemental avocation, then as his primary means of supporting his family. He used it to express themes of spiritual and historical community events that interested him, generally in simplified landscape settings that emphasized narrative and symbolic messages rather than exact proportions and details.

In some works, though, the difference in correspondence to natural appearance can be due to the artist's very different purpose for the work. *The Yellow Cow* by Franz Marc (1880-1916, Germany) clearly does not slavishly reproduce natural appearances but instead seeks to convey through abstraction a sense of light-hearted lyrical expres-

Figure 4.4 | *The Residence of David Twining*
Artist: Edward Hicks
Source: Wikimedia Commons
License: Public Domain

Figure 4.5 | *The Yellow Cow*
Artist: Franz Marc
Source: Wikiart
License: Public Domain

sion for the animal. (Figure 4.5) To achieve this end, Marc took great liberty in creating an image that went far beyond what he saw, to make an expression that carries messages of what he thought and felt about his subject. Marc created a great many images of animals in nature that were metaphorical reflections of his views of mankind and the human spirit. Such a movement towards abstraction often derives from the artist's wish to express an emotional or intellectual commentary on the subject, or to use the subject as a starting place to diverge from visual appearances of the purely

Figure 4.6 | *Composition (The Cow)*
Artist: Theo van Doesburg
Source: MoMA
License: Public Domain

physical phenomenal world in order to create a statement of some other ideas.

Another artist bearing investigation in this regard is Theo van Doesburg (1883-1931, Netherlands), who used his own philosophical probing to frame a systematic path from naturalism in his renditions of the cow to an abstraction that is visually quite far removed from what most of us see in the phenomenal world. (Figure 4.6) Beginning with a series of exploratory sketches, he sought to reduce the linear forces of a cow's form to the three he thought were essential components of the physical and metaphysical world, that is,

vertical, horizontal, and diagonal, while reducing the three dimensions of the cow's form to the painting's two-dimensional surface. At the same time, he tried to simplify the forms and volumes, progressively creating a strongly abstracted picture that few of us would likely recognize as of

a cow if we were not led through the process by which he developed the image. Indeed, we have evidence of the process and its result in *Composition VIII (The Cow),* a fully developed instruction that provides us with great insight into Van Doesburg's train of thought and work, as well as his process of abstraction. (Figure 4.7)

Representation, then, shows us some broad vision of what we see in the original, be it a person, landscape, interior, event, or such, with some level of detail. To one degree or another, all art is ab-

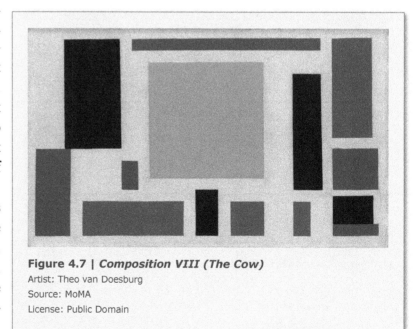

Figure 4.7 | *Composition VIII (The Cow)*
Artist: Theo van Doesburg
Source: MoMA
License: Public Domain

stract in that it is not the original form but instead the artist's response to the original form rendered in artistic terms—although, clearly, not all of it is so strongly abstracted that we lose the plainer references to the physical world.

4.4.2 Idealization

Sometimes artists create an **idealized** version of a natural form rather than truly reflecting its actual appearance. This was the norm, for example, in depictions of royal figures in ancient Egypt. There was a **canon**, or set of principles and norms, for the representation of royals that was very specific about just how they must look, including norms for the proportions of the different parts of the body to one another, their stance, and other details. The canon also set standards for their garments, headgear, the false beard, the arm and fist positions, and other details. The canon was remarkably conservative and unchanging, altering very little over the many centuries that ancient Egypt existed.

The figures of the Pharaoh Menkaure (r. c. 2530-c. 2510 BCE) and his Queen Khamerernebty are shown as being well proportioned, physically fit, and in young adulthood. (Figure 4.8) Because the king was regularly assessed with regard to his favor with the gods and fitness to rule, he was required to be in top physical condition—or so he must appear in any official imagery. This necessity resulted in the **idealization** of the natural physical form. So, while it is a representational image of the royal body, the need to depict him as a fit and worthy ruler meant that he

Figure 4.8 | Statue of Menkaura and Queen Khamerernebty II
Author: Keith Schengili-Roberts
Source: Wikimedia Commons
License: CC BY-SA 2.5

was generally shown as being in the prime of life, with a trim and perfectly proportioned physique, and with no apparent hint of weakness or vulnerability. By contrast, the image of an Egyptian state official, Ka-Aper, who was not of royal rank, was created with a different idea. (Statue of Ka'aper: http://www.museumsyndicate.com/item.php?item=27334) As a commoner, he is shown with a very different physique—rather pudgy and more relaxed, certainly not governed by the rules for the royal imagery. It is more naturalistic, not idealized like the royal works.

To study idealization further, we will explore the evolution of nude male sculptural forms in ancient Greece. We know Greek sculptors began with ideas they gleaned from the Egyptian forms

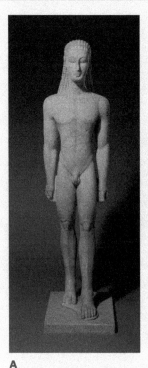 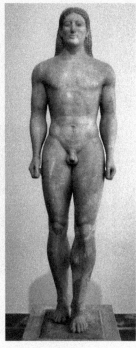 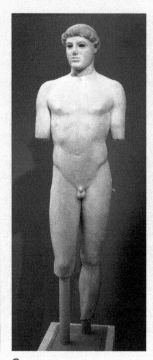 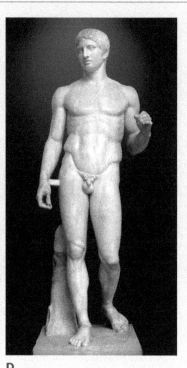

A　　　　　B　　　　　C　　　　　D

Figure 4.9 | Scultpures of the human form demonstrating anatomical accuracy

Photo A | Marble statue of a kouros
Source: Met Museum
License: OASC

Photo B | The Kroisos Kouros
Author: User "Mountain"
Source: Wikimedia Commons
License: Public Domain

Photo C | Kritios Boy
Author: User "Tetraktys"
Source: Wikimedia Commons
License: CC BY-SA 3.0

Photo D | Doryphoros from Pompeii
Artist: Polykleitos
Author: User "Tetraktys"
Source: Wikimedia Commons
License: CC BY 2.5

they knew but then altered them in some very significant ways that reflected their own distinctive culture. They presented the forms in the nude (only sculptures of males were nude at first, female sculpture remained clothed until the fourth century BCE) and, over time, they increasingly sought to capture more accurate physical details and the principles of movement in the body, rather than the static sense of permanence the Egyptians had favored.

From early on, Greek artists had the opportunity to observe the Olympic contests, athletic competitions that were held every four years in honor of Zeus, the ruler of their gods. The Olympics featured nude male athletes in a great many physical activities and diverse exercises, games, and sports. Over time, Greek artists developed a keen understanding of human physiognomy, how various movements and feats were achieved, and how bones, muscles, and tendons coordinated and functioned. They increasingly rendered the human form with great anatomical accuracy. When we look at the sculptures in Figure 4.9, we can see the evolution of depiction from the two figures dating to the Archaic period (800-480 BCE), when kinship with Egyptian work is apparent, to the Early Classical (c. 480-450 BCE), and then the High Classical period (c. 450-400 BCE), considered to be the epitome of naturalism in artistic depiction of the male physique.

The turning point in this evolution—the moment when the achievement of naturalism was pronounced—was with the creation of the *Kritios Boy*, c. 480 BCE. (Figure 4.9c) At that point, the beginning of the Classical period in Greece, sculptors captured the potential for naturalistic movement and the **contrapposto** or weight shift of the knees and hips that occurs when standing with one leg at ease or walking. This soon gave way, however, to a canon of art for the refined form. So, again, true naturalism gave way to a notion of the "perfect" or idealized form.

4.4.3 Non-Representational or Non-Objective

One further note is needed in consideration of the relationship of type to response to the phenomenal world. Recurrent strains of abstraction appear throughout the history of art, when artists elected to streamline, suppress, or de-emphasize reference to the phenomenal world. In the twentieth century, though, this approach took on different character in some instances, with a stated rejection of the art as related to the natural world and concerned instead with the art itself, to the processes by which it was made, and with the product as referring to these processes and artistic qualities rather than to some outside phenomenon: the observed world.

Still, the art is never completely independent of some reference: the viewer might respond to the color, painterly effect, line quality, or some other aspect that is not necessarily associated with recognition of a particular physical object or "thing" but that relates to the qualities of the art in some way, that is, to some recognition of refer-

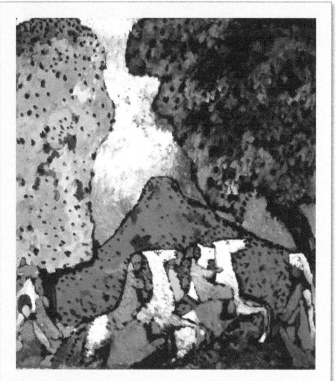

Figure 4.10 | *Blue Mountain*
Artist: Wassily Kandinsky
Source: Wikiart
License: Public Domain

ence—although this recognition may be ephemeral and may be nameless. The response might be quite visceral or intellectual, nonetheless. The development of this idea was perhaps an inevitable phase of the abstraction and explorations of the formal means that had been conducted by various movements that evolved in nineteenth and twentieth centuries.

Stories abound about the era in art and the push from abstraction to non-representation, with several artists claiming to have led the breakthrough. The first artist to use the term **non-objective art, however,** seems to have been Aleksandr Rodchenko (1890-1956, Russia), (*Spatial Construction no. 12*, Aleksandr Rodchenko: http://www.moma.org/interactives/exhibitions/1998/rodchenko/texts/spatial_construct_jpg.html;*Assembling for a Demonstration*,

Figure 4.11 | *Angel of the Last Judgment*
Artist: Wassily Kandinsky
Source: Wikiart
License: Public Domain

Figure 4.12 | *Red Spot II*
Artist: Wassily Kandinsky
Source: Wikimedia Commons
License: Public Domain

Aleksandr Rodchenko: https://www.moma.org/collection/works/45090?locale=en) and its most active early theorist and writer was probably Vasily Kandinsky (1866-1944, Russia, lived Germany and France). (Figures 4.10, 4.11, and 4.12)

The artistic climate fostered widespread experimentation, and the synergistic atmosphere was a seedbed for new ideas and modes of working. Rodchenko sought to affirm the independence of artistic process and the "constructive" approach to creating artworks that were self-referential, and he explored the possibilities in painting, drawing, photography, sculpture and graphic arts. Kandinsky, also Russian but working in Germany, wrote an important treatise entitled *Concerning the Spiritual in Art* (1912) that was widely popular and soon translated from the original German into many languages. He explored color theory in relationship to music, logic, human emotion, and the spiritual underpinnings of the abstractions that for centuries had been viewed and absorbed through religious icons and popular folk prints in his native Russia.

4.5 STYLES OF ART

In addition to looking at where along the spectrum from representation to non-representation a work of art may fall, we can examine the style of the work. Style can encompass the principles about form and appearance shared within a certain culture or era. Style can refer to a movement or group of artists and their work, where the commonalities can range from employing like elements and principles of design, to using certain materials or processes, to following a set of religious, political, or ideological beliefs. Style also indicates the visual characteristics of an individual artist's work. We conduct a stylistic analysis by examining the artistic elements and considering how they have used, and how they relate to other works by that artist, group of artists, or in a certain time frame, culture, or region.

In general, artistic styles tend to fall into three broad categories: Period, Regional, and Formal styles. Period styles are groups of art in which the works derive their characteristic structure from the culture prevalent during a particular time period. A good example of a period style would be Gothic Art or Ming dynasty Art. Regional styles are groups of art in which the works derive their structure from the culture prevalent in a particular place. A good example of a regional style would be Dutch Art or Latin American Art. Formal styles are groups of art in which the works derive their structure from principles that are not characteristic of either one place or one time. A good example of a Formal style would be Surrealism, Impressionism, or Modernism. Formal styles tend to be the "isms."

From the earliest times, we can see that some artists sought to make their depictions conform closely to what they saw in the world around them, but that for various reasons they often chose to emphasize certain aspects at the expense of great naturalism. It is a mistake, however, to assume that the degree of naturalism that you see in the artwork is necessarily and primarily related to the skill level of the artist.

Artistic and stylistic change is generally a matter of evolution, and often rather reactionary. The artistic choices about style (and other matters) made at any particular point are influenced by what other works of art look like at that moment. So the artist will likely try to create an expression that goes further in one direction, or changes directions in some way. Thus, art might become more naturalistic, as we have seen, or it might become less so, because the artist thinks the art might express the idea better by using a slightly different style or a radically different idea. The divergence is related to current "thinking" within the culture and other more specific circumstances.

4.5.1 Cultural Style

There are artistic choices with regard to style in every work. While these choices are generally made at the discretion of the individual artist today, for much of history style has been a reflection of the broader cultural currents that influence so much of life in any time and place. These cultural factors have often led to the general approaches to representation that art historians call "conventions of representation." To acquaint ourselves with these conventions and how they pertain to a cultural style, we will look at a few examples.

4.5.1.1 Ancient Near East

These conventions are evident to us when we examine a broad selection of works from those created in the ancient Near Eastern cultures during several centuries. Look at the way figures are depicted in a detail from the Standard of Ur (c. 2600-2400 BCE) from ancient Mesopotamia, today Iraq, a wooden box with scenes of war and peace made from inlaid pieces of iridescent shell, red limestone, and blue lapus lazuli. (Figure 4.13) We see the figures have sufficient naturalism to allow us to easily recognize the human body. But we also see that they include a range of naturalistic detail.

The figures appear static, even when they are shown to be moving through space. They are shown in a **composite view**, that is, with portions of the body shown in profile and others in frontal view

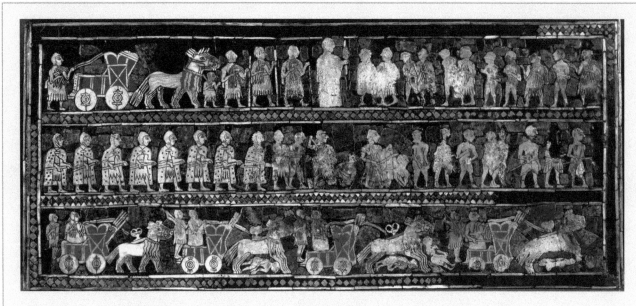

Figure 4.13 | Standard of Ur, 26th century BCE, "War" panel
Author: User "Dbachmann"
Source: Wikimedia Commons
License: Public Domain

Figure 4.14 | Music Stele
Author: User "Jastrow"
Source: Wikimedia Commons
License: Public Domain

so the artist can provide details that would not be visible in a strict profile. They turn the body in space so that the viewer sees the hips and shoulders, along with a twisted torso, turned slightly towards the viewer. For warriors and leaders, this is a heroic stance, showing power and command. The composite view is completed by giving a frontal view of the eye on the profile of the face and head shown.

This approach to figural forms continues in additional ancient Near Eastern works. The *Stele of Music* (c. 2120 BCE), depicting Gudea with attendants in one register and musicians below, shows the king ceremonially preparing to lay out a temple in the city of Girsu while accompanied by music and chanting. (Figure 4.14) In the relief of Sargon II, an Assyrian king who ruled 722-705 BCE, created approximately 1,400 years later, we see the use of these devices again, along with more variations of costume and headgear. (Figure 4.15)

These instances drawn from across many centuries but from the same geographical region that is today Iraq, show the persistence of a set of conventions of representation shared by the related cultural groups. We can also observe here that, when there is more emphasis on naturalism of the human body, it is at the service of conveying a sense of power, usually to give more detail to musculature—especially in the chest and shoulders. This slight abstraction or deviation from absolute naturalism is also used to create a sense of greater physical stature and presence, a manipulation of actual sizes known as **hierarchical proportion**, meant to show the figures' relative importance. These conventions of representation serve to convey dignity and significance within the broad cultural style shared by these associated groups.

As noted, **abstraction** is not a modern method of art, but has been used purposefully in many eras. Abstraction, simplification of naturalistic forms, appears in the conventions of representation in the ancient Near East; unlike most later instances of abstraction, however, these conventions did not follow upon and show a reactionary counter-movement to a naturalistic approach, nor were they a stage that further amplified certain features for purposes of expression or emotional exaggeration.

Figure 4.15 | Sargon II and dignitary
Author: User "Jastrow"
Source: Wikimedia Commons
License: Public Domain

4.5.1.2 Ancient Greece and Rome

We earlier discussed the progression of cultural style in ancient Greece from the Archaic period to the High Classical period. The latter was also the era when the Parthenon temple and the other structures on the Acropolis in Athens were rebuilt or renovated as a statement of the power of that city-state. (Figure 4.16) The work of this era of artistic pinnacle is called **classical**.

By extension, the ancient Roman work that was created to emulate the Greek Classical style is sometimes defined, as well, as classical art. Careful distinctions, though, need to be made amongst the strictly classical, the imitative, and the revival of classical form in later eras. Examining these styles further, let us first look at what happened after the Greek High Classical era. Art in Greece,

Figure 4.16 | Acropolis of Athens
Author: User "A.Savin"
Source: Wikimedia Commons
License: CC BY-SA 3.0

Figure 4.17 | Apollo Sauroctonus
Artist: Praxiteles
Author: User "Baldiri"
Source: Wikimedia Commons
License: Public Domain

Figure 4.18 | Hercules Farnese
Artist: Glycon of Athens
Author: User "Marie-Lan Nguyen"
Source: Wikimedia Commons
License: CC BY 2.5

in what are called the Late Classical (400-323 BCE) and Hellenistic (323-31 BCE) periods, shows changes that move away from the High Classical norms in becoming variously more dynamic, more expressive, more emotional, more dramatic. (Figures 4.17 and 4.18) That is, they are exaggerated in some way from the calm composure of the Classical style that had expressed the cultural value of complete balance achieved by "a sound mind in a sound body," a rather sober and self-contained ideal.

In later Greek culture, we can see changes in an expansive political spirit, the influx of foreign cultural forces, the development of drama in theater, increasing materialism, and other factors that change the artistic and aesthetic spirit, consequently requiring different modes of artistic expression. The Romans, although deeply admiring the classical Greek art, held different cultural ideas and ideals, so Roman art, unless directly copying the Greek, would express their different views of life and the world. These included especially Roman worldliness, their boundless interest in expansion (which brought in a great variety of additional influences), their great ingenuity and inventiveness in such arenas as engineering and architecture, and their stress on individualism.

The Roman Republican period (509-27 BCE) overlaps the Greek late Archaic, Classical, and Hellenistic periods. During the Republican period, Romans favored an anti-idealized approach to portrayal of people that went beyond simple naturalism to a very frank and unvarnished study of individuals, with a measure of veneration for the more mature citizens as models of an accomplished life. (Figure 4.19) The

Figure 4.19 | Togatus Barberini
Author: A. Hekler
Source: Wikimedia Commons
License: Public Domain

Romans honored their ancestors and kept their venerable images as portrait heads, which they carried in funeral processions and kept in their homes; they valued the accomplishments of old age, so their views on aging and the aged were often expressed through **veristic** or truthful renditions of their likenesses.

Figure 4.20 | Augustus of Prima Porta
Author: User "Till Niermann"
Source: Wikimedia Commons
License: CC BY-SA 3.0

However, the use of these unidealized depictions varied from one phase to another throughout ancient Roman history. It is especially noted that in the Early Imperial era (27 BCE-197 CE), with the rise of Augustus to Emperor, the practice of idealization in portraiture was again favored for the imperial likenesses, often seen clearly as part of the political propaganda used to promote the positive perception of the emperor and the promotion of his political goals and programs. The portrayal of the man Augustus, regardless of his age at the time of the creation of a portrait, was made to be the image of a powerful young man, heroic in stature, fit and fine. (Figure 4.20) Ensuing emperors varied their choices in this regard, some opting for a return to the age prior to the Imperial Age and notions of Republican virtue and the value of age and experience, others using the idealizing and propagandistic approach, to some degree.

In the late Roman Empire (284-476 CE), though, we see suppression and streamlining of natural detail in art that followed and was a reaction to that long period of naturalistic representations of the human figure. Scholars interpret this abstraction as a means of stressing other-than-natural features that are ideological, spiritual, or philosophical in character. For example, in the *Portrait of the Four Tetrarchs* from c. 300 CE, we see that the *idea* of the **tetrarchs**, or four co-ruling emperors, working together to rule the four divisions of the vast Roman Empire is more important than the *representation of likeness* of any one of these co-rulers as an individual. (Figure 4.21)

Naturalism has given way to uniformity, with nearly identical figures of men in the same costume, crown, armor, and stance, as they embrace one another to show their joint office and efforts in the service of the Roman citizenry. Even though there is considerable detail in their clothing that links their joint rule to Roman traditions of military rulers and leaders, the suppression of distinctive, individual physical characteristics is used convey the concept of how they will function as one.

A few years later, when the Roman Empire briefly returned to a singular rule under Constantine the Great, the

Figure 4.21 | The Tetrarchs
Author: User "Nino Barbieri"
Source: Wikimedia Commons
License: CC BY-SA 3.0

new Emperor opted for an even more abstract-ed and simplified portrait representation. (Figure 4.22) He thus removed himself even further from the tradition of imperial portraits that had each varied in its extent of naturalism and idealization—even though the head emulates some in being clean-shaven, with a fringed cap of hair, and having an air of imperial hauteur. But it is far less personal and less intimate in its address to the viewer, both in large part to its marked suppression of detail, than depictions of earlier rulers. Further, Constantine appears to be focused on the heavens above, towards which his gaze is directed. The portrayal has been read as being more spiritual, linking him to the emerging Christian faith. Thus, the portrait is associated with a societal and cultural turn from worldly to spiritual matters, and that is likely reflected in this change in artistic interpretation.

Figure 4.22 | Marble portrait head of the Emperor Constantine I
Source: Met Museum
License: OASC

4.5.1.3 Indian Subcontinent

Strictly speaking, Greece and Rome were the classical civilizations of antiquity in the West, and some would even limit the use of the term "classical" in art to the High Classical period in Greece. The same principles and conventions of representation, however, include numerous works from other times and places. The revival of characteristics associated with the cultural styles associated with ancient Greece and Rome recur repeatedly throughout history in the West, and also appear sometimes in non-Western cultures. Becoming familiar with a few examples will make more apparent the variations of a naturalistic style, whether subtle or quite pronounced, that can be further investigated with regard for the cultural and individual values that are influential at the moment of the work's creation and use.

In India, naturalism was not usually as restrained as those of the classical ideal we have been exploring. The Emperor Ashoka (r. 268-232 BCE), who reigned over most of the Indian subcontinent, oversaw the construction of 84,000 **stupas**, dome-shaped shrines, to house Buddhist relics. In this **Yakshi**, or female nature figure, guarding one of the fours gate at the Great Stupa at Sanchi, the emphasis is on fleshy form, voluptuous and prosperous, indicating a robust healthy physique with connotations of earthly blessing and prosperity. (Figure 4.23)

During Ashoka's reign and in the succeeding centuries, influenced by increasing contact with Western cultures and artistic styles that came with both friendly trade and aggressive military incursions by Greeks and Romans, many changes occurred in Indian art. A notable example is the Buddhist sculpture of Maitreya from Gandhara (today Pakistan), dating to the third or fourth century CE. (Figure 4.24) Maitreya, derived from the Sanskrit word for "friend," is a **bodhisattva**—a person who is able to reach nirvana but compassionately chooses to help others out of their human suffering. Maitreya, a successor to the current Buddha, will appear in the future.

Figure 4.23 | Elephants on North Torana, Sanchi, India
Author: User "Bernard Gagnon"
Source: Wikimedia Commons
License: CC BY-SA 3.0

The influence of Greek and Roman art can be seen in the treatment of drapery and the physical form. Although the figure is somewhat fleshier than Western counterparts, retaining the Indian penchant for more full-bodied physique, it is somewhat less substantial and certainly more concealed by the envelopment of abundant cloth than what had earlier been the norm for figural interpretation in India.

4.5.1.4 Romanesque and Gothic Eras in Europe

Returning to Europe, Romanesque art of the eleventh and twelfth centuries is noteworthy with regard to the idea of expressing a prevalent preoccupation among Christians about the ends of their lives and the end of time. For spiritual purposes, they often made a choice for greater abstraction and distortion, rather than the emphasis on a naturalistic depiction of the human form as seen in ancient Greek and Roman art. Their forms are not only simplified with suppression of naturalistic features in some ways, but are also twisted and turned in space, while their garments have a lot of linear detail that does not correspond well to the physical forms of the bodies they adorn. The effect is to remove their meaning from a focus on worldly phenomena, redirecting it to a sense of spiritual agitation.

Figure 4.24 | Standing Bodhisattva Maitreya
Source: Met Museum
License: OASC

Figure 4.25 | Last Judgement
Artist: Gislebertus
Author: User "Lamettrie"
Source: Wikimedia Commons
License: CC BY-SA 3.0

Many of the depicted scenes relate to the Christian expectations of the event of the Last Judgment, reflecting warnings to the devout that that their lives and deeds now will be assessed at that point in the future. At Autun Cathedral (1120-1132) in France, we see a graphic array of elongated figures in the Last Judgment within the **tympanum**, the space above the **portals**, or doors. (Figure 4.25) The scene and surrounding decorative reliefs, created by the sculptor Gislebertus (active c. 1115-c. 1135, France) between 1130 and 1135, are centered on the flattened figure of the judging Christ. He presides over the resurrection of

the dead and the ensuing assignment to a heavenly welcome or a grotesque greeting by the denizens of Hell. Despite the lack of naturalism, the messages are clear in reference to human experience and prevalent beliefs of the era.

Following the Romanesque style in Europe was the Gothic era, which spanned the twelfth to fourteenth centuries in Italy and continued into the sixteenth century in northern Europe. The Gothic style included a return to greater naturalism, as focus shifted back to the natural world in many ways. (Figure 4.26) Figural forms began to reflect the observation of physical facts, and a phase of artistic evolution began that would eventually culminate in the intense naturalism of the Renaissance, especially in Italy from the fourteenth to the sixteenth centuries.

Along the way, however, conventions of representation in Italy and in northern Europe diverged, producing increasing different cultural styles. For example, the "Court Style" was prevalent in the royal works of the Late Gothic era (late fourteenth to sixteenth centuries), particularly in France, and lingered into the early Renaissance of the late fifteenth century in northern Europe. The approach reflected the prominence of aristocratic tastes and the

Figure 4.26 | Saints Martin, Jerome, and Gregory
Author: User "Jedhunsaker"
Source: Wikipedia
License: Public Domain

exaltation of earthly rulers and the conception of God and the saints (especially the Virgin Mary) as the court in Heaven. (*The Virgin of Paris*, Notre-Dame, Paris: https://www.oneonta.edu/ faculty/farberas/arth/Images/arth212images/gothic/notre_dame_madonna_child.jpg)

While there is a clear change from the Romanesque style, the figures are not yet really naturalistic, with an emphasis on elegance and aristocratic attitude dominating the figural imaginings. As seen here, there is often abundant drapery falling in rich and graceful folds, so exaggerated that one cannot discern the space for a full figure beneath. The hips and knees, rather than showing the classical contrapposto positioning that the ancient Greeks developed, are gracefully swayed into an S-curve, connoting sophistication and refinement.

4.5.2 Stylistic Periods or Movements

In addition to examining style as a broad expression and embodiment of cultural beliefs and values, we can focus more finely upon stylistic groups and artistic movements as artists and works grouped together due to similarities in subject matter, formal approach, spiritual or political beliefs, or other commonalities. A stylistic movement can be based upon a pointed and conscientious revival of visual and philosophical traits of an earlier style. An artistic movement can also reflect the cyclical and recurrent evolution of style, with phases of moving gradually towards greater naturalism, and then rebounding towards some stylistic aberration that is less reflective of physical nature and instead expresses some other interest of human life and artistic attention.

4.5.2.1 Italian Renaissance

The first artistic era in the modern West that we can speak of as possessing more specific traits and commonalities than a more broadly defined cultural style is the period known as the Renaissance, which is French for "rebirth." Originating in Italy in the fourteenth century, the Renaissance was a period of conscious and purposeful revival of the ideas and ideals of the classical past. Within a shared cultural interest in **humanism**, the philosophical belief in the value of humans and their endeavors, artists of the Italian Renaissance sought ways to express themselves as individuals in their art. Through study of ancient art and close observation of the world around them, Renaissance artists as a group—but each characterized by singular traits—realized another pinnacle of naturalism in the human form. Italian artists of the fifteenth century would also invent linear perspective, so that all lines parallel to the viewer's eye recede to a vanishing point on the horizon line.

A good example of linear perspective is the fresco *The Holy Trinity* by Masaccio (1401-1428, Italy), the first painting in which the technique was systematically employed. (Figure 4.27) The work depicts the crucifixion of Christ, with God the Father behind and above him supporting the cross, and Mary and St. John the Baptist standing to either side. When we extend the **orthogonal lines** from the ceiling vault above the holy figures, we find they converge at a point on the floor where the images of the patrons kneel, below and outside the vaulted area. This line divides the fresco into two zones: the zone above that, which for Christians symbolized eternal life, and the skeleton beneath the line which symbolizes the waiting grave. The **vanishing point**—and the attention of the viewer—is on the line between them where the patrons kneel in prayer. It thus subtly but elegantly uses **linear perspective** to impart a message. The patrons and the viewer are "on the line between life and death" and have a religious decision to make.

During the preceding Romanesque and Gothic eras, philosophical thought was shifting from a focus on achieving everlasting life through devotion and considering humans and their feats to be weak and insignificant; however, the power of religion and religious beliefs had not diminished. Humanism of the Italian Renaissance both celebrated human intellectual and creative accomplishments—as can be seen in use of linear perspective in *The Holy Trinity*—and embraced the teachings of the Roman Catholic Church that emphasized the humanity of Christ.

As a result, there was a shift away from distinct physical and emotional separation of holy figures within works of art to depictions that emphasized their spiritual presence among the faithful. For example, in the *Madonna and Child Enthroned with Saints* by Raphael (1498-1520, Italy), a hierarchy of Mary as the Queen of Heaven seated high on her throne with a ceremonial canopy and hanging cloth emphasizing her majesty is maintained. (Figure 4.28) The steps before her, however, are open for the viewer to symbolically ascend through devotion, and the serene landscape behind her is clearly on this earth and not a vision of a celestial heaven.

Figure 4.27 | *Holy Trinity*
Artist: Masaccio
Author: Web Gallery of Art
Source: Wikimedia Commons
License: Public Domain

Subjects such as the Madonna and Child, which allowed the artist to accentuate human qualities such as the love, mercy, and tenderness which these holy figures had in common with the worshipper, were favored during the Italian Renaissance. Not only did the choice of subject matter reflect the new value placed on human empathy and agency, the myriad approaches to such subjects indicate the new freedom artists felt to abandon a broad cultural style as seen in earlier eras. Instead, they adopted stylistic traits that embodied a collective desire to "rebirth" the forms and philosophy of art as practiced in Classical Greece and Rome. This resulted in artists accentuating the individual in their art making within the agreed upon stylistic standards and ideals of the period.

As an example, compare Raphael's *Madonna and Child Enthroned with Saints* to *Madonna and Child* painted approximately six years later by Titian (c. 1488-1576, Italy). (Figure 4.29) Both artists stress the tender connection between mother and child. Looking closely at the faces of all three women in Raphael's work, however, we can see their features and the tilt of their heads are nearly identical, suggesting the artist chose to depict them in a similarly idealized manner. The Madonna in Titian's work, on the other hand, has more individualized facial features. Titian places a greater emphasis on the naturalistic folds and flow of drapery than Raphael does, highlighting

Figure 4.28 | *Madonna and Child Enthroned with Saints*
Artist: Raphael
Source: Met Museum
License: OASC

Figure 4.29 | *Madonna and Child*
Artist: Titian
Source: Met Museum
License: OASC

the transparency of cloth across Mary's lap, for example. Last, Titian brings the detailed landscape behind the figures closer to the picture plane, situating the figures in nature; Raphael focuses upon the grouping of figures in the foreground with a distant view of the land. In this way through their art, we have a front row seat to a changing cultural view about the proper relation of religious figures to the everyday physical world during the Italian Renaissance.

4.5.2.2 Realism

We have already discussed naturalism as an approach to depicting objects that exist in the physical world in representational art. Now let us examine the terms naturalistic and realistic. These terms are often (incorrectly) used interchangeably, but their meanings and implications in art differ. Works that are **naturalistic** are those in which the appearance corresponds to nature, that is, to how the subject of the work looks in the natural, phenomenal world, such as the cows of Rosa Bonheur. In distinction, those that are correctly called **realistic** relay information or opinions about the underlying social or philosophical reality of the subject matter: they go beyond the natural appearance to express additional ideas.

Works created with a view to such realism may also be naturalistic in appearance, but they go beyond the naturalistic appearance to include social commentary in the pictorial message. Examples include works such as those by Gustave Courbet (1819-1877, France, Switzerland) that were created to express the realities of the rural poor in mid-nineteenth-century France and that were partly artistic statements of rebellion

Figure 4.30 | A Burial at Ornans
Artist: Gustave Courbet
Author: Google Art Project
Source: Wikimedia Commons
License: Public Domain

against the prevailing norms of academically acceptable art. The ***École des Beaux-Arts*** was the nationally institutionalized body in control of training and exhibition of art in France, and its conservative tendencies went against such frank treatment of mundane subject matter. Rather, they promoted lofty subject matter, refined treatments, and their most highly prized works dealt with topics like history, religion, heroic narratives, and the like. Here, in the *Burial at Ornans,* Courbet presented not a grand ceremonial event, but an ordinary country funeral. (Figure 4.30) The scene includes a disparate group of common folk standing awkwardly in disarray—even though the grand size was associated with a more elevated subject and treatment.

The academic norms would have dictated that such a ritual event be presented with a greater sense of formality and pomp, emphasizing the coordination of activities in an uplifting and reverential manner. Since Courbet had trained and achieved mastery in the official French system, the painting was shown in the annual Salon, the official venue of the *École des Beaux-Arts*; nevertheless, it was widely criticized as lacking decorum and having too much **realism.**

Another of Courbet's works, *The Stone Breakers,* also shown at the Salon in 1851, garnered its share of the same sort of criticism, for it presented the hard labor of rural peasants as though it were a heroic activity. (Figure 4.31) Courbet again used realism to make a strong visual statement of the nobility of people and tasks that lay far outside the refined academic definitions of art. By doing so, he condemned not only the Academy but also the societal standards that supported such judgment and ranking of art and human activity. Thus, the art movement known as Realism was begun. Many works created in this vein were condemned and refused for exhibition in the official Salons, resulting in an anti-Academic movement among artists and the quest of many for independence from the state-con-

Figure 4.31 | *The Stone Breakers*
Artist: Gustave Courbet
Author: The Yorck Project
Source: Wikimedia Commons
License: Public Domain

trolled system for training and exhibition.

Such subject matter and approach to making art appeared in many different places throughout the nineteenth and twentieth centuries. Such artwork invariably was associated with other signs of social change and upheaval, frequently reflecting the lives and interests of the peasantry—both rural and urban—and highlighting the oppressive conditions of their lives. In Russia, among other places, the movement included a spirit of probing and of artists expressing the distinctive cultural characteristics and specific social issues of their countrymen. Ilya Repin (1844-1930, Russia), in *Barge Haulers on the Volga,* pre-

Figure 4.32 | *Barge Haulers on the Volga*
Artist: Ilya Repin
Author: User "Thebrid"
Source: Wikimedia Commons
License: Public Domain

Figure 4.33 | *Three Women in Church*
Artist: Wilhelm Leibl
Author: The Yorck Project
Source: Wikimedia Commons
License: Public Domain

sented a realistic view of the arduous labor of men bringing the river barges to shore for unloading; the artist took great care to present each of them as an individual to be respected. (Figure 4.32) He also defined them in terms of age, physique, stature, and ethnicity, conveying the group as a sort of cross-section of Russian peasantry of the day.

In Germany, the influence of Courbet's Realism, coupled with study of portraits by Old Masters (European painters of renown c. 1200-1800), appears in a study by Wilhelm Leibl (1844-1900, Germany) called *Three Women in the Church.* (Figure 4.33) In this painting, the detail of the individual women is remarkable, delineating as it does their rustic costumes, their strongly individual characters, their large work-worn hands, and their other physical features. Leibl had rendered these peasants with realistic attention to the effects of their hard life at their different ages, while conveying a great sense of respect for their traditions of family and faith. He sought to counter the legacy of glorified German history and myth with unflinching views of the ordinary people he knew.

Stylistic components of and ideas behind Realism were also used by American artists, notably in the early decades of the twentieth century, when the crowded urban centers fostered harsh living conditions for the poor working class citizens. One important group within that stylistic movement, known as the Ashcan School, included painters such George Bellows (1882-1925, USA), whose *Cliff Dwellers* shows the crowding and chaos in a Lower East Side New York City neighborhood on a hot summer day. (Figure 4.34)

These artists were often making commentary on the undesirable effects felt by newly arrived immigrants and the rural poor who had been lured into large metropolitan areas in hopes of better prosperity and lifestyle, especially as many remained on the lower rungs of the industrialized and commerce-oriented society. Again, the overall definition of form may be seen as naturalistic, but his efforts for realism led Bellows to a rather painterly, brushy approach that does not have definitively naturalistic detail throughout.

One further particular point needs to be made about the idea of realism in art. It is a mistaken notion to believe that photographic works are inherently or necessarily more realistic than any other work because they record some actuality. The artist who uses photography has as many opportunities for choice as one who works in any other medium and can make choices that alter that actuality or its appearance. The photographer selects the subject matter and then can choose viewpoint, lighting, compositional field, a variety of photo processes and materials, and exposure time. The process of development and printing offers further options for manipulating the imagery, and sometimes changes are made after the printing process is complete. There is not necessarily any more "truth" or "realism" in a photo than in any other type of art.

For example, in the works of some photographers such as Edward Steichen (1879-1973, Luxembourg, lived USA) and Lucas Samaras (b. 1936, Greece, lives USA) we see that the artists have manipulated the photographs to alter their

Figure 4.34 | *Cliff Dwellers*
Artist: George Bellows
Author: User "Achim Raschka"
Source: Wikimedia Commons
License: Public Domain

Figure 4.35 | *Moonlight: The Pond*
Artist: Edward Steichen
Author: User "DcoetzeeBot"
Source: Wikimedia Commons
License: Public Domain

appearances. Steichen used layers of **gum bichromate** to add color and to create a sense of hazy atmosphere for a mysterious nocturnal landscape. (Figure 4.35) Samaras, on the other hand, created a type of photography he called **Photo-Transformation** by using his fingers and a stylus to move and smear the dyes of a Polaroid print while still wet. (*Photo-Transformation*, Lucas Samaras: http://www.metmuseum.org/art/collection/search/265049) Leaving the protruding hand untouched, Samaras altered the spatial relationships in his photograph by blurring the surrounding imagery, including his own face, which became quite indistinct in the process. The stages of creating photographs offer innumerable opportunities for altering the imagery from its "natural" appearances, while still often retaining the sense of "authenticity" of the photograph itself.

4.5.2.3 Expression(ism)

As we have seen, choices made to move away from naturalism can reflect both the culture at large and the issues with which artists concern themselves as they seek to express ideas and/or feelings of the moment. **Expression** has been sought for many purposes related to thought, belief, emotional impetus, and any human concern that might prompt the creation of artistic articulation, in its various forms and media. Often, though, the idea of **expressionism** in art is more narrowly used to define the idea of foregoing a measure of naturalism in favor of the emotional content, emphasizing how the culture and the artist felt about the subject matter. This may be used in the West or East.

Examples are numerous in the illustrations of narratives, such as the Indian mythological story of the Hindu Goddess Durga, who dramatically slays the Buffalo Demon, using weapons borrowed from the male gods. (Figure 4.36) Such a story lends itself well to a dynamically expressive interpre-

Figure 4.36 | The Great Goddess Durga Slaying the Buffalo Demon
Author: User "DcoetzeeBot"
Source: Wikimedia Commons
License: Public Domain

tation in art, as does the sort of devotional idea presented in the German works called ***andachtsbilder***, devotional images used to aid prayer, as seen in Figure 4.37. These works were created on both small and large scale to provoke contemplation of the sufferings of the Virgin Mary and Jesus Christ as prompted by the stories of the Passion of Christ. Such works were further inspired by the relation of the holy figures' sufferings to the physical effects of the Black Plague, rampant from Asia to Europe during the fourteenth century.

A more specific movement of Expressionism in Germany arose in the early twentieth century to give artistic form to the emotional and societal reactions to unrest caused by political and cultural upheavals. Reflecting the desire for social reform that was part of Realism as well as the long history of expressiveness in German art, the group was named the New Objectivity (*Neue*

Figure 4.37 | Pieta Liebieghaus
Author: User "FA2010"
Source: Wikimedia Commons
License: Public Domain

Sachlichkeit). In the aftermath of World War I (1914-1918), these artists presented harsh and piercing glimpses of the effects of the war's devastation on German society in the 1920s and of the ensuing societal unrest accompanying the emergence of the Nazis and the Third Reich in the 1930s. Artists such Max Beckmann (1844-1950, Germany, Netherlands, USA) and George Grosz (1893-1959, Germany) used their craft to level harsh and cynical criticism against what they saw in the society around them, at home and across Europe.

In *Paris Society,* Beckmann showed a group of businessmen, aristocrats, and intellectuals (many of whom emigrated to Paris to flee conditions at home) gathered for what ought to be an evening of social pleasantries, but was instead one clearly pervaded by a sense of foreboding and gloom. (*Paris Society*, Max Breckmann: http://www.guggenheim.org/new-york/collections/collection-online/artwork/503) The realism here shows the lack of connection among the partygoers, even to the extent that they apparently avoid or ignore one another, crowded as they are into an uncomfortable space. Beckmann himself, once a celebrated artist in Germany, became an object of censure and ridicule by the time of the Nazi regime, and his artwork is often full of a sense of the malaise of the age.

Grosz, also despised by the Nazis, tended to make much more specific use of his critical realism, delineating especially harsh condemnations of the military and governmental establishments. For example, in *The Hero,* Grosz used graphic realism to convey his view of the anti-heroic treatment of individuals—especially World War I veterans—that he saw all around him. (*The Hero*, George Grosz: http://www.moma.org/collection_ge/object.php?object_id=72585) In the work of these two artists, we can note that the realistic approach sometimes moves away from strong naturalism. The artists seem to have deliberately chosen to make their renditions somewhat abstracted and unrefined—even crude—for the sake of expressive emphasis.

4.5.2.4 Abstract Expressionism

We examined differences between representational and abstract art when we explored Van Doesburg's exploration of cows and the work of other artists who manipulated form by reducing its visual components or altering its appearance so that the form did not conform to the ways it might appear in nature. These artists chose to limit the degree to which they would carry the investigation of abstraction, opting to avoid losing references that were more or less clearly recognizable.

In the middle of the twentieth century, based in New York City, a movement called **Abstract Expressionism** included works of drawing, painting, print, and sculpture that were focused on the physical properties of the medium used as opposed to pictorial narrative, although not all of them were without reference to the figure or the phenomenal world altogether. In the work *Untitled* of 1957 by Clyfford Still (1901-1980, USA), we see how the imagery can remind us of a jagged crevice in a mountain landscape, but without definitive representation, and the artist himself denied that there was such a subject there. (*PH-971*, Clyfford Still: https://www.sfmoma.org/artwork/75.35)

Other artists associated with Abstract Expressionism used less sense of representation in their work. Included in the category were Jackson Pollock and Mark Rothko (1903-1970, Latvia, lived USA). (*The Deep*, Jackson Pollock: http://www.wikiart.org/en/jackson-pollock/the-deep-1953; *No. 61 (Rust and Blue)*, Mark Rothko: https://en.wikipedia.org/wiki/File:No_61_Mark_Rothko.jpg) Abstract Expressionist artists were more concerned with artistic process and formal means than with the creation of narrative pictures. In examining a small cross section of work by the Abstract Expressionist artists, we can see that it may not be appropriate, after all, to call this a stylistic category, as there is not really a stream of visual similarities among them; rather, they are characterized as much by their freedom from the constraints of stylistic rules and their lack of unifying visual features.

4.5.3 Individual Style

Johannes (or Jan) Vermeer lived in the seventeenth century, a time of artistic flowering often referred to as the Golden Age of Dutch art. During his lifetime, Vermeer was a painter of some renown in his hometown of Delft whose work was purchased by a small number of collectors. After his death in 1675 at the age of forty-three, however, he and his work were largely forgotten, in part because the few works he painted were in private collections and rarely seen. For example, Vermeer's painting *The Geographer* was in the hands of more than two-dozen private owners before it was sold to the Städel Museum (Städelsches Kunstinstitut) in Frankfurt, Germany, in 1885. (Figure 4.38) And, Vermeer himself was not

Figure 4.38 | *The Geographer*
Artist: Johannes Vermeer
Author: User "Hkgeogphr"
Source: Wikimedia Commons
License: Public Domain

"re-discovered" until 1860, when museum director Gustav Waagen recognized a work attributed to another artist as a painting by Vermeer. Working with Waagen, art critic Théophile Thoré-Bürger published a **catalogue raisonné**, a detailed, comprehensive list of the artist's work, in 1866, launching Vermeer toward the fame he and his thirty-four known paintings enjoy to this day.

After such a long period of obscurity, it is all the more interesting that Vermeer is considered today to have such a distinctive style. As in *The Geographer*, the great majority of his works are set in a

Figure 4.39 | *Wheat Field with Cypresses*
Artist: Vincent van Gogh
Author: Met Museum
Source: Wikimedia Commons
License: Public Domain

domestic interior, strongly lit by a multi-paned window to the left. Sunlight washes across the table at the window and the figure standing there, to the floor and the wall behind. The objects in the room are both those commonly found in a Dutch household of the day and specific to the occupation of a geographer, namely, the celestial globe, charts, and compass the man holds. Vermeer achieved the luminosity of the scene, with small details warmly highlighted to a fine glow, by applying multiple layers of translucent glazes of paint. The palette of earth tones interspersed with the vivid blue of ground lapis lazuli and brilliant vermilion of powdered cinnabar provide a richness, clarity, and stillness that are distinctively Vermeer's, as well.

The life and work of Vincent van Gogh also provides us with a good example to talk about the individual style of an artist. In addition to what can be learned about the artist through his drawings and paintings, the more than 800 letters Van Gogh wrote to his brother, Theo, other family members, and friends, provide valuable information about his artistic intentions and thoughts about his art and life. After a childhood the artist described as troubled and lonely, he found happiness in 1869 at the age of sixteen when he took a position with the art dealer Goupil & Cie, first in the Dutch city of The Hague and then in London, England. After leaving the firm in 1876, however, he spent the next seven years in a series of vocational and romantic pursuits that left Van Gogh disillusioned and adrift. In 1883, he began to pursue drawing and painting, for which he had shown promise as a child. The two years he spent in Paris, 1886-1888, provided him with seemingly endless opportunities to study and grow as an artist. Overwhelmed by the pace of life there, however, in 1888 he settled in Arles, a small town in the south of France, where he spent the last two years of his life.

Largely based on the prolific artistic output during and biographical details about those last two years, Van Gogh is well known as an emotionally troubled artist who struggled artistically, financially, and socially. His work from that period does not look like that of any of his contemporaries, so we feel confident that his choice of subject and technique reveals something personal and intimate rather than polished, distant, and conventional. (Figure 4.39) His swirling brush strokes and vivid colors seem to indicate the chaotic and emotionally turbulent life he was experiencing. His choice of cypress trees as symbols of eternity reveal a concern with the spiritual that is well documented in his letters of the time. His passion, dedication to painting, and perhaps even a kind of desperation all seem to drive Van Gogh's individual stylistic approach.

4.6 BEFORE YOU MOVE ON

Key Concepts

Visual art can be usefully interpreted using a variety of approaches to discovering meaning in the elements, principles, and relationships present in works of art. A structured approach using description, analysis, interpretation, and evaluation is presented and exemplified as one mode for understanding how works of art can carry meaning.

Other modes of interpretation recognize many approaches to art-making. Works of art may be idealized, representational, non-objective, or abstract. Issues of historical and personal style also become important in understanding what artists hoped to communicate with their artwork.

Types of art revolve primarily around representation, abstraction, idealization, and non-objective art, which is a rejection of representation.

The historical progression of artistic style simultaneously relies on and is limited by technology, socio-cultural, and religious constraints. Examples of cultural or Regional style are drawn from the ancient Near East, Ancient Greece and Rome, and the Indian sub-continent. Examples of period styles exemplified include the Romanesque and Gothic periods of Europe and the Italian Renaissance. Examples of formal styles, i.e., the "isms," include nineteenth century realism, expressionism of Weimar Germany, and the Abstract Expressionism of the New York School.

Test Yourself

1. Discuss the difference between the categories of representational art, abstract art, and non-representational art.

2. Cite and briefly describe the four phases of critical analysis presented in this chapter.

Phase	Description
a. _____	_____
b. _____	_____

      c. _____   _____

      d. _____   _____

3. Cite one example of an idealized work of art and discuss potential reasons for and goals of this idealization, especially as relates to the work's culture of origin.

4. Restate the three types of art historical **style** mentioned in this chapter, citing one example of each, and illustrate this example with a specific work of art

Style	Example	Artwork
a. _____	_____	_____
b. _____	_____	_____
c. _____	_____	_____

4.7 KEY TERMS

Abstract: in art, the property of representing selected essential features of a particular subject instead of relying on objective appearance alone.

Andachtsbilder: a German term to denote devotional images used to aid prayer.

Bodhisattva: in Buddhism, an enlightened person who remains in the world in order to help others attain enlightenment.

Catalogue Raisonné: a published collection of all the works of a given artist or art exhibition.

Composite view: the construction of a human figure from both profile and frontal views, for example, as in ancient Egyptian art.

Contrapposto: an asymmetrical arrangement of the human figure in which the line of the arms and shoulders contrasts with and balances the line of the hips and legs.

École des Beaux-Arts: an influential art school in France.

Expressionism: one of several art movements of the twentieth century that were concerned with conveying emotional and mental responses through art (German Expressionism, Abstract Expressionism, Neo-Expressionism).

Gum Bichromate: a photographic print process which uses gum Arabic and bichromate.

Hierarchical proportion: the condition in which the size of figures is determined by social importance rather than observation.

Humanism: the belief that people are naturally good and that problems can be solved using reason instead of religion.

Idealized: an image that is represented as being ideal or perfected.

Linear perspective: a geometric system for representing the illusion of receding space.

Naturalistic: of or pertaining to the appearance of nature, without idealization.

Non-objective: unrelated to or exclusive of perceptions of objective external reality.

Non-representational: artwork which intentionally avoids the strategy of representation, instead selecting only novel and original experience as subject matter.

Orthogonal lines: in linear perspective, diagonal lines that recede into fictive space.

Photo-transformation: a type of photography created by Lucas Samaras which uses fingers and a stylus to move and smear the dyes of a Polaroid print while still wet.

Portals: in Gothic architecture, doorways, traditionally embellished with sculptural decoration.

Representation: in art, the use of signs or images which stand in for or take the place of something else.

Stupas: in Buddhist religious architecture, rounded mounds which contain religious relics, mark sacred places, or are used as sites of meditation.

Tetrarch: in Roman political history, the term for one of four co-emperors of the Roman Empire installed by Diocletian in 293 CE.

Tympanum: in Gothic Architecture, the semi-circular area above the Portal, traditionally embellished with sculptural decoration.

Vanishing point: in linear perspective, the point on the horizon to which orthogonal lines converge.

Yakshi: in Hindu and Buddhist mythologies, female counterparts to male Yaksha, who are both mythical beings that guard treasure hidden in the Earth.

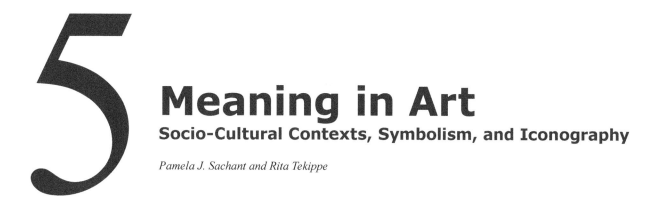

5 Meaning in Art
Socio-Cultural Contexts, Symbolism, and Iconography

Pamela J. Sachant and Rita Tekippe

5.1 LEARNING OUTCOMES

After completing this chapter, you should be able to:

- Place works of art in historical, social, personal, political, or scientific contexts.

- Define and distinguish between symbolism and iconography.

- Identify changes in symbols and iconographic motifs over time and in different cultures.

- Relate iconography to visual literacy.

- Describe connections between symbolism, iconography, and storytelling.

- Recognize metaphorical meanings in art.

5.2 INTRODUCTION

The process we go through when we look at a work of art to determine if we recognize and can make sense of its content is not just a visual one. It is a mental process as well, largely based on the elements within and about the work we can identify and categorize. As we look and think, we may be given clues about what the work means by where it is, when it was made, what culture it came from, who created it, or why it was made. Any information we can gather helps us understand the work's context, that is, for what historical, social, personal, political, or scientific reasons the work of art was made. And then, using all the contextual information we have gathered, we interpret the work of art's content to discover what it means or symbolizes.

5.3 SOCIO-CULTURAL CONTEXTS

5.3.1 Historical Context

We can learn about the historical context to help us interpret the content and understand the meaning of two seventeenth-century Dutch paintings. Willem Claesz. Heda (1594-1680, Nether-

Figure 5.1 | *Still Life with Gilt Goblet*
Artist: Willem Claeszoon Heda
Author: Web Gallery of Art
Source: Wikimedia Commons
License: Public Domain

Figure 5.2 | *Vase of Flowers*
Artist: Jan Davidszoon de Heem
Author: User "DcoetzeeBot"
Source: Wikimedia Commons
License: Public Domain

lands) created *Still Life with a Gilt Cup* in 1635, and Jan Davidsz. de Heem painted *Still Life with Flowers* around 1660. (Figures 5.1 and 5.2) Heda lived in his native Haarlem his entire life; de Heem was born in Utrecht but traveled in the Netherlands and then lived in Antwerp for the majority of his career, c. 1635 to 1667. He briefly returned to Utrecht but settled back in Antwerp in the 1670s where he remained until his death.

Although depicting different types of things, each of these paintings is a **still life**, an arrangement of objects both made by humans and found in nature, such as flowers, fruit, insects, sea creatures, and animals from the hunt. A still life falls into a subject category known as **genre** subjects or scenes of everyday life. Both Heda and de Heem specialized in painting still lifes that were beautifully arranged and stunningly lifelike. Each was well known for his ability to depict a variety of textures and surfaces often displayed side-by-side, as we can see here, to create a dazzling and sumptuous visual array.

There are a number of things going on in the Netherlands in the 1600s—known as the Dutch Golden Age—that can help explain why Heda and de Heem included some of the objects in their paintings. What is today the Netherlands (or Holland) and Belgium were together ruled first by the Dukes of Burgundy, the Burgundians, beginning in 1433 and then by Charles V of the Habsburg family in 1506. Charles V left the Netherlands in 1515, however, to become King of Spain. Tension created by family members who remained in place to rule led to friction with the Dutch and eventually to revolt beginning in 1566. At the same time, the Protestant Reformation that originated in Wittenberg, Germany, under Martin Luther in 1517 had spread through much of northern Europe, including parts of the Netherlands. Followers of the new Protestant faith were at first tolerated by the Catholic Spanish rulers, but they were soon treated as heretics, and their faith was seen as a rebellion to be crushed. William I, Prince of Orange, a Dutch nobleman, turned away from his position in the court of the Habsburg rulers to lead his country into the Dutch War for Independence from Spain, more commonly known as the Eighty Years War (1568-1648). In 1581, the seven northern provinces of the Netherlands were declared independent, forming what we still know as Holland today. The southern area that remained under Catholic Spanish rule was known as Flanders and is modern Belgium. Fighting continued on and off between the Dutch and Spanish until 1618 when they both became embroiled in a larger European War known as the Thirty Years War (1618-1648). With the signing of the Peace of Westphalia in 1648, the Spanish crown officially acknowledged the republic of Holland.

In the midst of this ongoing turmoil over politics and religion, as well as decades of disruption and destruction caused by war, the Netherlands also experienced a time of tremendous economic growth, revolutionary scientific exploration, dominance in worldwide trade, and flourishing of the arts. The rise of the merchant class (equivalent to today's middle class) led to the spread of education and wealth among new segments of society. Their knowledge of and appreciation for art, along with their discretionary income, in turn led to increased patronage. Patrons of art were not looking to purchase sculptures and paintings for churches, however, as Protestants do not embellish their houses of worship; they do not adorn the word of God as found in the Bible. This led to interest in new subjects in painting, such as genre and still life painting, as well as landscapes, city views, portraits, and religious subjects in works meant to hang in the home.

The subject of Heda's painting, *Still Life with a Gilt Cup,* is ostensibly the remains of a meal of oysters and bread, but it is even more about all the objects accompanying the food. (Figure 5.1) The tin plates and open-lidded pewter pitcher are relatively simply fashioned and could have been made by local craftsmen. But the remaining items, including a spiral ribbed clear glass cruet for oil or vinegar behind the tin bowl of oysters, the green glass wine römer, or goblet, decorated with **prunts** (applied blobs of molten glass, here drawn into points), and the tall, heavily ornamented, and gilded vessel topped by a lid with a figure of a warrior, are all luxury goods. They indicate wealth and good taste, and they allude to Holland's importance as a nation of traders who import beautiful objects from around the world.

We are not meant to look at this feast for the eyes and simply congratulate ourselves on our success and prosperity, though. The fact is the feast is over, and all we have here are the remains of what has too quickly passed. The richly decorated silver berkemeier, a wide-mouthed drinking vessel with a slender stem, is overturned. The oysters are a delicacy that retain their freshness and appeal only briefly, and the lemon, while beautiful, is actually bitter and will soon dry out. These are reminders that life is fleeting. No matter what material riches and comforts one accumulates on earth, it is more important to prepare one's soul for life everlasting.

In a similar fashion, in *Still Life with Flowers* de Heem sets before us, teeming with life and in abundant disarray, the beauty and bounty of nature. (Figure 5.2) But he also shows the swift passing of the seasons by depicting flowers, fruits, and vegetables that bloom and ripen throughout the year. The tulips—from highly prized and costly bulbs imported by the Dutch from the Ottoman Empire (modern Turkey)—honeysuckle, roses, carnations, peas, grapes, and corn—introduced to Europe from the Americas—are among the profusion of colors and forms that de Heem unrealistically depicts as all in season at the same time. The viewer would instead know that long before the orange carnation blossomed in the fall, the blood-red striped tulip would have withered in the spring. De Heem is reminding us in this **vanitas** (Latin: vanity) still life of our own mortality and the transience of life in the face of certain death.

Both paintings' messages reflect the importance in the Protestant faith, as practiced in Holland at the time, of the believer's direct connection to God without the need for intercessors. The faithful do not need the word of God to be interpreted for them, and the messages of God are everywhere. Both paintings are celebrations of riches and pleasures of life, but they are also reminders of its brevity and the unimportance of earthly possessions and human achievements in the face of eternity. So, while the works demonstrate the Dutch viewers' pride in themselves and their young nation's accomplishments in the face of tremendous obstacles, they also carry a word of caution and a reminder to be vigilant.

5.3.2 Social Context

Lilly Martin Spencer (1822-1902, USA) painted *Conversation Piece* around 1851-1852. (Figure 5.3) A **genre painting**, it depicts an everyday scene of a mother holding her infant in her lap while the father stands beside them playfully dangling some cherries above the baby's eager grasp. It is a quiet scene of family life, a moment of contentment and peace, with the dining table not yet cleared after a meal adding an even greater sense of intimacy and informality. Spencer was the only prominent female painter at that time in the United States, and the majority of her works are narrative genre pieces such as this one. They are scenes of domestic life, often suggesting a story told through the setting, the arrangement and gesture of the figures, and their facial expressions.

Elements in Spencer's work often seem to reflect her personal life. The artist depicted herself and her husband

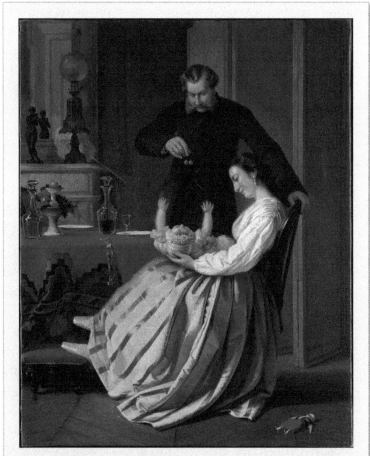

Figure 5.3 | *Conversation Piece*
Artist: Lilly Martin Spencer
Source: Met Museum
License: OASC

in *Conversation Piece,* as she did in many of her paintings. Not only was it unusual that she was a successful professional painter, when she married Benjamin Rush Spencer, he took on the household duties and aided his wife in pursuing her career. Over the course of their long (and what is believed to be happy) marriage, while also bearing thirteen children and raising seven to adulthood, Spencer remained the breadwinner of the family.

By the middle of the nineteenth century, a number of changes had been introduced into American industry and commerce that had far-reaching effects on the roles women, men, and children played in the home and in the labor force. The advent of new machinery and production methods in the textile industry, for example, generated a need for mill workers that in turn fostered the growth and spread of urban centers. At the same time, both those who owned and managed the mill factories as well as those who worked in them became part of a wage-based economy, and the demand for goods and services to support them rose accordingly. In New England, the majority of the mill workers were young women who had been recruited from rural areas; the wages they earned were often saved in anticipation of marriage or to supplement their family's income. But critics feared the economic and social independence these young women gained would turn them against the often hard and isolated farm lives they left behind, and indeed many chose not to return. The greatest apprehension, however, was these women would turn away from their rightful place in the private sphere of home.

The growing industrialism of American society impacted men and their roles within and outside the home, as well. Men primarily worked in the public sphere, that is, outside the home in areas such as manufacturing, business, or commerce. Their roles were in sharp contrast to the domestic duties and roles of wife and mother played by women. This separation of obligations and expectations led to rigid gender roles in which both women and men were contained. The roles confined the woman to the protective environment of home, while the man sheltered her as he faced the harsh demands outside.

In Spencer's painting, the woman represents the feminine ideal of a nurturing and content mother. But rather than showing a father who holds himself apart from the womanly, domestic sphere—as was far more common at the time—Spencer depicts the man in an equally caring and warm role. An oval is formed by the mother's bent head and arm which extends from her hand supporting the baby's head through the baby's upraised arm to the father's bent arm, his bowed head, and his left arm resting on the back of the mother's chair. At odds with many at the time who believed men and women existed in separate spheres, Spencer draws the family into one circle.

American industrialism worked hand-in-hand with American ingenuity. Steamboat routes on the Mississippi River and its tributaries substantially contributing to the growth of settlements and cities from New Orleans to Pittsburgh began in 1811. The first steamboat to make that run was the *New Orleans* designed by Robert Fulton and Robert Livingston, both key figures in the development of steamboat design and travel. As would be the case with the thousands of steamboats that would traverse the Mississippi over the next century, it was made of wood and propelled by a paddlewheel that was powered by a steam engine; the steam was made by heating water in boilers which had to be watched to avoid pressure building to the point of explosion, a very real and constant danger. In attempts to better travel time between landings or by engaging in races with

Figure 5.4 | *The Champions of the Mississippi - "A Race for the Buckhorns"*
Artist: Frances Flora Bond Palmer
Source: Met Museum
License: OASC

other steamboats, however, it was not uncommon for the engineer to stoke the fires while keeping the boilers' safety valves closed, allowing steam pressure to build past safe levels.

Although 230 boats were destroyed due to boiler explosions between 1816 and 1848 with the loss of nearly 1,800 lives, one of the great attractions of steamboat travel remained its speed.[1] The excitement and the danger of a steamboat race are captured in a print published by Currier & Ives in 1866, *The Champions of the Mississippi: A Race for the Buckhorns*. (Figure 5.4) Nathaniel Currier (1813-1888, USA) and his brother-in-law James Merritt Ives (1824-1895, USA) formed the company Currier & Ives in 1857. They published black-and-white and hand-colored lithographs on numerous subjects meant to appeal to a broad spectrum of the American public, including landscapes, genre scenes, portraits, depictions of politics and current events, and the latest innovations in science, industry, and the arts.

---

1   "Steamboats." American Eras. 1997. Encyclopedia.com. (June 22, 2015). http://www.encyclopedia.com/ doc/1G2-2536600971.html

The firm of Currier & Ives hired well-known artists of the day to create the drawings from which their lithographic prints were made. The artist who drew the *Champions of the Mississippi* was Frances Flora Bond Palmer (1812-1876, USA). Palmer, like Lilly Martin Spencer, supported her family as a full-time artist. Palmer produced hundreds of original drawings in the seventeen years she worked for Currier & Ives, more than any other artist they employed. She printed and hand-colored many of her own works, as well, parts of the lithographic process generally reserved for artists in the firm with less training and expertise. For example, the prints were usually painted in an assembly line, with one artisan applying a single color and passing the work on to the next for another color. That Palmer took part in all phases of creating the prints was an indication of her great skill and versatility.

As was the case with the majority of scenes Palmer created, she did not witness the race between the steamboats *Queen of the West* and *Morning Star* or the cheering crowd on the shore. She depicted numerous such scenes, however, as competitions such as this were commonplace and prints commemorating them were popular and sold well. The races and the steamboats were a source of pride and a celebration of American ingenuity, competitiveness, and success. For those who owned a print such as *The Champions of the Mississippi*, the vast majority of whom had never seen the river or a steamboat competition, it represented the open possibilities of America's greatest waterway and indomitable spirit. As described by Mark Twain, who grew up in a town on the river's shore and spent four years as a riverboat pilot (1857-1861), there was a nearly magical quality to the allure and excitement of life on the river, especially when a steamboat race was coming. He related in his memoir *Life on the Mississippi* (1883):

> In the "flush times" of steamboating, a race between two notoriously fleet steamers was an event of vast importance. The date was set for it several weeks in advance, and from that time forward, the whole Mississippi Valley was in a state of consuming excitement. Politics and the weather were dropped, and people talked only of the coming race.
>
> The chosen date being come, and all things in readiness, the two great steamers back into the stream, and lie there jockeying a moment, and apparently watching each other's slightest movement, like sentient creatures; flags drooping, the pent steam shrieking through safety-valves, the black smoke rolling and tumbling from the chimneys and darkening all the air. People, people everywhere; the shores, the house-tops, the steamboats, the ships, are packed with them, and you know that the borders of the broad Mississippi are going to be fringed with humanity thence northward twelve hundred miles, to welcome these racers.[2]

5.3.3 Personal or Creative Narrative Context

Charles Demuth (1883-1935, USA) painted *The Figure 5 in Gold* in 1928. (Figure 5.5) Demuth met poet and physician William Carlos Williams at the boarding house where they both lived in Philadelphia while studying at the Pennsylvania Academy of the Fine Arts. Demuth's painting is one in a series of portraits of friends, paying homage to Williams and his 1916 poem "The Great Figure":

2   Mark Twain, *Life on the Mississippi* (Boston: James R. Osgood & Co.), 1883. Accessed from: http://www.gutenberg.org/files/245/245-h/245-h.htm

Among the rain
and lights
I saw the figure 5
in gold
on a red
firetruck
moving
tense
unheeded
to gong clangs
siren howls
and wheels rumbling
through the dark city.

Williams described the inspiration for his poem as an encounter with a fire truck as it noisily sped along the streets of New York, abruptly shaking him from his inner thoughts to a jarring awareness of what was going on around him. Demuth chose to paint his portrait of Williams not as a likeness but with references to his friend, the poet. The dark, shadowed diagonal lines radiating from the center of his painting, punctuated by bright white circles, capture the jolt of the

Figure 5.5 | *I Saw the Figure 5 in Gold*
Artist: Charles Demuth
Source: Met Museum
License: OASC

charging truck accompanied by the clamor of its bells. The accelerating beat of the figure 5 echoes the pounding of Williams's heart as he was startled. It was the sight of the number in gold that Williams was first aware of at the scene, and Demuth uses the pulsing 5 to symbolically portray his friend, surrounded by the rush of red as bright as blood with his name, Bill, above as if flashing in red neon.

For Demuth, that connection between his friend and his poetry told us far more about who Williams *was* than his physical appearance. A traditional portrait would show us what Williams looked like, but Demuth wanted to share with the viewer the experience of the poem the artist closely identified with his friend so that we would have an inner, deeper understanding of the poet. Demuth gave us his personal interpretation of Williams through the story, the narrative, that he tells us with the aid of "The Great Figure."

Georgia O'Keeffe gives us a portrait of the American landscape in a similar way in her painting *Cow's Skull: Red, White, and Blue* from 1931. (*Cow's Skull: Red, White, and Blue*, Georgia O'Keeffe: http://www.metmuseum.org/collection/the-collection-online/search/488694) Throughout the nineteenth century and into the first decades of the twentieth century, the majority of artists depicted the American land through its mountains and forests, farmlands and prairies, rivers and waterfalls: the vast stretches, immense heights, bounty, variety, and majesty of the seemingly endless continent. In this painting, however, O'Keeffe chose to portray the beauty of the United States not through its fertile grasslands or rocky peaks but in the austerity and simplicity of the desert of the American Southwest that she had come to appreciate, as symbolized by the sharp lines of a bleached cow's skull set against patriotic red and blue.

O'Keeffe was born in 1887 near Sun Prairie, Wisconsin. After studying art and working as an art teacher in several areas of the United States, including Chicago, Illinois, Amarillo, Texas, and Columbia, South Carolina, O'Keeffe moved to New York City in 1918.

Alfred Stieglitz (1864-1946, USA), a photographer, publisher, and art gallery owner who was instrumental in introducing audiences to and helping them appreciate European and American modernist art in this country in the first decades of the twentieth century, had exhibited O'Keeffe's drawings in his gallery 291 in 1917. The following year she accepted his offer of support so that she could devote herself to painting full-time. After more than ten years in New York, depicting streets and buildings of the city and at the Stieglitz family home on Lake George in upstate New York, O'Keeffe decided to spend the summer of 1929 with friends in Santa Fe and Taos, New Mexico.

Painted after that trip, *Cow's Skull: Red, White, and Blue* shows the artist providing a contrast to traditional and popular landscape views. She is inviting the viewer to contemplate how nature can be daunting and uninviting and to remember the flinty strength of the pioneers who moved across and settled in the demanding climate and terrain of the Southwest. The harshness of that life can be seen in the jagged lines of splintered bone in the skull, a reminder of inevitable death—similar to a seventeenth-century Dutch *vanitas* piece such as de Heem's *Vase of Flowers*. But, the skull was also an object representing life to O'Keeffe:

> To me they are as beautiful as anything I know. To me they are strangely more living than the animals walking around…The bones seem to cut sharply to the center of something that is keenly alive on the desert even tho' it is vast and empty and untouchable—and knows no kindness with all its beauty.[3]

5.3.4 Political Context

As was the case with the painting *Pear Blossoms* by Qian Xuan (Figure 1.10), *Bamboo and Rocks* by Li Kan (1245-1320, China) was painted during the Yuan Dynasty when the Mongols ruled China. (Figure 5.6) There are similarities but also important differences between the works. *Pear Blossoms* was painted in 1280, shortly after the Mongols took power, and *Bamboo and Rocks* was painted nearly forty years later in 1318. During that period, the Mongolian leaders made substantial changes in the government, thrusting out those in imperial power and scholar officials, including painters. Those who had been at the top of the social and political hierarchy were now turned away from government positions and looked upon with distrust and distaste.

---

3   Georgia O'Keeffe, "About myself" in *Georgia O'Keeffe: Exhibition of oils and pastels* (New York: An American Place: 1939).

Figure 5.6 | *Bamboo and Rocks*
Artist: Li Kan
Source: Met Museum
License: OASC

Although the Mongols appreciated Chinese painting and artists were commissioned to make (or appointed to produce) works for those in power, many were unwilling to paint for the foreign leaders. Kan's painting is interpreted as a reflection on China, its people, and its traditions under Mongolian rule. *Bamboo and Rocks* is a pair of scrolls painted with ink and color on silk meant to be hung side-by-side. Unlike *Pear Blossoms*, which is a scroll meant to be unrolled in approximately twelve-inch segments on a table then rolled again to reveal the next segment and finally stored away between viewings, *Bamboo and Rocks* would remain in view hanging on a wall. Both are ink paintings capturing the simplicity of beauty in nature. But the objects depicted also have symbolic meaning going back to ancient Chinese culture. Bamboo symbolizes virtue, grace, and resilience, while rocks symbolize strength and power to endure. In Kan's painting, their contrasting forms, low and curvilinear against upright and angular, balance each other. The artist is indicating that

during the Yuan Dynasty, under the rule of the Mongol, the Chinese people would be like bamboo; they would bow but not break in the uncertain climate of the rocky landscape of occupation.

Francisco de Goya y Lucientes (1746-1828, Spain) was court painter to King Charles IV from the beginning of his reign in 1789 until Napoleon ousted Charles from his throne in 1808 during the French invasion of Spain. Goya was hired the same year to make a visual record of the bravery of the Spanish people against the onslaught of the French invaders. The impact of

Figure 5.7 | *Plate 15 from "The Disasters of War" (Los Desastres de la Guerra): And there is nothing to be done (Y no hai remedio)*
Artist: Francisco de Goya y Lucientes
Source: Met Museum
License: OASC

what Goya saw, however, changed the direction and tone of the series of prints he made from the unflinching courage of his fellow citizens to despair over the barbarous atrocities committed and merciless suffering endured by all who are trampled in the path of war. He created the series of eighty-two etchings, *The Disasters of War*, between 1810 and 1823. *Y no hai Remedio (And There's Nothing to Be Done)* is the nineteenth print in the series; it reflects the hopelessness of war. (Figure 5.7) There is no escape, nor is there justice. Both civilians and soldiers become de-humanized and numb in the endless slaughter, here in the form of a firing squad.

The print series was not published until 1863, thirty-five years after Goya's death. There are theories why: the artist was fearful of political repercussions, the scenes were too graphic, or the wounds were too painful for public release in the immediate decades after the war. The artist himself gave no explanation. By the time *The Disasters of War* series was printed, the French and Spanish governments that had participated in and ruled immediately after the Peninsular War (1808-1814), as it came to be known, had both been superseded. Goya's documentation of and cry against human self-destruction had no impact at the time of the disasters themselves, but they are still among the most powerful images of political protest ever made.

5.3.5 Scientific Context

Art and science are inextricably linked. The words "technique" and "technology" both originate from the ancient Greek word **tekhne**, which means art. For the Greeks, both art and science were the study, analysis, and classification of objects and ideas. Through the study of math and art, they arrived at the **golden ratio**: when dividing a line in two parts, the longer part divided by the smaller part is also equal to the whole length divided by the longer part. Expressed algebraically, that can be written as a/b = ab/a. The visual representation of the golden ratio, the Greeks determined, results in the most visually pleasing proportions within and of an object or figure. (Figure 5.8)

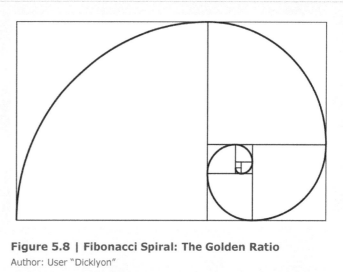

Figure 5.8 | Fibonacci Spiral: The Golden Ratio
Author: User "Dicklyon"
Source: Wikimedia Commons
License: Public Domain

Leonardo da Vinci was fascinated by how things work. The mechanics of nature, machinery, and the human body were all worlds to be explored deeply in order to be understood at their most essential, truthful levels. Although he was interested in human anatomy throughout his career, he spent the last twelve years of his life systematically studying and documenting his findings. He began in the winter of 1507-08 with a series of pen-and-ink drawings that he made of a dissection he carried out on an old man. In the winter of 1510-11, he completed additional dissections, probably working with anatomy professor Marcantonio della Torre at the University of Pavia. (Figure 5.9)

Leonardo intended to include his more than 240 drawings in a treatise on anatomy, but following Marcantonio's death from the plague in 1512 and political upheaval in the city of Milan where Leonardo lived, his focus shifted and he never completed and published his book. When he died in 1519, his drawings and notes on human anatomy along with approximately 6,500 pages from his other notebooks were dispersed and effectively lost to the world for 400 years. Leonardo's insights into such areas as the functioning of the heart and growth of a fetus, all completely accurate, had to be laboriously re-discovered by other artists and scientists in the succeeding centuries.

Questions that had long intrigued artists and scientists but could not be answered by observation with the naked eye, such as details about a planetary body in space, a specimen under a microscope, or an animal in motion, were finally being answered in the nineteenth century with the invention of photography. Leland Stanford, head of the Union Pacific Railroad, former governor of California, and racehorse

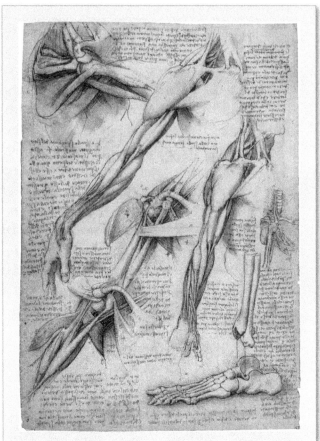

Figure 5.9 | Anatomical studies of muscles of the arm and shoulder, bones of the foot
Artist: Leonardo da Vinci
Author: User "Discovering da Vinci"
Source: Tumbler
License: Public Domain

owner, in 1872 accepted the challenge to prove whether all four feet of a horse left the ground when galloping. He hired photographer Eadweard Muybridge (1830-1904, England, lived USA) to conduct a study of the sequence of movement that is too rapid to be captured by the human eye. Muybridge experimented with setting up cameras along a track to photograph the horse and rider at evenly spaced intervals. He was soon able to prove that indeed all four hooves are in the air when the horse's legs are under its body—not when the legs are fully extended to the front and rear as many had thought. (Figure 5.10)

While the first set of photographs Muybridge took for Stanford were lost, the industrialist (who with his wife Jane would found Stanford University in 1885) encouraged the photographer to continue his studies. Muybridge published his findings on the galloping horse in *Scientific American* in 1878. In the aftermath, Muybridge spoke frequently throughout the United States. He was invited to continue his studies at the University of Pennsylvania where his work was valued for the information it would provide in the areas of technology, science, and art. He conducted his photographic experiments there from 1884 to 1887, and the following year he published his

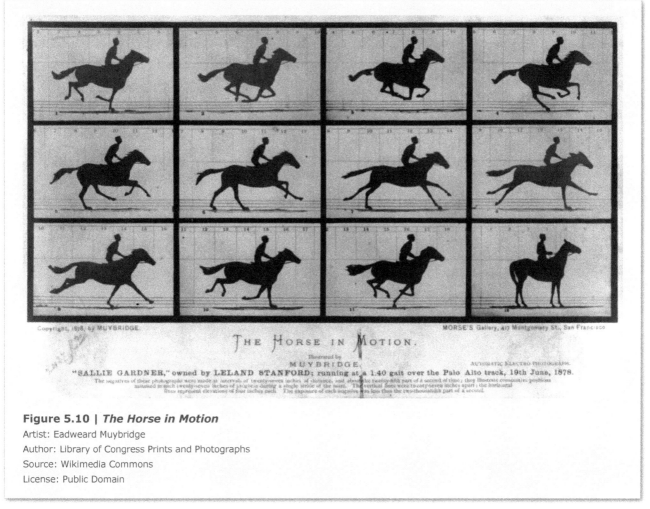

Figure 5.10 | *The Horse in Motion*
Artist: Eadweard Muybridge
Author: Library of Congress Prints and Photographs
Source: Wikimedia Commons
License: Public Domain

book *Animal Locomotion,* which contained 781 photographic plates of a wide variety of motion studies including men, women, children, horses, lions, bison, ostriches, cranes, and cats.

5.4 SYMBOLISM AND ICONOGRAPHY

Symbolism refers to the use of specific figural or naturalistic images, or abstracted graphic signs that hold shared meaning within a group. A **symbol** is an image or sign that is understood by a group to stand for something. The symbol, however, does not have to have a direct connection to its meaning. For example, the letters of the alphabet, which are abstract graphic signs, are understood by those who use them to have individual sounds and meanings. The users have assigned meaning to them, as letters have no meaning in and of themselves. An example of a naturalistic image is a rose, which in most Western civilizations symbolizes love. When one person gives a rose to another, it is a symbol of the love the person feels.

Iconography is the broader study and interpretation of subject matter and pictorial themes in a work of art. This includes implied meanings and symbolism that are used to convey the group's shared experience and history—its familiar myths and stories. Iconography refers to the symbols used within a work of art and what they mean, or symbolize. For example, in different cultures a snake may stand for evil, temptation, wisdom, rebirth, or the circle of life. A depiction of a snake in a scene with Adam and Eve has specific meanings for those of the Christian faith or others who understand the snake stands for temptation within the context of that subject or story. In Chinese culture, however, a snake represents the power of nature and is said to bring good fortune to those who practice the snake's restraint and elegance of movement.

5.4.1 Changes in Meaning of Symbols and Iconography

While a symbol might have a common meaning for a certain group, it might be used with variations by or hold a different significance for other groups. Let us use the example of a cross. At its core, a cross is a simple intersection of vertical and horizontal lines that could refer to the meeting of celestial and terrestrial elements or forces or could lend itself to other variations of meaning. The cross most frequently associated with Christianity is the Latin Cross, with the long vertical bar intersected by a shorter horizontal one—believed by many to be the form of the cross upon which Jesus Christ, the central figure of the faith, was crucified. (Variants of the Cross: http://wpmedia.vancouversun.com/2010/02/1346.crosses1.png) But its simplicity of conception lends itself to various other readings, as well, and in pre-Christian use it was related to sacred and cosmic beliefs.

Within Christian usage, the cross has taken a great number of different of forms, including the equal-armed Greek Cross, favored by the Byzantine Christians; Celtic crosses, with a circular addition to the crossing; X's and upside-down crosses associated with specific Christian **martyrs**, individuals who died for their faith, on such instruments of torture; and many others. In art, we might see them as simple flat graphic works, or decorated in two-dimensional renditions, or as fully developed three-dimensional interpretations, like the numerous grave markers in Irish cemeteries, where they are further embellished with intricate motifs and iconographic depictions of Bible stories. (Figure 5.11)

The Ankh, another cross form, with a looped handle, seems to have been devised by the ancient Egyptians as a symbol of the life-giving power of the Sun. (Figure 5.12) It was one of the numerous pictographic symbols they used both as a

Figure 5.11 | Celtic Cross
Author: User "Sitomon"
Source: Wikimedia Commons
License: CC BY-SA 2.0

Figure 5.12 | Ankh
Author: User "Alexi Helligar"
Source: Wikimedia Commons
License: CC BY-SA 2.0

separate sign and as part of the hieroglyphic system of writing they developed.

Clearly, many other symbols have various meanings, especially when they are represented as more abstract graphic signs. To read their implications in any particular application will require your considering where it was made and for what specific purposes, as well as how it might have been adopt-

Figure 5.13 | Hindu Swastika
Author: User "Masturbis"
Source: Wikimedia Commons
License: Public Domain

Figure 5.14 | Tian Tan Buddha
Author: User "Henry_Wang"
Source: Pixabay.com
License: CC0 Public Domain

Figure 5.15 | The Emblem of the Nationalsozialistische Deutsche Arbeiterpartei (NSDAP also known as the Nazi Party)
Author: User "RsVe"
Source: Wikimedia Commons
License: Public Domain

ed and turned to different use at that time or later. Sometimes the shifts in meaning may be radical, as in the form of the swastika, an ancient sacred sign used in many different cultures, including India and others throughout Asia, as well as the Near East, and Europe. (Figures 5.13, 5.14, and 5.15) It has historically been a very auspicious sign with implications of good fortune and positive movement, and was therefore adopted for the ground plan for Buddhist stupa worship centers. Of course, in the twentieth century, its appropriation by the Nazi Party as a symbol of the superiority of the Aryan heritage led to very different and now generally negative connotations.

Iconography is often more specific and definitive, with concrete reference to world experiences and, beyond that, to some form of narrative for the group involved.

Again, analysis of the pictorial form requires examination of the context in which the artwork was created. We can and must look at the underlying narrative, but, as we shall discuss in the next several chapters, the pictorial expressions evolve both independently of the narrative sources and in response to narrative and artistic change.

For example, Christians (more specifically that branch now known as Roman Catholics) debated the "true nature" of the Virgin Mary, the Mother of Jesus Christ.

Figure 5.16 | West Portal of Notre-Dame Cathedral
Author: User "Clicsouris"
Source: Wikimedia Commons
License: CC BY-SA 3.0

Among the points of debate was whether Mary was bodily in Heaven with her Son or whether she had to wait until the end of time when the whole of mankind would experience bodily resurrection, that is, at the time of the Second Coming and the Last Judgment, when everyone would have their lifetime of deeds assessed for purposes of learning whether they would spend eternity in Heaven or Hell. These Christian ideas are among those a great amount of art has been devoted to over time.

To illustrate, we can look at differences between two works about Mary and her place and role in Heaven that appeared in church relief sculpture during the twelfth and thirteenth centuries. These differing ideas focused on the implied elevation of Mary to a divine status, or to her not being seen as divine herself, in which case, the faithful needed to keep a view of her as being in a more subordinate or secondary status. The questions included consideration of Mary as the "Queen of Heaven," who might be ruling alongside her son. At Senlis Cathedral (1153-1181) in France, she was depicted as apparently a co-ruler with Christ, but ensuing theological discussion took issue with this possible over-elevation. (Figure 5.16) So, while the renditions of Mary as the celestial queen continued in popularity, they made it clear that she was only considered to be there at the bidding and will of Christ. This can be seen at Chartres Cathedral in France, where she bows her head to Jesus. (North Portal of Notre-Dame Cathedral: https://www.bluffton.edu/~sullivanm/chartresnorth/cportal.html)

What we see here, again, is that our full analysis of the artworks we encounter needs a complex approach that includes a variety of visual clues and a wide range of research on the contextual details of its creation and use. In contrast to the longstanding assertion that "beauty is in the eye of the beholder," the appropriate interpretation according to the intended symbolism and/or iconography must take the society, culture, and related circumstances into account to accurately reflect its intended meaning or original meaning for viewers. We will be exploring these ideas in greater detail in the next several chapters.

5.4.2 Symbolism, Iconography, and Visual Literacy

Symbols like the cross or the swastika will only have shared meaning for those who agree upon and affirm a specific interpretation, which can be positive or negative for any particular group of people. This specific meaning in symbols is always going to be the case for viewing of any visual expression, whether in simplified graphic sign form or a more detailed pictorial rendition. Additionally, the viewers must also often have some measure of instruction about how to view a particular work so they can understand its meaning more fully.

Also noteworthy is that members of any group use art as a means of sharing ideas and sentiment, as well as for expressing and teaching ideology. While the didactic uses of art have often been discussed in terms of instruction for the non-literate, we should recognize that the meanings of pictorial content and the tools used to create the picture must be learned as well. The apparent superficial meanings that are evident through unschooled visual examination do not produce the level of comprehension available in a more fully developed illustration of a tenet of a faith, political message, history lesson, or chart or graph of economic trends. So "visual literacy" should be considered a skill related to verbal and reading literacy for any didactic function. Only members of a group who have been led to understand and perceive the underlying principles will know how to "read" an illustrated message.

For example, we can look at the *Ritual Vase from Warka* (today Iraq) or the *Seven Sacraments Altarpiece* by Rogier van der Weyden. (The Warka Vase: http://dieselpunk44.blogspot.com/2013/08/the-warka-vase.html) (Figure 5.17) One

Figure 5.17 | Seven Sacraments Altarpiece
Artist: Rogier van der Weyden
Author: Web Gallery of Art
Source: Wikimedia Commons
License: Public Domain

could likely identify the basic pictorial content of either work, but further knowledge would be needed to analyze them further. If you were a member of the intended audience, you might have a bit more insight into what each artist had created in pictorial terms, but even the initiated viewer would likely have a limited "reading" of the work.

In the case of the *Ritual Vase from Warka*, even if you had lived in ancient Sumer and had been a devotee of the goddess Inanna, you would likely need further instruction about how the carvings on the different registers of the vase were arranged to show the cosmological conception of the created world. That is, one starts at the bottom with the primordial earth and waters, moves to the plants and animals above them drawing sustenance so that they could be harvested and herded by the humans, who then offer part of their gleanings to the goddess serving them from the temple as seen in the upper realm of the middle photograph. This design would be further explained as a neatly **hierarchical** arrangement, in which the levels of the created world were presented in different sizes, according to their relative importance. Additional meanings could be layered upon this cursory explanation with repeated teaching occasions and viewings.

The *Seven Sacraments Altarpiece* was painted by Rogier van der Weyden in a region and an era of tremendously complicated iconography: Flanders during the Late Gothic/Northern Renaissance period. The presentation here includes detailed pictorial description of each of the seven sacraments that marked the stages and stations of Christian life. This symbolism again developed over time, and often in response to theological writings that informed the artist and the viewer about specific meanings. The written sources are detailed and complex, with the pictorial rendition richly reflecting what the well-instructed Christian would know about these important rituals and their effects.

The larger central panel of the **triptych**, or three-part, format was used by the artist to emphasize the Crucifixion as the dominant overarching event that is related to each of the sacraments. Additionally, he provided angels with scrolls to identify them as if speaking to the viewer. So, here the messages are both pictorial and inscribed, and the iconography is a complex program that relates all these ritual events to the whole of the Christian life and faith. Truly, the viewer must be an initiate to discern the meanings behind all the symbolism or a scholar to discover them. Nonetheless, even the casual or uninitiated can read much of what is present in the painting and can identify both familiar elements and those that might lead you to further investigation. This is often the task and the path in interpretation of iconography in art.

5.4.3 Symbolism and Iconography in Mythology and Storytelling

From early on, art contained expressions of mythical accounts that people shared about their beliefs and ways of living. From the time of the first great civilizations, for example, in Egypt, the Near East, China, Japan, and India, artwork related to the stories of the people. The degree to which any contemporary written sources confirm these interpretations varies, but that these myths had commonly understood meanings for the people for whom they were made is confirmed by both their frequent appearance and their apparent places in their culture's artistic traditions, sometimes over centuries. Artistic iconographic traditions therefore show strong relationships to

Figure 5.18 | Belt Buckle from Sutton Hoo ship burial
Author: User "Jononmac46"
Source: Wikimedia Commons
License: CC BY-SA 3.0

beliefs and practices known from written sources—although written documentation sometimes does not appear until later times.

Because early stories were often passed along through oral tales, we do not always have a literary record of them until later times, even after the ideas had been expressed symbolically in pictorial art. An example of this symbolism may be found in the rich **hoard** (a collection of objects) known as the Sutton Hoo Ship Burial, found in England and deriving from the early Middle Ages era known as the Migration period (300-700 CE). Although the wooden ship itself has disintegrated, the burial hoard it contained provides details that confirm and broaden our incomplete understating of the adventurous societies of that time and their beliefs about needs for the afterlife. The diverse objects also lend certain insights into the epic tales of such warrior kings as Beowulf, whose story seems to have been a long-standing oral tradition, one perhaps re-told for centuries before being committed to written form. The lavish ornaments, such as this belt buckle and purse cover, give visual testimony to the tales of dragons and heroes like Beowulf through their expressive and intricate patterns and rich materials. (Figures 5.18 and 5.19) The fine metalwork on the purse cover is **cloisonné**, which is created by affixing gold or metal strips to the back

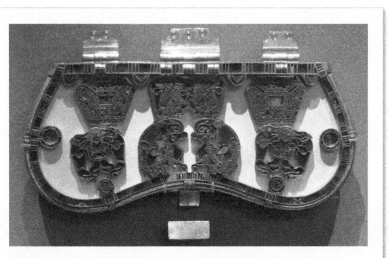

Figure 5.19 | Purse Lid from Sutton Hoo ship burial
Author: User "Jononmac46"
Source: Wikimedia Commons
License: CC BY-SA 3.0

Figure 5.20 | Terracotta Amphora (jar)
Artist: Andokides
Source: Met Museum
License: OASC

Figure 5.21 | The Column of Trajan
Artist: Apollodorus of Damascus
Author: User "Alvesgaspar"
Source: Wikimedia Commons
License: CC BY-SA 4.0

surface, making compartments, that are filled with powder (in this case, ground garnets) and heated to 1,400-1,600 degrees F.

The art of ancient Greece often showed great concern with the stories of Greek mythology as well. Tales of the gods and warriors abound, including those about great physical or intellectual contest, such as the well-known struggles of Herakles (known as Hercules under the Romans) one of which is seen on this amphora. (Figure 5.20) Such tales were very familiar, and viewers were expected to supply the details of the rest of the story through the parts that were shown. However, the skillful artist can enliven the presentation of the figures with posture, gesture, expression, and such symbolic props as the club and the tripod Herakles holds.

As with literary accounts, the artworks associated with historical and legendary events often include a very wide range of symbols and imagery to help convey ideas. These range from mundane details to grand historical moments, as in the Column of Trajan, nearly 100 feet in height, which commemorates the military campaigns of Roman Emperor Trajan (r. 98-117 CE) against the Dacians (101-102 and 105-106 CE) in 155 scenes. (Figure 5.21) Or

as appear in the Bayeux Tapestry, an embroidered cloth 230 feet in length that pictorially recounts the events of the Norman Invasion and Battle of Hastings in 1066. (Figure 5.22) Each of these works shows decisive points in their respective historical events in army operations and in the details of the hard work involved in preparing for battle. (Figures 5.23 and 5.24) In this way, they provide us with glimpses of everyday life in the respective eras alongside specific details about the particular campaigns, the cultures in which they were significant, and the

Figure 5.22 | Section of the Bayeux Tapestry depicting the Battle of Hastings
Author: User "Thincat"
Source: Wikimedia Commons
License: Public Domain

individuals who were key players in the historical events. The details of arms and armor, organized troops and chaotic fighting, building of defensive structures and devices, moments of victory and defeat, and innumerable other items and activities—all are individually and collectively efficient means of recounting the evolution of the events which, in each of these works, is dramatically developed across a long scrolled compositional field that further emphasizes the lengthy narrative each one progressively disclosed.

Figure 5.23 | Detail of Plate XLVI, The Column of Trajan
Artist: Apollodorus of Damascus
Author: User "Gun Powder Ma"
Source: Wikimedia Commons
License: Public Domain

Like many works of public art of the Roman Imperial era, the column glorifies not only Trajan (the base of the column was designed to contain his ashes) and his deeds, but also the ideas of imperial rule, the role of conquest in expanding the Empire, and the skilled work of Roman soldiers in battlements and tactics. By contrast, the Bayeux Tapestry has more emphasis on the actual tumultuous battle scenes—replete with mounted cavalry in chain mail and elaborate helmets—but it also includes a great deal more sense of historical context: events leading up to the 1066 Battle of Hastings after the death of King Edward the Confessor (r. 1042-1066) and his burial in the newly refurbished Westminster Abbey he had adopted as his royal church. Both of these works also include inscriptions that explicate ideas and events, as well as serve to further present the political messages about the battles—presented on the tapestry in a sort of scene-by-scene narrative—again, for each, underscoring the relationships between literary and pictorial presentations of ideas.

Figure 5.24 | Detail of the Bayeux Tapestry depicting Odo, half brother of William the Great, in battle
Author: User "LadyofHats"
Source: Wikimedia Commons
License: Public Domain

5.4.4 Exploring Symbolic and Iconographic Motifs

Such items as arms and armor are obvious sorts of symbols that clearly depict their purposes, but much symbolism that we see in other artworks has more veiled and variable meaning. Such simple items as flowers and candles can be used in very complex ways in pictures that carry diverse meanings, thus requiring careful study and even deep research in order to discern their implications in a particular work.

For example, the *Merode Altarpiece* by Robert Campin (c. 1375-1444, Belgium) depicts the Christian story of the Annunciation to the Virgin Mary by the Angel Gabriel that she will become the Mother of Christ, the son of God. (Figure 5.25) This work is full of symbols that have been widely studied to discern and interpret their messages. The lilies are generally interpreted to symbolize the purity and virginity of Mary—in other pictures, though, they might have other meanings, including reference to death, resurrection, birth, motherhood, or other events or conditions. Within this one work, the use of the candle, just extinguished with a trail of smoke, is given several different meanings by diverse viewers and scholars. It might show the moment of acquiescence, when Mary agrees to bear the Christ child, in which God takes human form. It has also been read as a foreshadowing of Christ's death, of human death in general, and of the fleeting nature of life for all.

In the time and place of the altarpiece's creation, symbolism in paintings was particularly apt to be rich and varied, offering the viewer/believer a lot to see and to contemplate further. In this way, if the symbols could be read in different ways, they could then provide ongoing stimulus for meditative reflection on the diverse levels of meaning.

Figure 5.25 | *Annunciation Triptych* (Merode Altarpiece)
Artist: Robert Campin
Source: Met Museum
License: OASC

Figure 5.26 | Terracotta Bobbin
Artist: Attributed to the Penthesilea Painter
Source: Met Museum
License: OASC

And some symbolic **motifs**, distinguishing features or ideas, carry different meaning in one context from what they might in another. Most symbols are not universal, although they often bear related meanings in diverse contexts. For instance, the sort of figure you might identify as an angel, that is, a winged creature with a human-like bodily form, has appeared in the art of many different cultures. They generally represent beings that can travel between the terrestrial and celestial realms, but their more specific roles can vary widely, for good or evil purposes. The Angel Gabriel, just seen in the *Merode Altarpiece,* was a messenger from God, according to the Christian tradition. This motif was built upon the Jewish tradition of angels sent from God for bringing news or instructions, or intervening as needed. Islamic interpretations, also building on the same traditions, are similar—although the figural representation is less common in Muslim artwork.

Prior to such figures, winged creatures known as Nikes were depicted by ancient Greek and Roman artists to show a moment of victory, sometimes, as is the case here, further symbolized by the award of a fillet, a band wrapped around the head, or laurel wreath. (Figure 5.26) These winged figures were sometimes gods or goddesses. The genie figures that adorned palace walls in the ancient Near East, including horses, bulls, lions, and other animals, were also winged to show their superior and sometimes god-like powers or origins. (Figure 5.27) Other examples include the goddess Isis of ancient Egypt, and the Persian god Ahura Mazda. (Figures 5.28 and 5.29)

Another set of prominent Christian iconographic motifs are the winged symbols which often represent the Four Evangelists in art: Matthew is the winged man or angel; Mark, the winged lion; Luke, a winged ox; and John, an eagle. (Figure 5.30) At the same time they refer to four key events in the life of Christ: the Incarnation, Passion, Resurrection, and Ascension. Interpretations

Figure 5.27 | Lamassu
Author: User "Trjames"
Source: Wikimedia Commons
License: CC BY-SA 3.0

Figure 5.28 | The Egyptian Goddess Isis
Author: The Yorck Project
Source: Wikimedia Commons
License: Public Domain

of these evangelist symbols are rooted in the Old Testament Vision of Ezekiel and the New Testament Book of Revelation, as related by the writings of St. Jerome in the fifth century CE. They accrued additional iconographic details over the centuries, with implications of their status as the special creatures who surround the celestial throne of God—again, signifying that the wings facilitate movement between the realms traditionally ascribed to a **deity**, a god or goddess, and divinely related creatures. This use of wings clearly reflects human contemplation of the abilities that birds have to defy gravity and to express artistically the lofty aspirations of the earthbound.

Another frequently used iconographic motif that appears across the ages and across cultures is the **halo**, usually a circular area of light appearing behind the head of a person or creature. One example is the halo that appears behind the heads of Christ and the symbolic winged creatures in Figure 5.30. Note that Christ's halo has a cross form embedded in it, and his entire body is surrounded by a circle of light (made up of four arcs) known as an **aureole** or **mandorla**. Such devices, in many related forms, indicate a radiance that surrounds certain figures, showing their sanctity, divinity, or divine favor. It indicates their aura of holiness, with implications of their being infused with warmth, inflamed with divinity or with divine love. In some of the Asian versions, notably Hindu or Buddhist, the radiance is literally comprised of flames.

Frequently seen, as well, are such items as crowns, thrones, regalia like scepters, garments like official capes, monks' robes, or uniforms of all varieties—indications of a person's belonging to a specific group, class, or office that lead the viewer to identify

Figure 5.29 | The Egyptian Goddess Isis
Author: The Yorck Project
Source: Wikimedia Commons
License: Public Domain

Figure 5.30 | The Four Evangelists
Author: User "AnonMoos"
Source: Wikimedia Commons
License: Public Domain

some specific aspect of who the person might be and what role they have in the depiction. The positioning of figures relative to one another should also be read in order to discern meaning, interactions, relative rank, and other implications. The types of garb, accompanying items, and positioning often relate the message to a specific time and place by giving historical and cultural context through details of style or motifs used.

For example, on the stele depicting his victory over the Lullubi, the Akkadian ruler Naram Sin (r. c. 2254-2218 BCE) wears a horned helmet and is

much bigger than the men around him. (Figure 5.31) He ascends the mountain as his enemies beg for mercy under the watch of astral deities, and that shows his relationship to them as the source of his power and right to rule. In the *Ghent Altarpiece* by Jan van Eyck (c. 1390-1441, Belgium), we can also see a variety of such motifs: Christ, wearing the papal tiara as a crown; Mary, richly dressed and humbly reading; and John the Baptist, in his garment of penitence, and preaching. (Figure 5.32) Adorned with jewels and gold on his clothing, the throne on which he sits, and the crown at his feet, Christ is here being shown as the king of Heaven as well as Earth.

Figure 5.31 | Victory Stele of Naram Sin
Author: User "AnonMoos"
Source: Wikimedia Commons
License: Public Domain

Figure 5.32 | The Ghent Altarpiece
Artist: Jan van Eyck
Author: Web Gallery of Art
Source: Wikimedia Commons
License: Public Domain

5.4.5 Metaphorical Meanings

The metaphorical meanings of specific artworks also depend upon a certain level of viewer knowledge and insight. A **metaphor** is a figure of speech in which one thing symbolically stands for another, perhaps unrelated, thing or idea.

In *1550 Chairs Stacked Between Two City Buildings* by Doris Salcedo (b. 1958, Columbia), we see a metaphorical treatment of life change. (*1550 Chairs Stacked Between Two City Buildings*, Doris Salcedo: http://www.mymodernmet.com/profiles/blogs/doris-salcedo-1550-chairs-stacked) It is a view of displacement resulting from a 1985 uprising in her Colombian homeland that left many migrants displaced or dead, as well as similar catastrophic events in locales across the globe. The jumbled mass of furniture alludes to the upheaval of lives that are overturned by mass violence and terrorism, often of those already without roots, community, or stable lifestyles. The victims, frequently anonymous and relatively invisible in the site of such a revolt, nonetheless left some hints of their presence in the chaotic remnants of their fleeting existence, in a place where they had established so little sense of their individual identities. Her metaphorical expression gives a probing glimpse of the devastation such events have wrought around the world.

5.5 BEFORE YOU MOVE ON

Key Concepts

Another way that we can consider art is to consider the context of its creation and use. Any work of art will reflect, to some extent, the cultural moment in which it appeared. This means that the artist and/or patron made choices that reflect the physical place and the cultural or subcultural group in which they lived and worked and the shared ways of being, living, or thinking that defined that group. The group's defining features might be national, regional, racial, ethnic, religious, economic, or related to gender, age, occupation, avocation, class, condition, or some other aspect(s) they have in common, by choice or by chance.

The artworks we encounter are filled with iconographic reference, symbols, and metaphorical allusions that give us clues to the broader and deeper meanings that were intended by the artist or patron. These prompt us to further investigation and/or contemplation that can lead us to those meanings. At the same time, they can also prompt insights beyond the original meaning, especially when they are presented as a partial statement of a larger myth or narrative we already know and understand or we might discover through further research. It is important for us to distinguish between those types of reading as we explore—to carefully differentiate between what we can learn about the original meaning and our own responses to what we see. This is true of all sorts of symbolism, as we should avoid the temptation to ascribe a truly universal idea or meaning for a symbol or motif. This makes both the discovery process and the viewing experience endlessly interesting.

Some works purposefully oppose prevailing issues in the culture, and pointedly so. We will see these oppositions in detail when we look at works concerned with religion, war, race, gender, and other themes. Thus, in order to understand and analyze the full meaning of any specific artwork, we must take into account just where and when it was made and what socio-cultural, symbolic, and iconographic features and meanings might be considered as relevant factors in its creation and use.

Test Yourself

1. How are seventeenth-century Dutch still life paintings related to historical events in the Netherlands at that time?

2. How did Lilly Martin Spencer counter social conventions of behavior at the time she was painting?

3. Describe an example of how industrial advances in the nineteenth century impacted art in the United States.

4. Give an example of how personal identity might be expressed in art.

5. Give an example of symbolism used and its meaning in Chinese painting during the Yuan Dynasty.

6. Give an example of art being used in scientific discoveries.

7. Give an example of a symbolic object and its meaning.

8. Define symbolism and iconography, and describe the difference between them.

9. Describe the relationship between symbolism and visual literacy.

10. What did objects found at the Sutton Hoo Ship Burial visually communicate?

11. What are some commonalities in what is represented in the Column of Trajan and the Bayeux Tapestry?

12. Describe changes in the symbolic motif of winged creature in human form (today an angel) prior to Christianity.

13. Describe how symbolic motifs can be used to indicate divinity or a ruler.

14. Give an example of metaphoric meaning in art.

5.6 KEY TERMS

aureole or mandorla: a pointed circle of light or radiance surrounding a holy figure.

cloisonné: decorative work created by affixing metal strips to a surface, making compartments, that are filled with powdered material and melted at high temperatures.

deity: a divinity, a god or goddess.

genre: subjects or scenes of everyday life.

golden ratio: a relationship of parts achieved when the longer part divided by the smaller part is also equal to the whole length divided by the longer part; the golden ratio in art and architecture provides the most harmonious and visually pleasing proportions.

halo: usually a circular area of light appearing behind the head of a holy person or creature.

hierarchical arrangement: where the hierarchy or ranking of people or objects is represented by their different sizes, according to their relative importance.

hoard: a collection of objects.

iconography: the study and interpretation of subject matter and pictorial themes in a work of art.

mandorla: (see aureole).

martyr: individual who died for their faith.

metaphor: a figure of speech in which one thing symbolically stands for another, perhaps unrelated, thing or idea.

6 Connecting Art to Our Lives

Peggy Blood, Rita Tekippe, and Pamela J. Sachant

6.1 LEARNING OUTCOMES

After completing this chapter, you should be able to:

- Identify the purposes art serves in society

- Understand the philosophy of aesthetics in the visual arts

- Understand the function of art as a means of communication

- Understand how architectural forms contributed and enhanced to religious cultures

6.2 INTRODUCTION

Art has been described as humankind's most enduring achievement. From the time of early cave dwelling to contemporary society, art has served as a vehicle for translating our insights into understanding others and ourselves. The creation of art may have different aims, for example, to make something beautiful, to be broadly expressive and emotional (without connection to beauty) for personal reasons, to illustrate concepts and beliefs of great importance to its creators, to show ways in which a group is unified, or to make a social or political statement. These disparate aims have one thing in common: they each seek in some way to connect art to our lives.

6.3 AESTHETICS

Aesthetics, the study of principles and appreciation of beauty, is linked to our thinking about and connections to art. During the eighteenth century in Europe, philosophers and other thinkers began to question the interrelationship of art, beauty, and pleasure. German philosopher Immanuel Kant characterized the appreciation of beauty as the "judgment of taste," which is comprised of two parts: subjectivity and universality. Subjectivity, as the term suggests, is based on the feeling of pleasure or displeasure experienced by the individual viewer. Universality refers to views about art that are held in common, the "norm," so to speak. Kant believed the beauty of art can only be appreciated when the viewer is "disinterested," that is, when the viewer is deriving pleasure that is not based upon or produces desire. If the viewer's subjective judgment is disinterested, then a universally valid measure of taste can be rendered. Only if the viewer can separate the appreciation of art from the desire for it, and is instead interested in art for its pure beauty, or aesthetics, can the viewer be said to have achieved the judgment of taste.

Writers, composers, and artists who were part of the Romantic movement that emerged in Europe at the end of the eighteenth century soon questioned Kant's belief that aesthetics or the study of beauty in art, what he termed the judgment of taste, was both disinterested and universal. Turning away from categories and definitions based on rationality, Romanticism celebrated spontaneity, emotion, the individual, and the **sublime**: intellectual and imaginative sensations that defy measurement or explanation.

Figure 6.1 | _Death of Sardanapalus_
Artist: Eugène Delacroix
Author: User "Marianika"
Source: Wikimedia Commons
License: Public Domain

Romantic painter Eugène Delacroix (1798-1863, France) spent his lifetime seeking to express the extremes of human emotion and experience in his work based on history, literature, current events, and his own travels. With passages of brilliant color applied in thick, vigorous brush strokes, Delacroix depicted beauty, violence, tragedy, and ecstasy with equal passion, in waves of movement swiftly passing across his canvas. This quality can be seen in _The Death of Sardanapalus_ where the shadowed figure of the Assyrian king surveys the scene of carnage taking place before him with dispassion. (Figure 6.1) Although historical accounts indicate that Sardanapalus did have all of his possessions destroyed, including his concubines and horses, rather than surrender them to his enemies, Delacroix largely relied on his own imagination for his frenzied interpretation and embellishment of the scene.

John Dewey, an American philosopher, psychologist, and educational reformer, in 1934 wrote _Art and Experience_. He described the aesthetic experience in ways that somewhat reflect the process Delacroix brought to his painting. Dewey stated, however, that although it begins with the art object, the experience of art extends far beyond that one element to produce an ongoing exchange between artist, viewer, and culture at large that culminates in an experience that is a "manifestation, a record and celebration of the life of a civilization."[1] The "sudden" pleasure one feels when engaging with a work of art or architecture is, in fact, the product of a long process of growth and engagement. For example, walking around and through a grand structure such as Reims Cathedral (1211-1275) in France, with its High Gothic façade, lavish sculptural decoration, extreme verticality, and expansive windows, is breathtakingly impressive because object (building) and experience have coalesced. (Figure 6.2) Further, we continue learning from the experience of observing art or beauty—what, why, and when depends on how much we receive from the experience and from successive encounters.

The movement in thinking about aesthetics from Kant's judgment of taste, with its assumption of an intellectually-based universality, to Dewey's claim that the aesthetics of the work of art are found in the viewer's experience of it, at that moment and over time, mirror substantial changes that have taken place in all aspects of scientific and intellectual thought over the past

Figure 6.2 | Cathedral of Reims
Author: User "bodoklechsel"
Source: Wikipedia
License: CC BY-SA 3.0

three centuries. What we can learn from their theories is that we can examine ideas about "fine arts," "beauty," and "aesthetics" and perhaps come up with similar definitions conveying ideas of pleasure, temporary enlightenment, and human experience—but, we may not.

For example, Miami-based artist Jona Cerwinske (USA), began his career making graffiti art and street murals and considers any surface a ground for art. In 2007, he covered a Lamborghini car with an intertwined network of organic shapes and geometric lines. (Lamborghini Art, Jona Cerwinske: http://www.dubmagazine.com/home/cars/item/8746-jona-cerwinske-exotic-art) This work of art could be described as an example of disinterested contemplation: you look at the Lamborghini and contemplate the beauty and elegance of the car and its design. In this way, the car's aesthetic appeal stems from admiration of the object and the delight it gives; it is a judgment of taste. Conversely, it could be described as an aesthetic experience: looking at the Lamborghini produces a response of pleasure, perhaps at its beauty, its place in the history of fine motor cars, or the thought of owning and driving such a prestigious and fast vehicle. In this case, appreciation of beauty is both a broadly intellectual as well as an individual emotional response.

---

1   John Dewey, *Art as Experience* (New York: Minton, Balch, and Co., 1934), p. 326.

6.4 EXPRESSION (PHILOSOPHICAL, POLITICAL, RELIGIOUS, PERSONAL)

Art has important functions in facilitating various types of human expression. Both creating and viewing art can provide us means of stating or affirming our personal and collective feelings, thoughts, ideals, and attitudes. Often we learn values and philosophical ideas and themes through artistic means.

Among the many philosophy-based art movements of the late nineteenth century was the French group who called themselves *les Nabis*, or the prophets. Their task as artists, they believed, was to revive ideals of painting, to prophesy modern modes, and to affirm spiritual goals by envisioning nature's roles in life and creating a new symbolism. Among the movement's leaders was Maurice Denis (1870-1943, France), who often

Figure 6.3 | Wave
Artist: Maurice Denis
Author: User "Dcoetzee"
Source: Wikipedia
License: Public Domain

depicted landscape settings imbued with biblical or mythical themes. (Figure 6.3) His paintings are abstracted statements about his philosophies of faith and of the need for honesty in art. With willowy figural forms that were lyrically flattened in space, he asserted the two-dimensionality of the picture plane, seeking to avoid the delusions of depth and emphasizing the surface of the work and the beauty of color.

Political statements are often wed to philosophical principles in the ways that they are given artistic expression. Such was the case with grand American landscape paintings such as *Emigrants Crossing the Plains* by Albert Bierstadt (1830-1902, Germany, lived USA). (Figure 6.4) This painting was associated with the nineteenth-century philos-

Figure 6.4 | Emigrants Crossing the Plains or The Oregon Trail
Artist: Albert Bierstadt
Author: BOCA Museum of Art
Source: Wikimedia Commons
License: Public Domain

Figure 6.5 | Ara Pacis in Rome, Italy
Author: User "Manfred Heyde"
Source: Wikimedia Commons
License: CC BY-SA 3.0

ophy of Manifest Destiny which promoted the idea that the assimilation of land and the use of the natural resources of the western parts of the United States were God-given rights and duties for the people who had settled here. Essentially, the settlers (who were mainly of European descent) were destined to occupy and civilize the lands from one coast to the other. This philosophy justified the political actions that took away the Native Americans' rights and also led to the Mexican-American War (1846-1848).

The history of art is replete with instances of political statements and political propaganda, as we have seen. In ancient Rome, the Emperor Augustus not only presented himself as very young and fit in his portrait (see Figure 4.20), but also promoted his political agenda through such public monuments as the *Ara Pacis*. (Figure 6.5) This altar dedicated to the goddess of peace is adorned with messages about the peace and prosperity Augustus was bringing to the citizens through his many virtues and achievements, including his conquest of foreign lands, association with the Roman deities, role as chief priest, promotion of the family as the cornerstone of the empire, wisdom of the imperial/senatorial rule, and alleged ancestry leading back to the legendary founding of Rome by Romulus and Remus. All these pictorial messages served to characterize the ways that Augustus wanted his relationship to the people to be perceived. With its enclosed altar table, the *Ara Pacis* also carried religious messages about the practices of making sacrifices to the pagan deities, carried out by Augustus in his role as chief priest.

Such public artistic expressions have been common throughout time, but there have also been many statements of personal belief, sentiment, or feeling. Personal statements can also reflect on a person's status or occupation. Painter Adélaïde Labille-Guiard (1749-1803, France) portrays herself as highly positioned in society by virtue of her own skills in portraiture and her role as a teacher. (Figure 6.6) John Singleton Copley (1738-1815 USA, lived England) created a portrait of *Mrs. Ezekiel Goldthwait* that conveys her

Figure 6.6 | *Self-Portrait with Two Pupils*
Artist: Adélaïde Labille-Guiard
Source: Met Museum
License: OASC

wealth and status through clothing and setting. (Figure 6.7) At the same time, by having her reach for the fruit on the table, he alludes to her other accomplishments, including being the mother of thirteen children, a gifted gardener, and a wealthy landowner with orchards in colonial Boston.

6.5 UNIFICATION/EXCLUSION

Art and architecture can be used as a means of bringing together a group of people with like beliefs or views, and emphasizing what they have in common. In demonstrating how they are alike, such objects and places can also indicate how others are different, which can lead to the exclusion of those who hold different beliefs or views. The Dome of the Rock is such a place.

The events that have been agreed upon as having occurred, and their relative importance, are key to understanding the Dome of the Rock or Qubbat as-Kakhrah in Jerusalem. (Figure 6.8) Its site, origins, and various past and present uses are all fac-

Figure 6.7 | *Mrs. Ezekiel Goldthwait*
Artist: John Singleton Copley
Source: Museum of Fine Arts Boston
License: Public Domain

tors in the shrine's meaning and significance to the people of different backgrounds and faiths for whom it is a holy place. The Dome of the Rock was completed in 691 CE as a shrine for Muslim pilgrims by the Umayyad caliph, or political and religious leader, Abd al-Malik. The sacred rock upon which the shrine is built marks the site where Muhammad ascended to heaven on a winged horse. Part of the Temple Mount or Mount Zion, the rock is said to have great importance before Muhammad, as well, by those of the Jewish, Roman, and Christian faiths. It is the site where Abraham prepared to sacrifice his son, Isaac; according to the Hebrew Bible, Solomon's Temple, also known as the First Temple, was later erected there; Herod's Temple, completed during the reign of the Persian King Darius I around 516 BCE was next built; and it was destroyed in 70 CE under Roman Emperor Titus, who had a temple to the god Jupiter built on the site.

Figure 6.8 | The Dome of the Rock
Author: User "Brian Jeffery Beggerly"
Source: Wikimedia Commons
License: CC BY 2.0

As Christianity grew in the succeeding centuries, the city of Jerusalem, then part of the Byzantine Empire (c. 330-1453), became a destination for pilgrims visiting places Jesus was said to have lived or traveled to in his lifetime. But, the city came under Muslim rule in 637 CE, and it is thought that Caliph Abd al-Malik had the Dome of the Rock built on the holy site to demonstrate the lasting power of the Islamic faith, and to rival the Byzantine Christian churches in the region. As a young faith, Islam did not yet have a "vocabulary" of architectural forms established. Muslim builders and artisans instead borrowed from existing structures—houses of worship, palaces, fortifications—throughout the Mediterranean and Near East.

One of the inspirations for the Dome of the Rock is the dome of the Church of the Holy Sepulcher, also in Jerusalem, that was built in 325/326 CE on what is believed to be Calvary,

where Jesus was crucified, as well as the sepulcher, or tomb, where he was buried and resurrected. (Figure 6.9) While the overall plans of the two buildings are markedly different, the domes are nearly the same shape and size: the dome of the Church of the Holy Sepulcher is approximately sixty-nine feet in height and diameter, while that of the Dome of the Rock is sixty-seven feet. Each of the eight outer walls of the Dome of the Rock is sixty-seven feet, as well, giving the octagonal structure the balance of relative proportions, and rhythmic repetition of forms found in many Christian **central-plan** churches, that is, with the

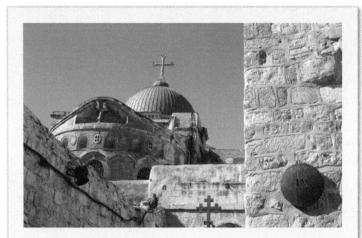

Figure 6.9 | Exterior view of the Church of the Holy Sepulchre
Author: User "Anton Croos"
Source: Wikimedia Commons
License: CC BY-SA 4.0

primary space located in the center. (Interior Diagram of the Church: https://classconnection. s3.amazonaws.com/815/flashcards/923815/jpg/picture101324161178159.jpg)

The Dome of the Rock has passed between the hands of Muslims, Christians, and Jews many times since it was built. Today, Jerusalem is part of Israel, but the Dome of the Rock is maintained by an Islamic council within Jordan's Ministry of Awqaf (religious trust), Islamic Affairs, and Holy Places. Since 2006, non-Muslims have again been allowed on the Temple Mount, during certain hours and after having gone through security checkpoints, but Muslims only are allowed into the Dome of the Rock. Some Orthodox Jews believe it is against their faith to visit the holy site at all.

The Dome of the Rock is one example of a holy site upon which a building or a succession of buildings devoted to different religious beliefs has been erected. Such a structure may have been used for hundreds of years by a group following a faith dissimilar to those before or after who claim ownership of it, and the structure may share architectural elements with houses of worship from other religious systems. Those things are not necessarily important to the believers, although there are numerous occasions in history when destruction of a holy building with the intention of replacing it with a place of worship sacred to the new regime symbolizes a conqueror's defeat of a people and their religion.

Key, however, is the conviction that the site is hallowed: the holiness of the place is believed without question. Keeping that in mind, recognizing the long, varied, and sometimes contentious history of the Temple Mount, the Dome of the Rock, and the city of Jerusalem, as well as the significance of events that have taken place there to people of the Jewish, Islamic, and Christian faiths, what is remarkable is the site is not one of exclusion. There is tension and at best a parallel existence of religious ideologies, but considering the divergent meanings and strong significance of the site as a place of pilgrimage and worship to so many, while the Dome of the Rock is far from being a model of unification, it is not an example of rejection.

On a more individual level, Winslow Homer (1836-1910, USA) was born in Boston, Massachusetts, and started his career there as a printmaker before moving to New York City in 1859. He opened his own studio and did freelance work for *Harper's Weekly*, making sketches that he and other illustrators produced as wood engravings for the journal. Once the Civil War began in 1861, Homer became an artist-correspondent for the magazine, sometimes traveling to capture scenes on battlegrounds, in soldiers' camps, and other newsworthy locales. He often created informal narratives about both military and civilian life, the war as experienced by those on the battle lines as well as the home front. His images and the stories they told were about the people, their efforts, bravery, sacrifices, and attempts to maintain a semblance of normalcy in the midst of a war that was tearing the nation apart.

In addition to his drawings and prints, Homer began painting Civil War subjects in 1862. He showed a number of these paintings to critical and popular acclaim in the annual exhibitions at the National Academy of Design in New York between 1863 and 1866. One of the last Civil War paintings he created was *The Veteran in a New Field*. (Figure 6.10) He started it shortly after the war ended and President Abraham Lincoln was assassinated, both events occurring in April 1865. Homer depicts a soldier who has returned to his farm. Having cast aside his Union jacket, the soldier-farmer has taken up his scythe and, with broad horizontal

Figure 6.10 | *The Veteran in a New Field*
Artist: Winslow Homer
Source: Met Museum
License: OASC

sweeps, harvests a bountiful crop. This quiet scene is a reminder of the never-ending process of life, death, and rebirth. Homer captures the sense of anxious relief, deep sorrow, and tentative hope individuals and nation alike were experiencing at that time of transition.

Homer was quietly calling for a healing of the Union, seeking grounds for unification of a bitterly divided and sorely wounded nation. He saw this recovery as being possible through the continuity of meaning found in the land and commonalities of work.

6.6 COMMUNICATION

In past societies in which art played a central role, people communicated through their creativity. In societies where many people were illiterate, they understood and learned more from symbolism and images than from words. One such example is the *Snake Goddess* discovered by archaeologist Arthur Evans and his team in 1903 at the Palace of Knossos on the island of Crete. (Figure 6.11) Part of the Minoan civilization (c. 3650-c. 1,450 BCE), this **deity** is believed to be a fertility symbol, also known as a "Mother Goddess," a religious symbol that appears from prehistoric eras until the Roman Empire. The snake held in each of the figure's upraised hands is associated with fertility and symbolizes the renewal of life due to the fact that it periodically sheds its skin. The object tells us about the type of culture from which it is derived, articulating their beliefs, traditions, and customs. For the Minoans, there was no need to explain or interpret this image because it was easily understood by their community.

For Chinese art, different periods in history have given way to different meanings attributed to its imagery. Although numerous textiles, calligraphy, ceramics, paintings, sculptures, and other objects and works from China are thousands of years old, the idea of grouping them under the description of "Chinese art" has a short history. In this sense, art in China is not really that old. This is because the vast majority of people in China did not see the artifacts that are the artistic heritage of that country before the twentieth century—when the Nantong Museum, the first built by the Chinese and not colonial occupiers, opened in 1905—despite the existence of a sophisticated tradition of creating art and of collecting and showing art to the elite.

Figure 6.11 | Snake Goddess
Author: User "C messier"
Source: Wikimedia Commons
License: CC BY-SA 4.0

Categorizing Chinese art allowed statements to be made about the art and people. The various ways in which different meanings have been read into Chinese art at different periods of time is well illustrated in this jade *gui* tablet. (Jade Tablet: http://culture.teldap.tw/culture/images/collection/20120807_NPM/jade04.jpg) A ***gui*** is a ritual scepter, held by a ruler during ceremonies as a symbol of rank and power. According to researcher Tsai Wen Hsiung, the history of using jade can be traced back seven thousand years. Looking at jade plaques unearthed from the Stone Age and Neolithic period, it is evident that the Chinese people were the first to carve jade for ornaments. This jade tablet is from the Late Shandong Longshan Culture (c. 2650-2050 BCE). Located in Shandong province, it *was the last Neolithic* jade *culture* in the Yangtze Valley River region, a land area rich in resources. The tablet is one of a large number of artifacts made from jade in that creative era, many of which replicated weapons and tools. Jade was the most precious material available in the Yangtze region at the time the jade *gui* tablet was made.

The tablet represents the excellent manufactured craftsmanship of the Shandong Longshan culture. The stone has a yellow tone with grey and ochre natural coloring resulting from aging over time. In low relief slightly below the middle of the tablet is a stylized face of a god shown in a typically flattened view. (Detail of Jade Tablet: http://culture.teldap.tw/culture/images/collection/20120807_NPM/jade05.jpg) There is an eighteenth-century inscription by a Chinese emperor who provides an explanation of the decoration. According to art historian Chang Li-tuan, the tablet was originally plain, but during the Ch'ien–lung reign two poems from different years were engraved on it; the last engraving in 1754 was by the Ch'ien–lung Emperor. The stone with its décor of symbolic images and incriptions represents the Chinese love of antiquity, depicting a people uniquely proud of interpreting their history. It also shows us the tradition in Chinese art of contributing to the meaning of a work by adding words and imagery to it over time. In doing so, both the symbolism and the status of the object are enhanced.

A more modern use of communicating through symbols in art can be found among the Ashanti people of Ghana, West Africa, and the Kente cloth woven by them and others in the region, including the Ewe people. Using silk and cotton, the cloth is woven on specially designed looms in four-inch strips that are then sewn together. (Figure 6.12) Kente cloth was tra-

Figure 6.12 | Kente Weaving
Author: User "ZSM"
Source: Wikimedia Commons
License: CC BY-SA 3.0

ditionally worn by kings during special ceremonies. The patterns and symbols woven into the cloth conveyed highly individualized messages that could not be reproduced by the weavers for any other individuals. Colors conveyed mood, with darker shades associated with grieving and lighter shades with happiness. Although the cloth was originally for political leaders, the design was not meant to convey a political message: it represented the culture's spiritual beliefs in symbols and colors.

In his conceptual art, Mel Chin (b. 1951, USA) does make a political statement. For example, he examines the psychological and social issues of imperialism in his black nine-by-fourteen-foot spider. In the stomach of the giant, intimidating spider is a glass case containing an 1843 china teapot on a silver serving tray. (*Cabinet of Craving*, Jesse Lott and Madeline O'Connor: http:// melchin.org/oeuvre/cabinet-of-craving) The sculpture symbolizes the destructive co-dependence of empires, depicting the English craving for tea and porcelain during the Victorian era and the Chinese desire for silver that led to the Opium Wars (1839-42, 1856-60). Although Chin takes an indirect approach in making his political statement, it is nevertheless powerful.

6.7 PROTEST AND SHOCK

Art also connects to our lives as a means of expressing protest, as can be seen in the work of Jaune Quick-to-See Smith (b. 1940, USA), a Native American who often sarcastically comments on the history of the treatment of her people by Americans in general and by the United States government in particular. The impetus for these two works was the 1992 celebration of the 500th anniversary of Columbus's discovery of the "New World." (*Trade (Gifts for Trading Land with White People)*, Juane Quick-to-See Smith: http://www.chrysler.org/ajax/load-artwork/26; *Paper Dolls for a Post Columbian World with Ensembles Contributed by US Government*, Juane Quick-to-See Smith: http://sam.nmartmuseum.org/view/objects/asitem/People$0040636/5/ primaryMakerAlpha-asc?t:state:flow=41dede4d-4192-4c2a-86e4-cd9d50f583c2) Her commentary includes the commercialization and stereotyping of her people, and their relegation to reservations, with forced cultural changes, as well as such harmful effects as the introduction of the deadly smallpox disease among people with no previous exposure to it. Her drawings and paintings are often very simple and straightforward in method and style but show masterful techniques that she developed through sophisticated artistic training.

Certainly, the category of shock could be applied to the works by Smith we have just seen, and shock has been used increasingly in contemporary art to bolster political statements of protest or just commentary on our expectations and frames of reference. Ron Mueck (b. 1958, Australia) has made a point of repeatedly challenging the viewer with questions about life and relationships in his hyperrealist sculpture. (*Mask II*, Ron Mueck: http://www.visualarts.qld.gov.au/mueck/ images/MUECKron_MaskII_EXHI010912_RGB.jpg) He often creates works of the human form that are exceptionally out of scale, unexpectedly undressed, or placed in unusual postures, thereby creating many surprises among gallery goers, especially those who approach these uncanny works at a close distance.

6.8 CELEBRATION AND COMMEMORATION

Figure 6.13 | The Wedding Party
Artist: Henri Rousseau
Source: Wikiart
License: Public Domain

The use of art to note the observance of particular life events for ordinary people, rulers, and officials of all sorts has been a frequent theme and appears in all eras and in myriad styles. The presentation of such an event can very effectively call attention to a distinctive new approach an artist takes. Such is the case for a painting in celebration of a wedding created by Henri Rousseau (1844-1910, France), a mostly self-taught artist. (Figure 6.13) Due to such stylistic traits as the lack of formal one-point perspective and simplified treatment of the human form, Rousseau was described by critics as a naive painter. His style was

Figure 6.14 | Funerary Stele of Hegeso
Artist: Kallimachos
Author: User "Marsyas"
Source: Wikimedia Commons
License: CC BY-SA 3.0

embraced by many **avant-garde** artists at the time, however, as boldly moving away from traditional methods and ideas taught in art schools at the time.

Artwork to express the grief of the living and to preserve and honor the memory of the deceased can be found in all ages and cultures. Funerary markers, some large and elaborate, have appeared in many eras. From ancient Greece, for example, we have a marble grave **stele**, or marker, carved with a portrait of a noblewoman seated on a Greek **klismos chair**, a curved-leg style then popular, while selecting a piece of jewelry from a young servant woman standing before her. (Figure 6.14) The jewelry, now missing, stood for the wealth of the individual, family, and society at large, and the state of well being that will continue for the group in spite of one individual's death.

6.9 WORSHIP

Perhaps the most frequent use of art as a means of connecting to viewers' lives through the ages has been for religious purposes, often entailing the aspects of worship whereby a deity, person, or narrative

Figure 6.15 | Rock Carving Depicting Vishnu
Author: User "Clt13"
Source: Wikimedia Commons
License: CC BY-SA 2.5

is presented for the viewer to use in order to express their devotion, as an occasion of worship, or to contemplate its meaning. Among the most formalized types are cult statues—images of deities, saints, or revered figures—such as Varaha, the boar-headed **avatar**, or physical form, of the Hindu god Vishnu. Here, Varaha is rescuing the goddess Bhudevi by slaying the demon that had trapped her in the ocean. (Figure 6.15) Dangling in mid-air as she holds his tusk, Varaha returned Bhuvedi to her rightful place on earth.

Other examples include the enormous altarpieces that were a central focus in churches during the Middle Ages, Renaissance, and Baroque (seventeenth century) eras in Europe, altarpieces such as *El Transparente* in the Cathedral of Toledo, Spain. Its elaborate carvings and gilding interplay with natural sunlight that streams in from strategically placed openings in the wall and ceiling. (Figure 6.16) Such works are designed to be awe-inspiring, presenting the viewer/believer with a spectacular visual expression of mysteries of the faith.

Figure 6.16 | El Transparente Altarpiece at Cathedral of Toledo, Spain
Author: User "Tim giddings"
Source: Wikimedia Commons
License: CC BY-SA 3.0

6.10 INFORMATION, EDUCATION, AND INSPIRATION

Art has often been used as a means to inform, to educate, and to inspire, and the religious works that we have viewed have been traditionally used for these purposes. In addition to those, we need to consider the many forms than have long been used to provide information for secular, or non-religious, purposes as well as those that have emerged more recently.

Perhaps the first would be the creation of scrolls and book forms, both of which occurred very early, the exact dates of which are indeterminate. We know the Egyptians created a form of paper made from flexible papyrus stems they rolled into scrolls and the Romans developed the **codex** form of books we use today, although each of these forms is also known to have been used by others. The Egyptians developed their system of writing in **hieroglyphs**, abstracted pictures that represent words or sounds, around 3,400 BCE. Literacy and writing was restricted among the Egyptians to highly educated scribes. (Figure 6.17) By around the first century BCE, the Romans had formalized a system of tiered education, that is, progressing through grades based on age and development of skills. Although formal schooling was generally reserved to those who could afford it, education was

Figure 6.17 | Haremhab as a Scribe of the King
Source: Met Museum
License: OASC

not restricted to any particular class or group. While the ancient Chinese used paper and printing methods from as early as the first century, these did not appear in the Western world for centuries afterwards. The invention of the printing press and movable type by Johannes Gutenberg in Germany in 1439 was truly momentous, as both written and pictorial forms could then be replicated and dispersed widely. (Figures 6.18 and 6.19)

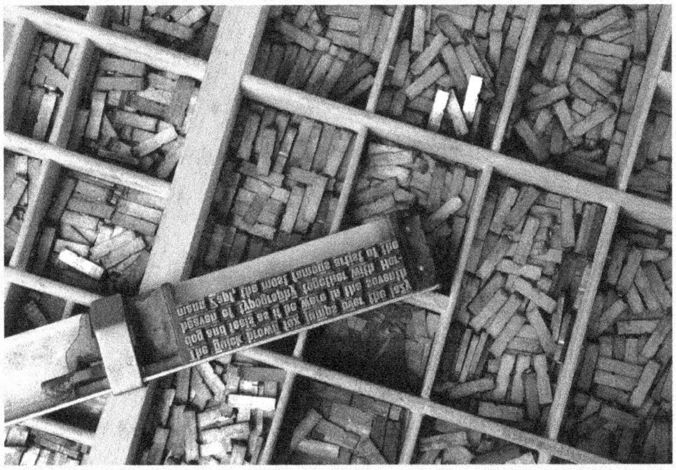

The advent of photography beginning in the 1830s considerably broadened the potential dissemination of information. Photography's use in

Figure 6.18 | Metal Movable Type
Author: Willi Heidelbach
Source: Wikimedia Commons
License: CC BY-SA 3.0

Figure 6.19 | Etching of 16th Century Printer
Artist: Jost Amman
Author: User "Parhamr"
Source: Wikimedia Commons
License: Public Domain

printed matter developed, and is notable for, the journalistic approach and documentary features it brought to newspapers and magazines in the early twentieth century that continue to this day. The graphic arts presented new means and a new arena for artists and also for the spread of information. Of course, at the same time, the potential for manipulation of these means resulted in the spread of a great wealth of material of dubious accuracy and purpose. Misinformation is spread as easily as information, so the need to critically evaluate the material and ideas you gather is increasingly important if you seek truth from art.

The early and mid-twentieth century brought us movies and television. From the late twentieth century to the present, the growth of visual media has greatly expanded the possibilities to the point that we are constantly bombarded with data we must assess with regard to its truth and value. The possibilities for gathering information and for using artistic means to inform are now broad and deep, and provide us with richly enticing and inspirational imagery for our viewing, thinking, learning, and art-making of all types.

6.11 BEFORE YOU MOVE ON

Key Concepts

We have observed in this chapter that art is like a mirror reflecting, communicating, and interpreting self, individuals, and society. Throughout history from primitive to modern, humans have been able to express a variety of ideas and feelings and even to evoke responses from neighbors through artistic markings and with the creation of structures. Those artistic expressions have been a major source in understanding each other and the world we live in. It has communicated in many different ways and styles the practical and abstraction, the cultural and the aesthetics of a people. As we have previously noted, Immanuel Kant characterized beauty or aesthetics and the practicality of it as a systematic way in understanding the range of the arts. We have noted that art can be an instrumental discipline, a powerful social or political force by which society interprets, controls, modifies, or adapts to their environment or to their personal taste and/or beliefs. Examples include the political and social statements of Jaune Quick—To—See Smith's "the Quincentenary Non-Celebration" or Jona Cerwinske's graffiti and murals, or the romantic and sacred aesthetic styles of Albert Bierstadt and Maurice Denis; the genre representation of cultural identity in the Ashante Kente cloth and the hyperrealist works of sculptor Ron Mueck; and in earlier years, a holy site like the Islamic structure The Dome of the Rock that is identified and recognized as a holy place by several diverse religious groups: Muslims, Jews and Catholics, thus representing several diverse groups all of which communicate powerful artistic messages. Each and all bring people together with like beliefs or views through an artistic structure of communicating: *creativity* (a substance of inventive, original , imaginative ideas); *disposition* (the character, temperament, formal structure qualities, and sequence); and *style* (communicating and delivering specific resources and physical attributes that send off a reaction).

Test Yourself

1. How did the development of photography impact social consciousness and awareness in the arts; cite examples. Discuss and show change and influence.

2. Historically, markings have been a means of delivering a religious message to different cultures. Identify and discuss at least three different early written religious art forms used to communicate a message. Explain the message and how it is influenced by the artist style in written form or imagery.

3. How have people used art to commemorate events in their lives throughout history? Show examples of images and elaborate on artist style and presentation of depicting the event.

6.12 KEY TERMS

aesthetics: the study of principles and appreciation of beauty.

Ara Pacis: an enclosed altar in Rome dedicated to Pax, the Roman goddess of Peace.

artifacts: a tool, weapon, or ornament created by humans that usually has historical significance.

avant-garde: works of art that are innovative, experimental, different from the norm or on the cutting edge.

avatar: physical form of the Hindu god Vishnu.

Bhudevi: a Hindu earth goddess and the divine wife of Varaha, an Avatar of Vishnu.

central-plan churches: are symbolic to reference the cross of Christ. Its round, cruciform, or polygonal design was popular in the West and East after the fourth century.

gui: a ritual scepter, held by a ruler during ceremonies as a symbol of rank and power.

hieroglyphs: abstracted pictures that represent words or sounds.

Kente cloth: woven silk and cotton wrap worn by Ashante kings during special ceremonies.

klismos chair: a curved-leg chair style popular in Ancient Greece.

les Nabis: a movement of Post –impressionist graphic and fine artists in France during the 1890s.

Neolithic period: known also as the Stone Age, is the last stage of prehistoric human cultural evolution. It is a period known for its polished stone tools, spread of architecture, megalithic architecture, and domestication of animals.

Palace of Knossos: the first Minoan monument located in Knossos. It was the residence of King Minos's dynasty, where he ruled.

Shandong Longshan Culture: Central China's Neolithic culture named after Longshan, Shandong Province. The culture is known for its production of black pottery.

Stele: grave marker.

Varaha: a Hindu god in the form of a boar during the Satya Yuga.

Form in Architecture

Rita Tekippe, Jeffrey LeMieux, and Pamela J. Sachant

7.1 LEARNING OUTCOMES

After completing this chapter, you should be able to:

- Understand the differences between function and form in architecture
- Understand how form and function work together in architecture created for different purposes
- Understand different types and uses of architecture

7.2 INTRODUCTION

So far, we have given very little consideration to architecture, yet it is one of the most culturally significant forms of art. Often, with structures that were built for group activities, they reflect the culture, its values, style, purposes, and preferences in the time and place more broadly and deeply than settings where individual choices might predominate. And decoration of such architectural settings, even if individual needs and ideals have been expressed through painting or sculptural themes, generally reflects the greater permanence of a structure expected to serve the group's purposes and needs.

The earliest buildings were likely designed to shelter a family or small group that lived together. Soon group needs came into play, and the community may have wanted to provide for joint activities of several types such as ritual/worship, group protection, government, markets, and other commercial needs. The types expanded as the societies grew, diversified, specialized, and sought ways to meet needs for both individuals and communities. The specific purposes led to diverse designs, and cultural values influenced both practical and stylistic choices. We will survey a small sample of landmark types from across the centuries from several different viewpoints, depending upon the significance of features for the individual examples. Our focus will sometimes be on the plan or layout of the structure, materials used in its creation, or spatial considerations as they relate to purposes and use. At other times, we will look at how the building is situated within a community, or how patrons, owners, and community members influence its construction and use. We will examine in greater detail the ritual uses, meanings, and significance of architectural settings and their decoration, in Chapter 10 Art and Ritual Life: Symbolism of Space and Ritual Objects.

Before we start our discussion, you should familiarize yourself with the basics of building, that is, how you might create walls and place openings in the walls while supporting the parts of the structure above. The most basic method is the **post-and-lintel** design in which two upright beams support a horizontal one to create a rectangular opening. (Figure 7.1) Before long, builders also devised a variety of

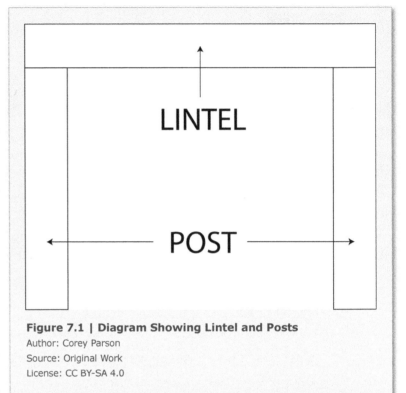

Figure 7.1 | Diagram Showing Lintel and Posts
Author: Corey Parson
Source: Original Work
License: CC BY-SA 4.0

arches, a curved or pointed structure spanning an opening and supporting the weight above, and then created further modifications of these techniques to develop **barrel vaults**, a series of circular arches that form a ceiling or roof, and **domes**, spherical-shaped ceiling or roof. (Diagram of Roman Arches: https://classconnection.s3.amazonaws.com/520/flashcards/1154520/jpg/untitled-13EF5EB39821CEF88AF.jpg; Domes: http://2.bp.blogspot.com/-jbiaW24DTZI/TVxCBDxx0TI/AAAAAAAAACk/VytZNRg0UK0/s1600/40-typology-dome.jpg) They also made variations that served decorative purposes. Over time, these have been imaginatively used for a tremendous variety of structural and decorative purposes, and you should keep them in mind as we investigate an array of buildings that reflect cultural concerns and human needs of all sorts. We will classify these buildings into several groups, although noting that a great number of them were multi-purpose: residential/housing, community needs, commercial buildings and centers, governmental structures, and those designed for worship.

7.3 RESIDENTIAL NEEDS

The earliest types of shelters were likely caves found by humans as they wandered to hunt and gather food and to find refuge from bad weather or pursuing creatures. The first independently standing structures were made of materials that were impermanent, that is, those found in nature—sticks, bones, animal pelts—and fashioned to create a covered space apparently as a protection from the elements. We have little evidence left for us to know fully how they were built and used, but some vestiges do remain that have enabled scholars to make reconstructions. (Figure 7.2)

Figure 7.2 | Reconstructed Jōmon period (3000 BC) houses.
Author: User "Qurren"
Source: Wikimedia Commons
License: CC BY-SA 3.0

Figure 7.3 | Recreation of a Celtic Roundhouse
Author: User "FruitMonkey"
Source: Wikimedia Commons
License: Public Domain

As people became more settled, domesticated animals, and cultivated crops, they developed such construction techniques as **wattle-and-daub** (sticks covered with mud), **rammed earth** (moist dirt and sand or gravel compressed into a temporary frame), and clay bricks (unfired and fired that developed alongside their evolving techniques for creating pottery vessels). (Drawing depicting architectural structure of Chinese round houses: http://arthistoryworlds.org/wp-includes/images/nhatau.jpg) (Figure 7.3)

They used these methods for communal living centers such as the village of Catalhöyük in modern Turkey (7,500-5,700 BCE), including common walls so that the clustered houses supported one another. (Figure 7.4) Such building methods addressed security issues by confining entry into living spaces to openings in the roofs, with ladders that could be retracted to foil trespassers. All of these types had certain common features to meet such everyday needs as warmth, cooking, sleeping, and storage, and were usually centered around a hearth with provision for smoke ventilation. Catalhöyük also included rooms that may have been for other common purposes, varying from shrines to serving as bakeries.

The use of stone for building structures began in prehistoric times,

Figure 7.4 | Çatalhöyük at the Time of the First Excavations
Author: User "Omar hoftun"
Source: Wikimedia Commons
License: CC BY-SA 3.0

Figure 7.5 | Old settlement Sjara Brae in Orkney Island, Scotland
Author: User "Chmee2"
Source: Wikimedia Commons
License: CC BY-SA 3.0

and an example of such a structure can be seen the Scottish village of Skara Brae (3,180-2,500 BCE). The walls were made of stacked stone while entryways and some of the furniture were created using the post-and-lintel method. (Figure 7.5) Because of the harsh northern climate, the structures were partially underground for protection from the elements. Additionally, covered walkways were created to facilitate movement among its eight units. Seven of these units apparently accommodated a family or small group, while the eighth was a common room, perhaps a workshop. In addition

Figure 7.6 | Inside a house at Skara Brae
Author: User "John Allan"
Source: Wikimedia Commons
License: CC BY-SA 2.0

to cultivating crops, these villagers likely herded, fished, and hunted for food. Stone furnishing such as seating, beds, storage spaces, and other items within the single-room units were around a central fire pit. (Figure 7.6)

With these basic methods, the humble shelter types of the Neolithic Age (c. 7,000-c. 1,700 BCE) and overlapping Chalcolithic (Copper) Age (c. 5,500-c. 1,700 BCE) provided a foundation for buildings of every sort used throughout history (with considerable elaboration of residential structures for the powerful and wealthy). Material choices eventually expanded to include first wood, brick, and stone, and later concrete and metal.

Residential palaces appeared by the time of the two great early civilizations of the Ancient Near East, Mesopotamia and Egypt, as well as those of the Aegean Sea: Crete, Cyclades, and mainland Greece prior to the development of the Greek Empire. The Palace at Knossos on the island of Crete was a grand residence for rulers of the Minoan civilization; the palace was built c. 1,700 BCE, after an earlier structure was destroyed by an earthquake, and abandoned between 1,380 and 1,100 BCE. (Drawing of Knossos: http://res.cloudinary.com/hrscywv4p/image/upload/c_limit,f_auto,h_900,q_80,w_1200/v1/245626/Palace_Complex_of_Knossos_vsyfng.jpg) The sprawling complex included residential areas, throne rooms, a central courtyard, and food storage magazines for crops and seafood used in the commercial trading, an important industry and mainstay in sustaining the people. (Floorplan of Residential Palace: https://classconnection.s3.amazonaws.com/16/flashcards/3907016/jpg/aafxpid0-1419F6BAD180C1BB19F.jpg) An island civilization, the Minoans were in the rare position of not having to protect themselves from enemies. The Palace at Knossos and similar structures on Crete were not fortified, that is, built behind solid walls and gates to hold off invaders. The palaces were instead built with windows and **colonnades**, or covered rows of columns, on their exteriors, allowing free circulation of light and air.

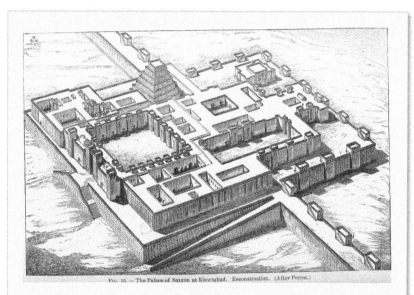

Figure 7.7 | Model of Palace of Sargon at Khosrabad
Author: Internet Archive Book Images
Source: Wikimedia Commons
License: Public Domain

Another palace complex, that of Neo-Assyrian King Sargon II (ruled 722-705 BCE) at Dur-Sharrukin, today Khorsabad in Iran, was clearly much more militaristic in character, evident by the surrounding defensive walls that strictly controlled access to the royal precincts. (Figure 7.7) Even after passage through a complex and imposing gateway, one had to cross guarded courtyards and passageways to approach the king's throne room. The structural presence was one of imposing power, as you can see from the enormous towered main portal. (Figure 7.8) To intimidate the visitor, interior decorations further asserted the mighty and ferocious nature of Sargon II with wall carvings depicting victorious battles. The complex also included temples for worship of the deities as well as quarters for high-ranking officials and servants.

Later developments for residences include apartment buildings for urban dwellers; such multi-family dwellings have taken many forms over time, and we can view an early type, from the second-century CE Roman port town of Ostia Antica, called an **insula**, which is Latin for "island."

Figure 7.8 | Palace of Dur-Sharrukin
Author: Encyclopedia Britannica
Source: Wikimedia Commons
License: Public Domain

Figure 7.9 | Ostian Insula
Author: User "Nashvilleneighbor"
Source: Wikimedia Commons
License: Public Domain

(Figure 7.9) In middle-class "apartments" such as these, there were stores and vendors' stalls on the ground floor facing the street. In some versions, the lower floors were for the wealthier people, while upper floors decreased in cost and desirability. The basic ideas of how to accommodate multi-family living were established by this time and have remained similar since. What has changed over time are the material and decorations used, styles adopted, provisions for electricity, water, and sewage management, and eventually zoning policies that would dictate locations, sizes, required provisions for safety, and density of occupation.

Private homes existed for the middle class and wealthy in towns and in the countryside; the latter were called villas whether they were primary residences or vacation homes. A private home in town might also have shops around its perimeter, but the accommodations for family life, entertainment, and conducting the owner's business were generally contained in a single floor layout. (Diagram of Roman Villa: http://michellemoran.com/CD/Roman-Villa.jpg) After passing through an entry from the street, one entered the **atrium**, a courtyard with a **peristyle**, a row of columns within a building often supporting a porch, left open to the sky with a pool in the center to catch rainwater. A private garden was in a second area open to the elements. The mild

Figure 7.10 | Scene from Lararium, House of the Vettii, Pompeii
Author: User "Patricio.lorente"
Source: Wikimedia Commons
License: CC BY-SA 2.5

climate led to provisions for a good measure of outdoor living as well as fresh air and sunlight during much of the year, even including indoor and outdoor dining rooms. There were rooms for sleeping, storage, and household work off the atrium and garden, as well as a space for worship, known as the *lararium*. (Figure 7.10) Here, two Lares, or household gods, flank an ancestor figure; the snake below symbolizes fertility and prosperity.

Roman royalty had grand palaces, and we have good evidence of such from the retirement compound created for the Emperor Diocletian (r. 284-305 CE) in Split set on the Bay of Aspalathos in the Roman province of Dalmatia, today Croatia. (Figure 7.11) The walled precincts with defensive watchtowers and fortified gateways included housing for his military garrison, a central peristyle courtyard, three temples, and his mausoleum, the building housing his tomb. The design, perhaps fitting for the aggressive persecutor of Christians and retired general, was quite militaristic in

Figure 7.11 | Diocletian's Palace
Artist: Ernest Hébrard
Author: User "DIREKTOR"
Source: Wikimedia Commons
License: Public Domain

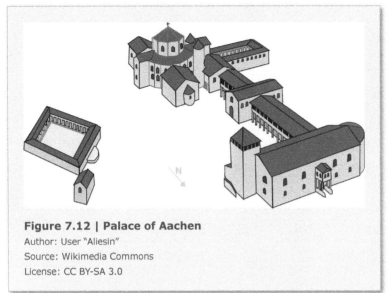

Figure 7.12 | Palace of Aachen
Author: User "Aliesin"
Source: Wikimedia Commons
License: CC BY-SA 3.0

many ways, resembling a Roman military encampment, or **castrum**. The private and public imperial areas were luxurious by contrast. Like most palace complexes, provisions were made to house soldiers and servants, and it was lavishly decorated throughout with frescos, sculptures, and **mosaics**, images or designs created on a wall or floor made up of small pieces of stone, tile, or glass.

While the locations for palaces were always strategically selected, the rationale was not always defensive in character. When Charlemagne selected Aachen, Germany, as the site for his main palace (he had several), among the attractions were its centralized site within his growing empire and the healing waters of the natural spa there. In examining the reconstruction of his complex, you will notice the baths, shown to the left of the palace complex, are an important feature, as they had been in Roman society. (Figure 7.12) He had a large audience hall, a grand portal, courtyards, housing, and an impressive palace chapel, which is the major structure still standing. (see Figures 3.13 and 7.64)

The church was an important statement for this model Christian ruler, and although it has been enlarged from its original central-plan design, the structure still carries notable features that were both impressive and influential for later medieval church architecture. Charlemagne's throne was positioned on the **gallery** level, an upper level overlooking the floor below. (Figure 7.13) The throne was above the entrance to the church, with an enormous "window of appearance" above the portal facing out into the atrium courtyard, where Charlemagne could address his Christian subjects gathered there. This emphasis on the western entryway was developed into the grand western facades of Romanesque and Gothic churches.

The Doge's (Duke's) Palace in Venice is another impressive statement of rulership wed to Christian leadership. (Figure 7.14) With its façade on the waterfront, the church of San Marco sitting directly be-

Figure 7.13 | The throne of Charlemagne and the subsequent German Kings in Aachen Cathedral.
Author: Bojin
Source: Wikimedia Commons
License: CC BY-SA 3.0

hind it, state offices located across from it, and the communal, open-ended **piazza**, or courtyard, between them, the palace literally connects the secular, religious, social, and political realms of Venetian life. (Figure 7.15) Public courtyards at the heart of cities became typical during the Italian Renaissance, as did private, interior courtyards in the center of Italian homes for rulers, wealthy aristocrats, and high church officials. As an official governmental center and residence, this Venetian palace included private quarters for the Doge along with meeting

Figure 7.14 | Doge's Palace and St. Mark's Tower, Venice
Author: User "Rambling Traveler"
Source: Wikimedia Commons
License: CC BY-SA 3.0

Figure 7.15 | Courtyard of Doge's Palace
Author: User "Benh LIEU SONG"
Source: Wikimedia Commons
License: CC BY-SA 4.0

rooms and council chambers, all richly decorated with marble, stucco, and fresco and including iconographic themes related to Venice, its history, and civic identity.

In Japan, the fourteenth-century Himeji Castle, built as a fort by the samurai Akamatsu Norimura, was situated dramatically atop Himeyana Hill. (Figure 7.16) Though a defensive posture was its primary motive, the great beauty and lyrical appearance of its curved walls and rooflines are its predominant effects. It has been called the "white heron" in response to the impression it gives of a great bird

Figure 7.16 | Himeji Castle, Japan
Author: User "Bernard Gagnon"
Source: Wikimedia Commons
License: CC BY-SA 3.0

about to take flight. The complex, again, has many purposes and comprises eighty-three different structures. The grounds include huge warehouses, lush gardens, and intricate mazes. Despite its fairytale looks, its defensive systems are complex and effective, including moats, keeps, gates, towers, turrets, and mounts and brackets for a variety of weapons. It has withstood numerous attacks and natural disasters over the centuries.

The final such royal complex we will explore is the Potala Palace in Lhasa, Tibet, established in 1645 by the fifth Dalai Lama; the palace functioned as the spiritual and governmental center for Tibetan Buddhism until the fourteenth and current Dalai Lama, Tenzin Gyatso (b. 1935), fled for political refuge in 1959. (Figure 7.17) The basic purpose of the palace was that of a Buddhist monastery; its original foundation was centered on two chapels of historical and spiritual significance to the order of monks. The palace is named after Mount Potalaka, the mythical abode of the Bodhisattva of compassion, Avalokiteshvara, and the paradisiac implications are meaningful to devotees.

Figure 7.17 | The Potala Palace in Lhasa, Tibet
Author: User "Xiquinho"
Source: Wikimedia Commons
License: CC BY-SA 3.0

Figure 7.18 | Chiswick House, London
Author: User "Patche99z"
Source: Wikimedia Commons
License: Public Domain

As at Himeji, the hillside is a striking component of its appearance, and the enormous complex makes a very dramatic presentation. Indeed, whether intended for defensive purposes or not, its imposing appearance is often a very important feature for royal architecture. The impression of this palace's organic relationship to the mountain is enhanced by its sloping walls, flat roofs, and numerous stairways that lead to its various structures. The complex includes living quarters for the Dalai Lama and the monks as well as governmental offices, a seminary, assembly halls, shrines, libraries, storage rooms, and numerous chapels. It includes statues and portraits of historical and spiritual leaders and many devotional and didactic depictions painted on walls and banners, and works for meditation and prayer. Burial mounds and tombs contain the remains of lamas and important scriptures.

The residential structures of the wealthy of previous eras have often been lost to us; however, we can examine some of the aristocratic family homes of the last several centuries to gain insight into some of the additional trends for creating dwellings that go far beyond the need for simple shelter and that show some of the design ideas devised by artists and architects. The house created for Lord Burlington in 1729 in Chiswick, England, is a good example of the Neo-Palladian style of architecture. (Figure 7.18) Andrea Palladio (1508-1580, Italy), a Venetian Renaissance architect, deeply studied ancient Greek and Roman architecture and architectural theory and developed new designs based on those but better fit to the means, methods, and needs of his day. His ideas were popular and have remained widely influential throughout the West to this day.

Lord Burlington created his neo-Palladian villa design under the influence of Palladio's ideas and those of other related designers. The basic idea here derives from a combination of a Greek temple front and a Roman dome, here supported by an octagonal **drum**, or circular or multi-sided base. Lord Burlington planned the house to showcase his fine collection of pictures and furniture and his architectural library as well as to provide comfort for his family living there. Great attention was paid to the surrounding gardens, and their design was very much a part of the overall scheme. Inspired by Roman gardens, they were designed by his friend William Kent (c. 1685-1748, England), an architect and early landscape architect, and included classicizing statues and miniature temples of a sort that were popular in English gardens of the day, thereby providing interesting and restful stopping points to a refreshing stroll outdoors. The logic and order of the layout of the building and grounds as well as the villa's sense of grandeur led to its admiration and emulation by other builders who sought a similar elegance.

The Neo-Palladian style was carried to the United States by Thomas Jefferson for the campus of the University of Virginia, the state capitol of Virginia, and his own home of Monticello,

Figure 7.19 | Monticello, Charlottesville, VA
Photographer: Matt Kozlowski
Author: User "Moofpocket"
Source: Wikimedia Commons
License: CC BY-SA 3.0

near Charlottesville, Virginia. (Figure 7.19) Jefferson adapted ideas he gathered while U.S. Ambassador to France by using humbler materials such as the red brick made from local clay that he considered a better choice for a less pretentious statement than marble or limestone. At Monticello, he also brought the structure lower to the ground and added a wooden **balustrade**, a railing supported by upright supports, to the roofline. Nonetheless, its Palladian design origins are clear. The interior of the house is full of provisions for Jefferson's notable intellectual and work habits such as his bedroom that opened into his office, his workrooms, and his collections of American artifacts.

In the United States of the late nineteenth-century Gilded Age (c. 1870-1900), a time of rapid technological, commercial, and economic expansion, wealthy industrialists built enormous

Figure 7.20 | The Breakers, Vanderbilt's mansion in Newport, RI
Author: User "Menuett"
Source: Wikimedia Commons
License: CC BY-SA 3.0

mansions in cities and at the seaside resorts or mountain retreats they favored. Among these, the Vanderbilt family (whose wealth came from shipping and railroads) commissioned several notable residences, mostly in the French-inspired Beaux Arts style, a period and style known in the U.S. as the American Renaissance (1876-1917).

One of these residences was The Breakers in Newport, Rhode Island, a lavish resort area replete with such structures. (Figure 7.20) The oceanfront house, designed by Richard Morris Hunt (1827-1895, USA), has seventy rooms on five floors and covers nearly an acre of

Figure 7.21 | The library at The Breakers
Photographer: Matt Wade
Author: User "UpstateNYer"
Source: Wikimedia Commons
License: CC BY-SA 3.0

land on a thirteen-acre lot with elaborate gardens. It was built with the most lavish material such as marble and wood from around the world and was decorated with rich and sumptuous furniture, fittings, and valuable artwork, as can be seen here in the library. (Figure 7.21) Clearly a residential structure of this type went far beyond the simple needs of housing to shelter a family from the elements and served to make a very grand and ostentatious statement of wealth and power.

By contrast to design ideas of the architects who catered to the wealthiest Americans, a new conception for providing living space came into being in the early twentieth century with Frank Lloyd Wright, who developed what he called the Prairie Style. He sought to counter the blocky forms that had become the standard for American homes with a structural sweep that hugged the ground, echoed the landscape, and fostered communication between the spaces in the house and the natural elements around it.

Perhaps the epitome of this thinking was realized in Wright's design for Falling Water, a western

Figure 7.22 | *Fallingwater*, Pennsylvania
Architect: Frank Lloyd Wright
Author: User "Daderot"
Source: Wikimedia Commons
License: CC0 Public Domain

Pennsylvania mountain home he created for the Kaufmann family of Pittsburgh. (Figure 7.22) At their request, he incorporated elements of their favorite recreation spot into the design: the rocky outcrop where they held picnics is in the living room, and the adjacent Bear Run waterfall pours out beneath the house's **cantilevered** terraces, self-supporting rigid structure projecting from the wall. Like most of Wright's houses, the place has flowing interior space, a great number of windows, and abundant natural light, as well as carefully coordinated use of stone and wood to incorporate the structure into the natural setting.

7.4 COMMUNITY AND GOVERNMENT

Clearly, many of the palaces and complexes we have explored included accommodation of community government needs. There were others throughout history that had somewhat more pointed community needs in mind for their creation but were often combined with other purposes as well. From the time of the rise of the earliest civilizations, the needs for government and religious expression often coalesced.

In the Mesopotamian Valley of the ancient Near East, today Iraq and Iran, we see this exemplified in the structure of the Ziggurat of Ur. (Figures 7.23 and 7.24) With

Figure 7.23 | Ziggurat of Ur, Iraq
Author: User "Hardnfast"
Source: Wikimedia Commons
License: CC BY 3.0

the idea that the deities resided in the heavens, the **ziggurat** was conceived as a man-made mountain that served as a base for the temple, raising it closer to the celestial regions where the deities were. The pathways to the temple at the summit were steep and the approach to the gods was appropriately aggrandized and formalized. At the same time, the basic platform structure was part of a complex that included the provisions for a variety of other community services, record keeping, and commercial and governmental functions. The compact complex was located at the center of the community and in many aspects became the hub of life.

The people of the ancient Near East built with mud brick, sometimes baked, that has not proven to be durable, so the remains of these structures, constructed from around 2,400 BCE until the sixth century BCE, are generally not well preserved. Still, there are sufficient clues in the ruins to reconstruct the ways they were built and used.

The Romans generally made provisions for community functions in the **forum**, an open public space at the center of each city; the cities were often laid out in a grid plan organized with areas dedicated to various types of industrial, commercial, communal, and residential needs. (The Master Plan of Verbonia: https://classconnection. s3.amazonaws.com/864/ flashcards/4000864/jpg/roman_ city_plan-141E58EF1FF4A4DE1CC. jpg) The number and types of buildings varied, but they often included temples, libraries, markets,

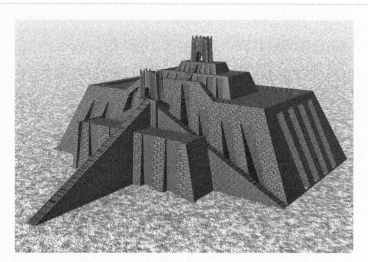

Figure 7.24 | Digital Rendering of the Ziggurat of Ur
Author: User "wikiwikiyarou"
Source: Wikimedia Commons
License: Public Domain

public baths (*thermae*), and judicial structures. The Forum at the heart of Rome was the site of numerous architectural statements and additions for the public good that were created by successive rulers.

One of the most influential of the buildings in the Forum of Trajan in Rome was the Basilica Ulpia, a center for law courts, business, and public gatherings. (Figure 7.25) The **basilica** included a long and broad open center space, a nave, flanked by aisles that fluidly expanded the area.

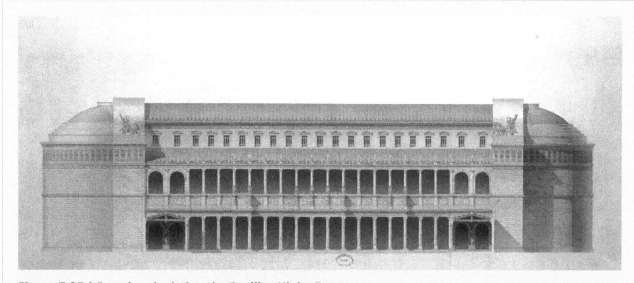

Figure 7.25 | Drawing depicting the Basilica Ulpia, Rome
Artist: Julien Guadet
Author: User "Joris"
Source: Wikimedia Commons
License: Public Domain

Figure 7.26 | Illustration Depicting the Basilica Ulpia
Author: Encyclopedia Britannica
Source: Wikimedia Commons
License: Public Domain

Figure 7.27 | National Mall and Washington Monument, Washington, DC
Author: User "Christoph Radtke"
Source: Wikimedia Commons
License: CC BY-SA 3.0

(Figure 7.26) This design provided a readily adaptable concept for other purposes, most notably perhaps the congregational space needed for Christian churches that would arise in later centuries as the Christian populace grew.

Significant community spaces sometimes have as their boundaries adjoining but separate architectural structures. These spaces are nonetheless important gathering places that need to be considered as such and in connection with the surrounding architecture that defines them. The National Mall in Washington, D.C., is one such place. (Figure 7.27) We identify it by its location within the capitol city and by its placement among all the government and other public/community buildings that line and define it. One only has to see it as a site for a presidential inauguration celebration or other large public gatherings to realize its significance as a community center.

Figure 7.28 | Theatre of Epidaurus
Author: User "Olecorre"
Source: Wikimedia Commons
License: CC BY-SA 3.0

Figure 7.29 | Colosseum in Rome
Author: User "Andreas Tille"
Source: Wikimedia Commons
License: CC BY-SA 4.0

Figure 7.30 | Wawadit'la, also known as Mungo Martin House, a Kwakwaka'wakw "big house", with heraldic pole.
Artist: Chief Mungo Martin
Author: Ryan Bushby
Source: Wikimedia Commons
License: CC BY-SA 2.5

Community needs for ceremony and entertainment have been addressed with specifically purposed architectural works since antiquity as well. Both the Greek and the Romans designed and built **theaters**, outdoor structures for dramatic performances, and **amphitheaters**, round or oval buildings with a central space for events, that provided models for such structures to this day. (Figures 7.28 and 7.29) While the basic concepts were devised by the Greeks to present reli-

Figure 7.31 | Whare at Waitangi Treaty House site
Author: User "Andy king50"
Source: Wikimedia Commons
License: CC BY-SA 4.0

gious festivals and ritual dramas, the Romans with their great ingenuity in engineering and material development added considerably to the potential for these designs to cater to changing needs and broader applications.

One of the most important contributions to the history of architecture was the Roman development of concrete for use as building material. Its greater strength, flexibility, and potential for adaptation made concrete far superior to the cut stone used to that point. These advances enabled the Romans to create new architectural forms by expanding the types of vaulting and means of spanning space they had previously used. Both of these important community structures, the theater and the amphitheater, were enlarged and put to new uses because of the Roman architectural contributions.

Pacific Island cultures, as do those of Native Americans, particularly venerate tribal heritage and so celebrate the communal events related to their heritage. Native North Americans of the Kwakiutl Nation created the clan **totems**, objects or animals that hold significance for a group of

Figure 7.32 | Waitangi in the Bay of Islands, New Zealand
Author: Phil Whitehouse
Source: Wikimedia Commons
License: CC BY 2.0

people, at the Wawadit'la, also known as the Mungo Martin House in honor of the chief and artist who built it in Victoria, British Columbia. (Figure 7.30) The recognition and celebration of their shared culture is expressed, as well, in the Meeting House of the Maori people at Waitangi, New Zealand, with its deep front porch and big open hall for group events. (Figures 7.31 and 7.32) Additionally, the carved and painted decorations inside and out have specific iconographic and symbolic significance for the individuals who gather together at such communal sites.

7.5 COMMERCE

Buildings for commerce have appeared over time. Early systems of trade and barter in some places eventually became formalized in ways that required marketplaces and commercial establishments with temporary or permanent housing. While open-air markets with vendor stalls continue to be used in many places, in others shops or full buildings evolved for commercial and service transactions.

Figure 7.33 | Church of the Holy Apostles and Museum of Ancient Agora
Author: User "A.Savin"
Source: Wikimedia Commons
License: CC BY-SA 3.0

Figure 7.34 | Carson, Pirie, Scott and Company Building, Chicago, IL
Author: User "Beyond My Ken"
Source: Wikimedia Commons
License: CC BY-SA 4.0

An early example appeared in ancient Athens, Greece, in the area where the open market or **agora**, was also located. The **Stoa** of Attalos, built by King Attalos II of Pergamon (r. 159-133 BCE), was comprised of a two-story covered walkway made of marble and limestone with columns on one side and a closed wall on the other. (Figure 7.33) Along the closed wall, there were twenty-one rooms on each level with each room providing space for a shop. These rooms were similar in character and purpose to those we noted on the ground floors of Roman villas and apartment buildings, but they provided for a more concentrated shopping area.

Our modern provisions for shopping centers and department stores were designed with different ideas about merchandising, sales, and consumerism but, as we have seen with the rapid rise of on-line shopping for durable and perishable goods, this scenario will likely be ever evolving. Indeed, grocery and department stores may become completely passé. But their development in the nineteenth and twentieth centuries presented new possibilities for architectural design.

An example is the Carson, Pirie, Scott and Company Store in Chicago, designed by Louis Sullivan (1856-1924, USA) and built in 1904. (Figure 7.34) One of the early applications for steel frame, or "skeleton frame," construction that made the development of skyscrapers possible, this sort of building also opened new possibilities for retail and office space. Here, the large ground-floor windows and corner entrance could provide a great deal of display space for attracting pedestrians while the expansive multi-story interior offered shoppers a wide array of goods, especially compared to the sorts of small shops and markets that had been its predecessors.

Figure 7.35 | The northwest entrance to the Carson, Pirie, Scott and Company Building
Author: User "Beyond My Ken"
Source: Wikimedia Commons
License: CC BY-SA 4.0

Not only the structure but also the decorative approach was innovative, as Sullivan combined Beaux Arts ideas with Art Nouveau motifs in the building's surface design. (Figure 7.35) The elaborate, curvilinear, plant-based motifs central to the Art Nouveau movement, c. 1890-1910, in cast metal relief panels above the doors and ground floor windows added to visual appeal for potential customers.

Figure 7.36 | User "Beyond My Ken"
Author: User "Extrawurst"
Source: Wikimedia Commons
License: CC BY-SA 3.0

New designs emerged for other commercial firms in this era as well. The Austrian Postal Savings Bank in Vienna, Austria, designed by architect Otto Wagner (1841-1918, Austria) has a huge multi-story façade covering a broad open interior space on the ground level; its sleek and modern aesthetic was startlingly new and different when it was completed in 1905. (Figure 7.36) One of Wagner's aims in the design was to create a sense of strength and solidity that engendered trust and a feeling of financial security in customers. The main banking customer area is filled with natural light. Wagner used marble, steel, and polished glass for the simplified decoration of the reinforced

Figure 7.37 | The Top of the Chrysler Building, New York City, NY
Author: User "Leena Hietanen"
Source: Wikimedia Commons
License: CC BY-SA 3.0

concrete building, turning away from the Art Nouveau aesthetic and replacing it with his sense of modernism.

The use of steel and reinforced concrete that facilitated the advent of the skyscraper truly revolutionized architecture and began a contest for height that continues today. Wealthy entrepreneurs and ambitious developers from around the world have joined in the competition for buildings of modern distinction. One example is the Chrysler Building in New York City, designed by William van Alen (1883-1954, USA). (Figure 7.37) Its décor in the Art Deco style (c. 1920-1940), including the ribbed, sunburst pattern made of stainless steel in the building's terraced crown, celebrates American industrialism and the automobile. At 1,046 feet, the Chrysler Building was for eleven months after its completion in 1930 the tallest in the world. (It was surpassed in 1931 by the Empire State Building at 1,454 feet.)

A more recent example is the Petronas Twin Towers in Kuala Lampur, Malaysia, designed by César Pelli (b. 1926, Argentina, lives USA). (Figure 7.38) Inaugurated in 1999, they were the tallest buildings for several years and remain the tallest twin towers to this day. The buildings' design motifs are inspired by Islamic art and culture; for example, the shape of each tower is the Muslim symbol of Rub el Hizb, or two overlapping squares that form an eight-pointed star. Both structures house commercial and business concerns and symbolize the architecture of modern business.

In the late twentieth century, architectural ingenuity, new materials, and the potential of computer design led some architects to develop radically innovative approaches to structures that might house any number of different types of needs. Among the most innovative in this regard is Frank Gehry (b. 1929, Canada, lives USA), who has designed buildings all over the world including museums, business towers, residences, and theaters.

In Los Angeles, he created the Walt Disney Concert Hall, completed in 2003. (Figure 7.39) Using titanium sheathing for multiform, swooping curvilinear forms and volumes,

Figure 7.38 | Petronas Twin Towers, Malaysia
Author: User "Morio"
Source: Wikimedia Commons
License: CC BY-SA 3.0

his buildings are sculptural in effect from a visual standpoint. Yet in each case, his buildings have proven effective and dynamic in creating spaces for the activities they house. The acoustics of the concert hall are widely praised as is the beauty of the architectural form in capturing the whimsical spirit of Walt Disney, the creator of so many American comics, cartoons, and movies.

Figure 7.39 | Walt Disney Concert Hall, Los Angeles, CA
Author: John O'Neill
Source: Wikimedia Commons
License: GFDL

7.6 WORSHIP

Structures for worship, as we have noted, were sometimes combined with or were near those created for other communal needs. We saw this with the ziggurat, in the Roman forums, and in palaces, among others. But we also have a considerable history of architecture intended solely for religious purposes. From early times, there were two distinctive conceptions for a sacred building: whether it was a house for the deity or a house for the worshippers. Beyond that, it might be for individual devotional activities or for accommodating a congregational group. We can keep these points in mind when examining the types of building designed for these goals.

Among the earliest examples are the pyramid complexes from ancient Egypt. (Figure 7.40) The **pyramids** were tombs composed of millions of

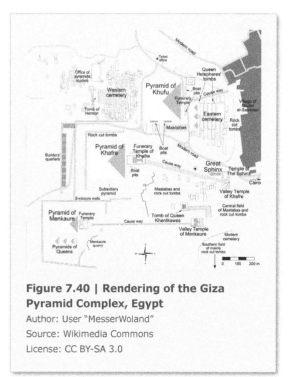

Figure 7.40 | Rendering of the Giza Pyramid Complex, Egypt
Author: User "MesserWoland"
Source: Wikimedia Commons
License: CC BY-SA 3.0

large stones in mathematically regular geometric structures carefully oriented to the
stars. Pyramids evolved over thousands of
years out of pre-Egyptian burial practices
that began with placing heavy stones over
gravesites to protect the occupants and their
grave goods buried within.

The Egyptians created these elaborate
and massive groupings of buildings for the
royal dead on the west bank of the Nile River,
creating a **necropolis**, or city of the dead. At
Giza, the body of the pharaoh or other royal
family member was brought down the river
from the palace to the valley temple on the
edge of the pyramid precinct. After priests

Figure 7.41 | Giza Pyramids
Author: Ricardo Liberato
Source: Wikimedia Commons
License: CC BY-SA 2.0

mummified the body of the deceased and prepared it for entombment, the body would be taken
to a mortuary temple near the pyramid. (Figure 7.41) That temple was the site where ceremonies
were carried out at the time of the mummy's placement within the pyramid, as were the perpetual
rituals required to honor the king in the afterlife.

There were also temples for the living that the king would have had commissioned and served.
One example is the Temple of Horus at Edfu, which has a number of typical features, although it was
built relatively late in Egyptian history. It is of the **pylon** type, so named for the two upright structures
that form its monumental façade and flank the main ceremonial portal. (Figure 7.42) The approach
to temples was often along an avenue of **sphinxes**, imaginative hybrid creatures, part human, part
animal, that led to the main door. Beyond the pylon wall was an open courtyard (Figure 7.43) and

Figure 7.42 | Temple of Horus, Edfu
Author: User "ljanderson977"
Source: Wikimedia Commons
License: Public Domain

Figure 7.43 | Inside the Edfu Temple
Author: User "Than217"
Source: Wikimedia Commons
License: Public Domain

Figure 7.44 | Temple of Hephaestus, Athens
Author: User "sailko"
Source: Wikimedia Commons
License: CC BY-SA 3.0

then a **hypostyle hall**, a structure with multiple rows of columns that support a flat roof, leading to the sanctuary. Typical of many sacred structures is this sort of staged progression by which one moves from the public or profane spaces through gradually more sacred, and often more restricted, areas that lead ultimately to the most sacred and reserved part. It is often the case that only priests or otherwise consecrated and dedicated persons are allowed in the **sanctuary**, the innermost and holiest space, while most of the congregation or worshipers are confined to less sacred parts of the temple, and the general public may be denied access to the premises altogether.

Greek temples like that devoted to Hephaestus in Athens, Greece, were not congregational at all. (Figure 7.44) They were designed as houses for the deity with a **cella**, or room, inside that was provided for the cult statue. Sometimes, there was also a cult treasury room within the temple, but ceremonies and sacrifices were conducted outside in the temple courtyard. Like the ziggurats, Greek temples incorporated the belief that the gods were on high, in the celestial realms, so they were often located in an **acropolis**, or sacred city high on a hill.

This can clearly be seen in the case of the Parthenon, dedicated to the goddess Athena, the patron of the city of Athens. (Figures 7.45 and 7.46) As in all Greek temples, a mathematical relation can be found ordering the size and relation of the Parthenon's elements. The length to width of the structure, the height to the width, the diameter of the columns, and their spacing all

Figure 7.45 | The Acropolis of Athens, Greece
Author: User "Salonica84"
Source: Wikimedia Commons
License: Public Domain

Figure 7.46 | The Parthenon, Athens, Greece
Author: Steve Swayne
Source: Wikimedia Commons
License: CC BY 2.0

Figure 7.47 | The Pantheon, Rome, Italy
Author: Roberta Dragan
Source: Wikimedia Commons
License: CC BY-SA 2.5

conform to the golden ratio of 4 to 9. This use of a single relation between the various elements of the structure gives it an aesthetically pleasing, unified, and more solid appearance, as does the use of several optical corrections. The columns lean slightly inward, and the **stylobate**, the base upon which the columns stand, bows upward slightly in the middle, both to give the appearance of being completely straight and flat.

Roman temples were often built in emulation of those of the Greeks, but they made many practical changes to the designs and often placed them in the center of the community, as opposed to the separated locations preferred by the Greeks. An important and very innovative temple design was created during the early Imperial era to honor the **pantheon** of nine planetary deities. To address the honor of the group, rather than individual gods, this temple, the Pantheon, took a different form. (Figure 7.47)

The building had a traditional temple front made up of columns supporting a triangular **pediment**. Rather than continuing into a rectangular, gable-roofed structure, however, the interior was an open circle with cult statues arrayed around its perimeter, each in a separate **niche**, or shallow recess in the wall. (Figure 7.48) That circular interior, acting as a drum, supported a huge domed space with an **oculus**, a circular opening, at its summit. Combining the circles of drum and dome creates a perfect sphere (diameter = height). (Figure 7.49) The whole of the structure was constructed using the ingenious Roman concrete, which allowed the creation of an unsupported dome—greatly facilitated by the use of **coffers**, or recessed squares, which tremendously reduced the dome's weight. The circle and square are not only featured in the ceiling construction, the repetition of those shapes is carried out in all of the architectural and decorative elements of the Pantheon's interior and exterior.

Figure 7.48 | Interior of the Pantheon, Rome
Artist: Giovanni Paolo Panini
Author: Google Cultural Institute
Source: Wikimedia Commons
License: Public Domain

In addition to these singular features, the Pantheon was the first temple structure the congregation was allowed to enter. Once Christianity supplanted the ancient Roman religions, spaces with large, open interiors would be needed to house the faithful attending mass. The Pantheon served the needs of a Christian church well, and it was converted in 609 CE. Its adaptation as a Christian church prevents our viewing it as it was intended to be used, but the Pantheon still stands in well-preserved condition and with little alteration to the structure

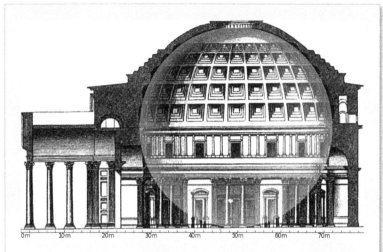

Figure 7.49 | Cross-section of the Pantheon in Rome
Author: User "Cmglee"
Source: Wikimedia Commons
License: CC BY-SA 3.0

and basic décor of fine marbles for the floor and interior columns, due to its continuous service as a house of worship since it was built in the second century CE.

Figure 7.50 | Lomas Rishi Cave
Author: User "Neilsatyam"
Source: Wikimedia Commons
License: CC BY-SA 3.0

Some of the earliest evidence of worship in India shows that it was conducted in caves; we also see attempts to create worship spaces by excavating the living rock and creating larger caves for this purpose. While rock-cut architecture exists in many places around the world, its extent in India over the centuries is unsurpassed and, due to its great durability, many fine examples of it are preserved.

A very early example is the Lomas Rishi Cave in the Barabar Hills from the third century BCE. (Figure 7.50) Because it is unfinished, we have a good idea of the methods and plans for the excavation, which included the addition of a large rectangular chamber leading into a smaller circular one. The sculptural treatment of the frame of the portal is a good example of the ways in which early architecture and decoration in stone imitated prior work in impermanent materials such as wood, as was the case for early architectural design around the world. Here, the designs simulate lattice, beams, and bentwood construction.

Later Indian worship structures such as the Brihadeshwara Temple dedicated to the Hindu god

Shiva, from the eleventh-century Chola Dynasty era, show the great complexity of conception of this type of worship space. (Figure 7.51) The tower at the far end is over the **garba griha**, or sanctuary, and as with the Temple of Horus at Edfu, there is staged progression from the profane (everyday) space to the most sacred. The whole is raised on a platform, a feature also seen in many sacred structures. Here, one must begin the approach by entering a gated courtyard, then ascend the stairs, and pass through the **mandapa**, or audience hall, before approaching the sanctuary. Outside the main temple but within the courtyard are subsidiary temples and shrines, as the worship is **polytheistic**, that is, with a great number of diverse deities.

Figure 7.51 | Brihadeshwara Temple, India
Author: User "Abhikanil"
Source: Wikimedia Commons
License: CC BY-SA 3.0

As is the case with most Hindu and Buddhist temples, although there are certainly ceremonial and ritual functions that are priestly duties, there is no restriction for lay people entering the sanctuary as the relationship to the deity is generally considered to be a personal one, not mediated by a priesthood.

The coexistence of Hindu and Buddhist deities evidenced by their shrines appears at many sites, though usually one or the other predominates at a given site. In addition to temples, another basic structure associated with Buddhism is the stupa. (Figure 7.52) One of the oldest stupas is in India where Buddhism first arose, at Sanchi in Madya Pradesh. Established in the third century BCE, it was conceived as a burial mound of a type, as it was believed to contain part of the earthly remains of Sakyamuni, founder of Buddhism. Surrounded by a tall stone fence, it is designed for the devotee to enter the fenced area and circumambulate, or walk around, the stone-faced, rubble-filled mound.

A great deal of symbolism is associated with the form including a **yasti**, or mast, rising from the center of the dome that stands for an **axis mundi**, or axis of the world, separating the earth from the sky above. The fence and gateways are also covered with mythological carvings related to Buddhist and Hindu beliefs. (see Figure 4.23) When the Buddhist stupa form

Figure 7.52 | Sanchi Stupa, Madhya Pradesh
Author: User "Ekabhishek"
Source: Wikimedia Commons
License: CC BY-SA 2.0

Figure 7.53 | Sultan Ahmed Mosque, Istanbul, Turkey
Author: User "Dersaadet"
Source: Wikimedia Commons
License: CC BY-SA 3.0

migrated to China, Japan, and elsewhere, the design evolved to include native architectural traditions resulting in the stupa form becoming the multi-tiered **pagoda**, a Hindu or Buddhist sacred building.

Centers for Islamic worship are housed in architectural structures known as **mosques**. While churches and temples associated with other faiths are generally oriented to the four cardinal directions, usually with the altar toward the east where the sun rises, the mosque will always be situated so that the worshippers face in the direction of the **qibla**, a fixed wall aligned to face Mecca, the city that is the epicenter for Islam. This orientation remains consistent regardless of where in the world the building is set. While several different standard architectural forms exist for a mosque, its most common distinguishing exterior feature is the **minaret**, the slender tower from which the call to prayer is issued. The Sultan Ahmed Mosque shows six minarets while four are common at other sites. (Figure 7.53)

The most basic architectural form for Christian congregational churches is the **basilica**, a structure of longitudinal plan adapted from the Roman public building form. (Figure 7.54) The Roman basilica had an entrance on one long side that led to the large open interior space, the nave. The **Christian basilica**, unlike that used by the Romans, has an entrance on one end, is divided into a center nave and side aisles along its length, and holds a semi-circular **apse**, or recess, containing the altar at the opposite end of the longitudinal building from the entrance. (Figure 7.55) As in other centers for worship we have seen, the holiest part of the church is farthest away from the most profane or public spaces. The progression from one end of the church to the other is a processional ritual, enhanced by the long rows of columns flanking the nave, the long exterior walls, that were often heavy wood or masonry structures until the Gothic era, and the filtered light that played among the structural components.

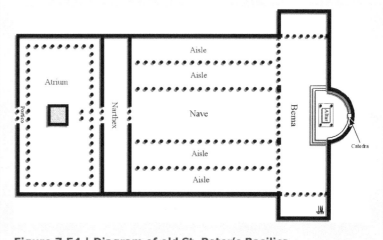

Figure 7.54 | Diagram of old St. Peter's Basilica
Author: User "Locutus Borg"
Source: Wikimedia Commons
License: Public Domain

Figure 7.55 | Basilica of Sant'Apollinare in Classe, Italy
Author: Angela Rosaria
Source: Wikimedia Commons
License: CC BY-SA 3.0

those in the Eastern Roman Empire, more commonly known as the Byzantine Empire, also employed the central plan, which had its origins in the circular plan, such as that used for the Pantheon. In the West, however, the circular, or central plan, church was used for a palace church such as Charlemagne's at Aachen, (Figure 7.57)

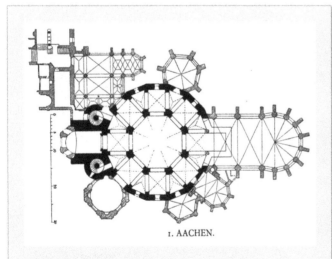

I. AACHEN.

Figure 7.57 | Floorplan of Aachen Chapel
Artist: Georg Dehio
Author: User "Fb78"
Source: Wikimedia Commons
License: Public Domain

This was the case in Old St. Peter's Basilica in Rome, (Figure 7.56) built in the fourth century CE on the model of the Roman basilica type. Also based on the Roman secular model was an atrium that was placed before the entrance. The original St. Peter's was the center of the Christian world for centuries and a model for church architecture, but it was replaced during the Italian Renaissance and Baroque periods with the much grander structure that exists today in Rome.

Christians in the Western Roman Empire used the basilica, or Latin cross, plan, but

Figure 7.56 | Drawing and reconstruction of the Constantinian Basilica, Rome
Artist: H. W. Brewer
Author: User "Lusitana"
Source: Wikimedia Commons
License: Public Domain

mausoleum (tomb building), or **martyrium** (site marking the death of a **martyr**, someone who died for their faith), where the placement of the altar does not need to address large crowds.

Perhaps the most familiar basilica or Latin Cross churches are those in the Gothic style in Europe that began in 1144. (Figure 7.58) When these structures were being built, they were not called "Gothic." Instead they were called "opus francigenum" or "work of

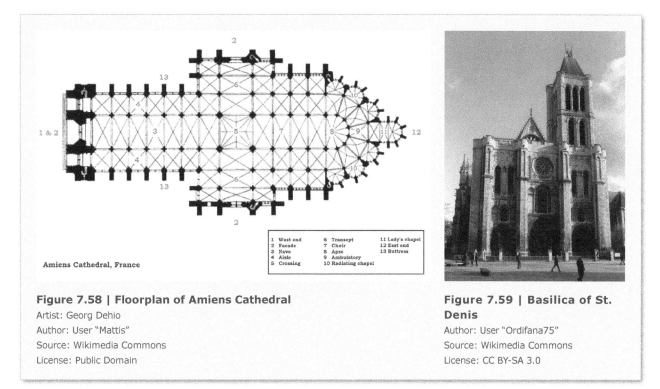

Figure 7.58 | Floorplan of Amiens Cathedral
Artist: Georg Dehio
Author: User "Mattis"
Source: Wikimedia Commons
License: Public Domain

Figure 7.59 | Basilica of St. Denis
Author: User "Ordifana75"
Source: Wikimedia Commons
License: CC BY-SA 3.0

the Franks" because of its origination at the Abbey of Saint-Denis. The term "Gothic" was coined in the sixteenth century, originally meant as an insult, by artist and historian Giorgio Vasari (1511-1574, Italy). He wanted to distinguish the architectural style, based on forms from ancient Greece and Rome at that time practiced in Italy, from medieval Christianity and its associations with the destruction of classical learning and culture. The Goths were Germanic tribes that he believed had invaded and destroyed the refined culture of ancient Rome. His pejorative name has persisted but without its originally negative connotation.

That first Gothic architecture was seen in the rebuilt choir at that Abbey Church of St. Denis, outside Paris, France, that was designed by the Abbot Suger and completed in 1144. (Figure 7.59) Several of the defining features of the Gothic cathedral were used there: the pointed arch, the ribbed vault, flying buttresses, and stained glass windows. Unlike the Roman circular arch, the **Gothic or pointed arch** is formed by two arcs with parallel sides. (Figure 7.60) A **ribbed vault** is formed at the intersection of two barrel vaults, with stone ribs sometimes

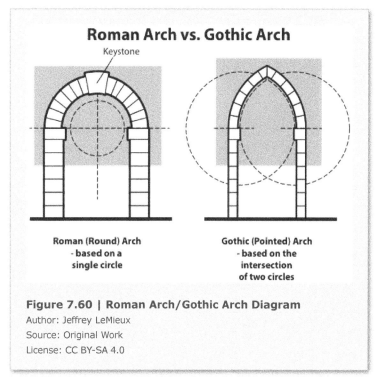

Figure 7.60 | Roman Arch/Gothic Arch Diagram
Author: Jeffrey LeMieux
Source: Original Work
License: CC BY-SA 4.0

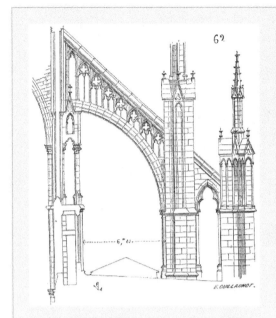

Figure 7.61 | Diagram of flying buttress of the Cathedral Basilica of Our Lady of Amiens
Author: User "BuzzWikimedia"
Source: Wikimedia Commons
License: Public Domain

Figure 7.62 | Bourges Cathedral
Author: User "sybarite48"
Source: Wikimedia Commons
License: CC BY 2.0

Figure 7.63 | Reims Cathedral, France
Author: Magnus Manske
Source: Wikimedia Commons
License: CC BY-SA 1.0

added to support the weight of the vaults. The **flying buttress** is a load-bearing component located outside the building, connected to the upper portion of the wall in the form of an arch. (Figures 7.61 and 7.62) The combination of the pointed arch, ribbed vault, and flying buttress allowed the height of the interior spaces to be dramatically increased and the thickness of the outside walls dramatically decreased. This development led to the widespread use of stained glass throughout the church and the addition of the **rose window**, a circular stained glass window dedicated to the Virgin Mary, usually found above the main portals. (Figure 7.63) The much larger number and size of windows allowed natural and multicolored light to flood the interior of formerly dark churches as was the case at St. Denis. (Figure 7.64)

Gothic churches were built throughout continental Europe and England, with regional variations, in the center of their communities usually, especially if they were cathedrals, or Bishop's churches. Whether viewed from a distance approaching a town or standing within the cathedral itself, the building soared above all others as it reached to the heavens. They were filled with architectural and sculptural ornamentation to teach the doctrines of the Church, Bible stories, and the accounts of Mary, the Apostles, and the other saints. Portals were especially the focus of sculptural effort. Standing figures in high relief of prophets, kings, and saints graced the sides of the **jambs**, or upright supports to either side of a door. (Figure 7.65) And many other sacred and secular figures, relief sculptures, often of Jesus and symbols of the Four Evangelists, Matthew, Mark, Luke, and John, were included in the tympanum above the doors. (Figure 7.66) The architects, masons, and sculptors responsible for these monumental buildings were highly skilled and creative, and Gothic cathedrals remained the dominating forms of the Western urban landscape until the late nineteenth and early twentieth centuries when the modern structural steel skyscraper surpassed them in height and scale.

The overall effect of walking into a Gothic cathedral is to be drawn upward into a vast, light, and airy space, and to be dislocated from the physical and drawn into the spiritual. (Figure 7.67) This effect is the epitome of the Gothic Christian view that the physical and sensual world is to be ignored or even disdained in favor of chastity, spiritual awareness, and religious devotion.

Figure 7.64 | Ambulatory of the Basilica of St. Denis
Author: User "Beckstet"
Source: Wikimedia Commons
License: CC BY-SA 3.0

Figure 7.65 | Martyrs, Chartres Cathedral
Author: User "Ttaylor"
Source: Wikimedia Commons
License: CC BY-SA 3.0

Figure 7.66 | Central tympanum of the Royal portal of Chartres Cathedral
Author: Guillaume Piolle
Source: Wikimedia Commons
License: CC BY 3.0

Christian churches of all denominations today generally follow the basilica model, but the sanctuaries vary considerably for diverse ceremonial practices. The **Gothic** type, with its pointed arches and glass windows that filter mystical light into the interior, is still common.

One example of an updated version is Thorncrown chapel, designed by E. Fay Jones (1921-2004, USA). Jones created a number of elegantly simple nondenominational chapels set into nature that let in diffuse light. (Figures 7.68 and 7.69) A pupil of Frank Lloyd Wright, Jones was inspired by Wright's principles of using simple, local materials to thoroughly integrate structure and setting. The most striking feature at Thorncrown, located in Eureka Springs, Arkansas, is the structure's light airiness. The whole of the interior for each of Jones's chapels is a small sanctuary that seems entirely at home in the forest.

Figure 7.67 | Nave of the Salisbury Cathedral, Wiltshire, UK
Author: User "Diliff"
Source: Wikimedia Commons
License: CC BY-SA 3.0

Figure 7.69 | Inside the Thorncrown Chapel
Architect: E. Fay Jones
Author: User "Bobak"
Source: Wikimedia Commons
License: CC BY-SA 2.5

Figure 7.68 | Thorncrown Chapel
Architect: E. Fay Jones
Author: Clinton Steeds
Source: Wikimedia Commons
License: CC BY-SA 2.0

7.7 BEFORE YOU MOVE ON

Key Concepts

We have seen architecture change throughout history in style, concepts, and purpose. However some aspects remain the same: its use for different purposes, expression of different types Specific in each instance to the particular patron or designer and to the purposes for the structure. Its uses for residential, commercial, communal or religious purposes, spiritual ideas, and sentiment.

This chapter allowed you to understand a broader range of methodologies in context of issues in modern art that evolved over time and with a world that became more complex. Architecture, other forms of art, has experienced great change in the designs of contrasting skyscrapers, incorporating more functionality and fluidity for the lives of modern people. Especially notable, perhaps, from our current perspective, are developments in art and architecture that occurred after World War II, when art's focus moved from Europe to New York. With the focus on the West, art changed to incorporate more freedom in technique and style as opposed to rules that governed art and structures. Artists and architects are now committed to societal issues and personal expression in art and architecture, using all aspects of society to define and explain. This new construct reflects tradition and non-tradition, gives more voice on societal issues, expresses more culture, and resonates individual expression and identity and society's aesthetic personality. Postmodern art focuses on public attention and its role in contemporary society by defining, questioning, and examining art's function, form, content aesthetics, and value.

Test Yourself

1. Describe at least three different examples of architectural work – each built for a different purpose, and discuss specific features of the work that are designed to meet certain distinctive needs.

2. Discuss two different structures built for religious use, explaining how form is related to purposes, and how the form is used by that religious group. Be specific about how it meets particular ritual or other needs of the group.

3. Select four different types of architectural structures and explain the type of architecture and the purpose of each building. Discuss characteristics of each façade, and how the façade addresses the user of the building.

4. Describe different features of temple/church structures that reflect specific beliefs about the deity/deities of the people who use it for worship. Discuss why those particular features are logical and suitable for the ways they are used.

7.8 KEY TERMS

Acropolis: "high city" – a hilltop setting such as that reserved for the temple complex in ancient Athens associated with Classical Greece, including several temples to Athena and other sacred sites and structures. The elevated location is associated with greater proximity to the gods who were believed to reside in the celestial realms.

Aesthetics: the branch of philosophy that concerns itself with the definition of beauty and with considerations of the purposes and value of art.

Aisle: one of the longitudinal divisions of a basilica building. Basilica form churches usually have either three or five aisles, the central one being called the nave.

Amphitheater: a round or oval building with tiers of seats around a central area used for performances and sport events.

Arcade: a colonnade with arched spaces between the columns.

Art Functionalists: believe that form follows function and that the value of art consists in its function or performance.

Avatar: an embodiment of a deity on earth.

Avant-garde: new, original, and experimental.

Basilica: a building of longitudinal plan, originally designed for Roman law courts and public meetings, later adopted for Christian usage because of its suitability for accommodation of large congregations and processional ritual.

Bodhisattva: a Buddha-to-be; a being who has achieved enlightenment but has postponed Nirvana in order to help fellow seekers in their spiritual quests.

Cantilever: a long beam or other horizontal prop projecting from a wall to support a balcony, stairs, or similar structure.

Castrum: a Roman military encampment or fortress, specifically designed on a grid plan, with specific zones related to activities/uses.

Colonnade: row of columns supporting a roof or entablature.

Deity: a religion's god or goddess.

Form: the structural components of a work of art or architecture.

Forum: open public space in Roman cities that served social, commercial, religious, and political needs of the residents.

Function: the meaning or purpose a work of art.

Gallery: a balcony or upper floor of a church or hall.

Garba Griha: Literally, the "womb" or most sacred precinct in a Hindu temple -- the sanctuary.

Gothic: a late medieval (12th-14th centuries) architectural style that may include pointed arches, ribbed vaults, and flying buttress. Gothic churches have very tall structures, high interior spaces and, increasingly, the walls are filled with stained glass windows that filter mystical colored light into the interior.

Hypostyle hall: structure consisting of a "forest of columns" arranged in numerous rows that support a flat roof.

Iconography: the subject matter and/or symbolism of an artwork, including reference to religious or other narrative meaning.

Insula: an apartment building in the ancient Roman civilization.

Logo: a design used by an individual or organization to identify itself or its products.

Mandapa: an audience hall in Indian architecture, often a porch-like ante-room to a temple, but also a free-standing gathering hall.

Mausoleum: a building containing one or more tombs.

Middens: refuse heaps, often of kitchen waste, but also for other discarded materials.

Minaret: a tower, usually tall and slender, associated with a mosque and signifying Islamic presence in a location.

Oculus: "eye"; an opening in an architectural structure, to let in light, located in a ceiling, a dome, or on a wall.

Peristyle: a row of columns that surrounds a space such as a courtyard.

Post-and-lintel: basic architectural means of creating an opening in a wall by placing two vertical members (posts) to either side of the opening and spanning the upper part of the space with a horizontal member.

Propaganda: biased, and sometimes misleading or hidden, information intended to influence views, beliefs, or behavior.

Qibla: a wall in an Islamic mosque that is situated so that prayer is oriented towards Mecca.

Rammed earth: dampened earth mixed with sand, gravel, or clay that is compacted into a temporary frame to create a wall.

Sphinx: a hybrid human/animal sculpture.

Stele: an upright stone slab often serving as a grave marker or public monument.

Stoa: a covered walkway in a public area, often fronting market stalls or other commercial spaces.

Stupa: a domed, hemispherical structure that functions as a Buddhist shrine. The conception is of a burial mound, designed for ritual circumambulation.

Tympanum: the semicircular area above a doorway, often decorated with sculptural artwork, especially as noted in Romanesque and Gothic church portals.

Wattle and daub: branches intertwined with twigs and straw, then coated with a substance such as plaster or clay to create a wall.

Ziggurat: a man-made mountain, designed to be the platform for a temple, raising it closer to the heavens where the gods were believed to reside.

8 Art and Identity

Peggy Blood and Pamela J. Sachant

8.1 LEARNING OUTCOMES

After completing this chapter, you should be able to:

- Name and categorize ways that artists explore the concept of identity
- Understand how art serves as a commentary on society
- Analyze how politics and societal concerns may influence art
- Understand how art expresses individual and group identity
- Understand how art preserves national culture and personal identity

8.2 INTRODUCTION

One of the more important themes emerging from the last century has been the individual's search for identity. For example, genealogical websites have proliferated and special television programs are devoted to the subject. Since it first aired on PBS in 2012, Henry Louis Gates Jr.'s *Finding Your Roots* has been a popular program. The British version, *The Guardian*, has been successful since 2006.

Some anthropologists suggest that the deep-rooted interest in identity or ancestry is partly shaped by evolutionary forces dating back to early humans supporting each other in extended family groups. Anthropologist Dwight Read theorizes that the Neolithic people were the first to understand the concept of the family tree and the perception of self in a family unit and in society.[1] If connected through blood, people have the tendency to be more willing to care for each other; a common interest and support system is readily realized within a clan or a group.

Early humans created two- and three-dimensional likenesses of themselves in their environment to help understand who they were in relation to the other members of their group. Contemporary humans do the same; they make records of themselves with family members, most

---

1   Ghose, Tia (Oct. 26, 2012). Why we care about our ancestry, Live Science. http://www.livescience.com/24313-why-ancestry.html

commonly in photographs and Selfies, and on Instagram. It is the same fundamental concept and placement in an environment that collectively identifies who we are in society, for example, in social gatherings, organizations, and religious settings. This means, above all, that we must place ourselves within the world in order to obtain identity. Children search for their identity at a very young age by observing and recognizing their parents and family members. Their markings within a simple drawing of self and family—similar to those of early humans—help them to vindicate and confirm who they are and how they are perceived by their family group.

Like children, artists sometimes explore their identity through self-portraits and symbolically in works of art that relate to ancestry or culture. Doing so allows them to take a look inside their core and see how they fit within their contemporary culture; this investigation of self plays an important role in how artists understand their environment and the world.

Vincent van Gogh is known as a person who spent much of his time in solitude. He painted more than thirty self-portraits between the years 1886 and 1889, placing him among the most prolific self-portraitists of all time. Indeed, some of his most respected works are his self-portraits that trace his image throughout the last years of his life, the most crucial to his career. (Figures 8.1, 8.2, and 8.3) While Van Gogh used the study of his own image to help develop his skills as an artist, these self-portraits also give us insights into the artist's life and well being, how he fit in society, and his place among the groups with whom he associated.

Like Van Gogh, Pablo Picasso painted a number of self-portraits. Throughout his career, Picasso painted various likenesses that reflected changes in himself, his style, his artistic development, as well as in his life style and beliefs—all of which may be viewed closely from the content of his

Figure 8.1 | *Self-Portrait with Straw Hat*
Artist: Vincent van Gogh
Author: Met Museum
Source: Wikimedia Commons
License: Public Domain

Figure 8.2 | *Selt-portrait as a painter*
Artist: Vincent van Gogh
Author: Web Museum
Source: Wikimedia Commons
License: Public Domain

Figure 8.3 | *Self-portrait with a bandaged ear*
Artist: Vincent van Gogh
Author: The Courtland Institute of Art
Source: Wikimedia Commons
License: Public Domain

Figure 8.4 | *Self-portrait*
Artist: Pablo Picasso
Source: WikiArt
License: Public Domain

Figure 8.5 | *Self-portrait*
Artist: Pablo Picasso
Source: WikiArt
License: Public Domain

paintings. (Figures 8.4 and 8.5) The first self-portrait, painted in 1901 while he was establishing himself as an artist in Paris, France, and still spending time in Barcelona, Spain, reflects the somber mode and tones of his Blue Period (1901-1904). The second, dated to 1906, at the very end of his Rose Period (1904-1906), Picasso depicts himself as the artist who by that time was moving in artistic circles, gaining respect, and acquiring patrons.

Frida Kahlo (1907-1954, Mexico) used the iconography of her Mexican heritage to paint herself and the pain that had become an integral part of her life following a bus accident at the age of 18 in which she suffered numerous injuries. She identified as a group member of her country, with Mexican culture and ancestry, and as belonging to the female gender. Kahlo's self-portraits are dramatic, bloody, brutal, and at times overtly political. (*Self-Portrait*, Frida Kahlo: https://upload.wikimedia.org/wikipedia/en/1/1e/ Frida_Kahlo_%28self_portrait%29.jpg) In seeking her roots, she voiced concern for her country as it struggled for an independent cultural identity. She spoke to her country and people through her art. Kahlo's art was inspired by her public beliefs and personal sufferings; she wanted her art to speak from her consciousness.

Although self-portraits of today may be slightly different from those of earlier decades, they still depict self-exploration and identity through society and groups that communicate who we are. Cai Guo-Qiang (b. 1958, China, lives USA) exploded small charges of gunpowder to create an image of himself. (*Self-Portrait: A Subjugated Soul*, Cai Guo-Qiang: http:// www.caiguoqiang.com/sites/default/files/styles/ medium/public/1989_SelfPortrait_0389_001ltr-web. jpg) Different from those by Van Gogh, Picasso, and Kahlo, Cai's self-portrait does not have any likeness or resemblance to his personal features, but it too sends a message about our society and how Cai relates to it. For example, the artist associates the lack of identifying information, rendering him anonymous, with contemporary society, and the fired gunpowder with both chaos and transformation.

Despite the distance in time that separates early and modern humans, the search for their place in society and who they are remains of fascination and a mystery to all humans regardless of their time in history.

8.3 INDIVIDUAL VS CULTURAL GROUPS

Often when one thinks of an artist, the image is of someone doing solitary work in a studio. During the Romantic period of the late eighteenth century until around 1850, artists, writers, and composers were associated with individualism and with working alone; this trend continued to develop up until recent times. The Romantic period valued and celebrated individual originality with musical and literary geniuses such Ludwig van Beethoven, Frédéric Chopin, Robert Schumann, John Keats, Edgar Allen Poe, and Mary Shelley. The visual arts boasted such geniuses as Francisco Goya, Eugène Delacroix, William Blake (1757-1827, England),

Figure 8.6 | *Oberon, Titania and Puck with Fairies Dancing*
Artist: William Blake
Author: Tate Britain
Source: Wikimedia Commons
License: Public Domain

Figure 8.7 | *The Battle of Abukir, 25 July 1799*
Artist: Antoine-Jean Gros
Author: User "DcoetzeeBot"
Source: Wikimedia Commons
License: Public Domain

and Antoine-Jean Gros (1771-1835, France). (Figures 8.6 and 8.7) Artists of the period exemplified the Romantic values of the expression of the artists' feelings, personal imagination, and creative experimentation as opposed to accepting tradition or popular mass opinion. Artists in the period broke traditional rules; indeed, they considered it desirable to break the rules and overthrow tradition.

From the Medieval to the Baroque periods, however, artists worked together in workshops and guilds, and schools were formed that stressed the importance of preserving heritage and history through rigorous and systematic artistic training. Large-scale commissions often required numerous hands to complete a work, emphasizing collaboration. Nevertheless, the artwork was expected to have a consistent style and quality of craftsmanship. To satisfy those various needs, artists often specialized in a particular type of subject matter. For example, Peter Paul Rubens (1577-1640, Germany, lived Flanders) and Jan Brueghel the Elder (1568-1625, Flanders) collaborated on more than twenty paintings over twenty-five years. (Figure 8.8) In their *Madonna in a Garland of Roses*, Rubens's celebrated skill as a figurative painter can be seen in the serenely glowing face of the

Figure 8.8 | *Madonna in a Garland of Flowers*
Artist: Peter Paul Rubens and Jan Brueghel the Elder
Author: The Bridgeman Art Library
Source: Wikimedia Commons
License: Public Domain

Virgin Mary and energetic cavorting of the cherubs surrounding the circular arrangement of flowers painted with accuracy and delicacy by Brueghel, who was known for his lively nature scenes.

A recent study by a Yale University researcher found the perception of high quality art today is that it is produced by a single individual. If produced by two or three people, as in a mural or public work projects, the value of the art drops. For creative works, perceptions of quality therefore appear to be based on perceptions of individual, rather than total effort. Nevertheless, a new trend across the world in general suggests that this tradition, which first arose in the West during the Renaissance, is not the norm around the globe; that is, the value of art as located in the single artist who produces art individually and alone may be more specifically based in certain cultures. Artists in the twenty-first century are collaborating with others through social media and/or face-to-face encounters. It is interesting to remember that the word "art" derives from a root that means to "join" or fit together. A whole constellation of ideas and practices can be accomplished through networking and collaboration as artists participate in group residencies and apprenticeships similar to workshop traditions of centuries ago to learn the customary methods and advanced techniques of their art.

8.3.1 Nation

The Kingdom of Benin, located in the southern region of modern Nigeria and home to the Edo people, was ruled by a succession of **obas**, or divine kings. It grew from a city-state into an empire during the reign of Oba Ewuare the Great (r. 1440-1473). From 1440, obas ruled the kingdom until

Figure 8.9 | Head of an Oba
Source: Met Museum
License: OASC

it was taken over by the British in 1897. Remarkably, the obas and people of Benin remained in control of their trading relations with Europeans and without interference from the rulers of the nations they traded with until the second half of the nineteenth century, prior to foreign rule. The city of Benin prospered and grew through trade with the Portuguese, Dutch, and British.

One of the benefits of dealing with merchants-sailors who traveled the seas was the variety of goods they brought with them and were eager to trade for foodstuff grown or refined by the Edo people. In particular, the Edo treasured brass and coral, along with the ivory they acquired through elephant hunts. Those materials were reserved for the oba and his court, and were used in abundance in the wide array of ceremonial and sacred objects created under each ruler. Kingship was passed from father to firstborn son, and, upon ascending to the throne, the new oba was expected to create an altar made of brass for his father, as well as one for his mother, generally in ivory, if she had attained the status of queen mother. The new oba also created a brass head to honor his predecessor. (Figure 8.9) Over time, objects such as plaques, bells, masks, chests, and additional altars made of brass or ivory, some adorned with coral, were added. Some were used to commemorate momentous events and honor heroes, but the majority of royal objects were used in ceremonial and symbolic support of the oba, his ancestors and subjects, and the kingship itself.

This nineteenth-century brass head of an oba, for example, is not meant to be a portrait of an individual king so much as a representation of the divine nature and power of being king. The oba derives his power from his interactions with and control over supernatural forces. He is allied with and assisted by his deified ancestors, whom he honors through rituals, offerings, and sacrifices. In stressing this continuity of kingship and his rightful place in that unbroken chain, the oba strengthens his own power and that of his people and nation.

The welfare of the kingdom rests on the oba's head, a heavy burden, which is emphasized in representations of him using a proliferation of objects weighing upon him (Oba Erediauwa: https:// olivernwokedi.files.wordpress.com/2015/02/10993492_326911840841133_13745743558468606 60_n.jpg). But, he does not bear the weight of ruling alone; he works with and relies on his advisors and subjects as they support him. That support is shown literally when the oba is in full ceremonial regalia. In this photograph of the current oba, Erediauwa, the King is shown in his royal garb, heavily beaded in coral with ivory bracelets and plaques at his waist; an attendant, supporting his right arm, is helping Oba Erediauwa bear the weight of kingship on behalf of the nation of Edo people.

Following George Washington's celebratory visit to Charleston, South Carolina, in May 1791, the Charleston City Council voted to celebrate the national hero by having John Trumbull (1756-1843, USA) paint a life-size portrait of the President and hero of the Revolutionary War (1775-1783) to "hand down to posterity the remembrance of the man to whom they are so much indebted for the blessings of peace, liberty and independence."[2] Having been Washington's aide-de-camp during the War of Independence, Trumbull chose to portray Washington as the steadfast and majestic general at the start of the Battle of Trenton, a pivotal engagement for colonial troops discouraged in the aftermath of several recent defeats. (Figure 8.10) The painting depicts clouds in a dark, overcast sky turning pink with the rising sun juxtaposed with the general's horse, frightened by the ongoing battle, held tightly by his aide. Washington stands with confidence, one glove off to hold a spyglass in his right hand, looking in the distance as if heeding a faraway call for victory.

Trumbull was pleased with "the lofty expression of his animated expression, the high resolve to conquer or to perish" that he captured in *George Washington before the Battle of Trenton*.[3] His patrons in South Carolina were not, though, and rejected the portrait when he presented it to them in 1792. Speaking on behalf of the people of Charleston, South Carolina Congressman William Loughton Smith "thought the city would be better satisfied with a more matter-of-fact likeness, such as they had recently seen him calm, tranquil, peaceful."[4]

This was not an isolated occurrence: the question of how a statesman and military hero should be represented had not been resolved to the satisfaction of artists or patrons in the eighteenth century, in the years both before and after the founding of the United States. As a representative democracy, the country's leaders should be depicted as a commander-in-chief who is also one of the people, many argued. But American artists unfortunately had no clear model for a "matter-of-fact likeness" in the portraits of European royalty and heads of state that they used as examples. Anthony van Dyck (1599-1641, Flanders), who was court painter to the King of England, around 1635 painted *Charles I at the Hunt*. (Figure 8.11) The informal yet

Figure 8.10 | *General George Washington at Trenton*
Artist: John Trumbull
Source: Art Gallery at Yale
License: Public Domain

Figure 8.11 | *Charles I at the Hunt*
Artist: Anthony van Dyck
Author: User "Tetraktys"
Source: Wikimedia Commons
License: Public Domain

2   *George and Martha Washington: Portraits from the Presidential Years*, exhibition, National Portrait Gallery, Washington, DC, 1999, accessed July 6, 2015, http://www.npg.si.edu/exh/gw/trenton.htm
3   Ibid.
4   Ibid.

dignified stance van Dyck adopted for his image of the sovereign, a gentleman out in nature, quickly became the favorite pose for aristocrats and other dignitaries sitting for a non-ceremonial portrait. The pose still remained a standard at the time Trumbull painted *George Washington before the Battle of Trenton*, but, as indicated by the painting's reception, it was not considered appropriate in a representation of the leader of a democratic nation. In addition, as the portrait was to commemorate Washington's visit to Charleston, townspeople thought the battle setting should be replaced with a view of that city.

Trumbull took note of his patrons' wishes and painted another version. (*General George Washington at Trenton*, John Trumbull: https://www.flickr.com/photos/35801169@ N00/6612343749) While Washington's pose remains virtually unchanged, Trumbull lightened the sky and inserted a view of Charleston Bay with the city on the far shore. Charleston leaders were satisfied and Trumbull promised delivery of the painting after some minor additions. The addition turned out to be the General's horse, but reversed from the original painting, with its hindquarters prominently displayed in the space between Washington's canary yellow breeches and his walking stick, and the distant city visible between the horse's legs. The painting still hangs in the Historic Council Chamber of Charleston City Hall.

8.3.2 Cultural Heritage and Ethnic Identity

One important aspect of cultural and ethnic identity is shared histories or common memories. Such histories are our heritage. However, heritage is not the full history. It connects to culture and ethnicity in order to convey the full story about who we were and who we have become as a society or individual. Self or national identity is built on its foundation. Defining terms will help in understanding how each interplay to identify who we are as an individual or nation.

Christian Ellers, a popular contemporary writer on cultures, defines identity as whatever a person may distinguish themselves by, whether it be a particular country, ethnicity, religion, organization, or other position. Identity is one way among many to define oneself. Ellers defines ethnicity as a group that normally has some connections or common traits, such as a common language, common heritage, and or cultural similarities. *The American Dictionary* defines culture as the way of life of a particular people, especially as shown in ordinary behavior, habits, and attitudes toward each other or one's moral and religious beliefs ("Culture"). We will look at these terms as they relate to artists, the visual documentarians of society.

Kimsooja (b. 1957, South Korea), a multi-disciplinary conceptual, reflects on her group identity by exploring the roots of her Korean culture. She draws upon tradition and history by selecting familiar everyday items such as fabric to communicate her message. Fabric wrapped into a bundle known as a "bottari" is commonly used to transport, carry, or store everyday objects in Korean culture. What is different is Kimsooja's use of fabric as an art form. Since 1991, Kimsooja has used fabric, sometimes in the form of a bottari, in an on-going series, *Deductive Objects*, exploring Korean folk customs, daily and common activities, and her cultural background and heritage in relation to her life and experience. (*Bottari Truck-Migrateurs*, "Je Reviendrai", Thierry Depagne and Jaeho Chong: http://farm8.staticflickr.com/7368/12236788126_2d99de3e56_z.jpg) In this example, she

Figure 8.12 | St. Basil Cathedral, Moscow
Author: User "Ludvig14"
Source: Wikimedia Commons
License: CC BY-SA 3.0

photographed figures draped in Korean printed fabric that conceals their ethnicity, culture, and identity. Their identity is left to the viewer's imagination, and their culture is left for the viewer to consider, using the print of the fabric as a clue.

A number of artists such as Kimsooja choose to communicate through their art who they are in relation to their culture and ethnicity. Their art becomes a means of validating their self-identity. Her Korean heritage represents a treasury of symbols that commemorates who they are as a people and a distinct culture with a common artistic sensibility. Their national self-image is, on one level, unambiguously defined by the convergence of territorial, ethnic, and cultural identities. The geographical conditions of the Korean Peninsula provide a self-contained nautical and continental environment with plenty of resources with which to create and be innovative. These conditions have given the people since prehistoric times a rich and unique culture to draw from and make contributions to humanity. Koreans take great pride in their homogeneous culture, and in their heritage.

Russia, similarly self-contained, for many centuries developed cultural characteristics and ethnic identities distinctly their own, as well. Russia's rich cultural heritage is visually stunning, from its vivid folk costumes to its elaborate religious symbols and churches. (Figure 8.12) Most Russians identify with the Eastern Orthodox (Christian) religion, but Judaism, Islam, and Buddhism are also practiced in Russia, making it a rich land of diverse ethnic groups and cultures. St. Basil's Cathedral, located on the grounds of the Kremlin in Moscow, and hundreds of other orthodox churches symbolize Russia's heritage; indeed, citizens proudly place pictures of the cathedrals in their homes and offices. The churches in Russia are astonishingly beautiful and very much a part of Russia's heritage.

Ironically, then, in light of such a rich internal history, why did Russia's rulers look to western European artists and artistic traditions to develop a new artistic identity in eighteenth century?

Carlo Bartolomeo Rastrelli (1675-1744, Italy, lived Russia), an Italian sculptor who moved to St. Petersburg, Russia, in 1716, is associated with the formation of Russia's "new" culture. As a young artist, Rastrelli moved from his native Florence during an economic downturn to Paris in search of greater opportunities. The lavish and majestic works he created there in the late Baroque style did not earn him the success he sought, but did bring him to the attention of Tsar (and

Figure 8.13 | Peter I
Author: User "shakko"
Source: Wikimedia Commons
License: CC BY-SA 3.0

later Emperor) Peter the Great (r. 1682-1725), who lured him and his son Francesco Bartolomeo Rastrelli (1700-1771, France, lived Russia) to the Russia court.

Peter the Great co-ruled with his brother, Ivan V, and other family members until 1696, when he was twenty-four years old. At that time, Russia was still very much tied to its internal religious, political, social, and cultural traditions. Peter the Great set out to modernize all aspects his country, from the structure of the military to education for children of the nobility. The Tsar traveled widely in Western Europe, implementing governmental reforms and adopting cultural norms he saw there. France was the model for sweeping changes he had carried out in court life, fashion, literature, music, art, architecture, and even language, with French becoming the language spoken at court over the course of the eighteenth century.

Carlo Bartolomeo Rastrelli and his son Francesco Bartolomeo Rastrelli were among the painters, sculptors, and architects, then, who were instrumental in introducing to Russia the new conventions and styles that supplanted Russia's cultural heritage and identity. For example, Carlo Rastrelli's portrait bust of Peter the Great bears a striking stylistic resemblance to a portrait bust of French King Louis XIV (r. 1643-1715) by sculptor and architect Gian Lorenzo Bernini (1598-1680, Italy). (Figures 8.13 and 8.14) Bernini's bust, created during a visit to Paris

in 1665, shows Louis XIV as a visionary and majestic leader who is literally above vagaries of human existence such as the wind that billows his drapery. Carlo Rastrelli's portrait of Peter the Great, completed posthumously in 1729, draws upon the same traditions—dating back to images of Roman emperors such as Augustus (see Figure 3.23)—of showing absolute authority through such devices as the lift of the head, eyes scanning the distance, and wearing of military armor.

His son Francesco Bartolomeo Rastrelli was an architect who also worked in the Baroque style. He received his first royal commission in 1721, at the age of twenty-one, but he is

Figure 8.14 | Bust of Louis XIV of France
Artist: Gian Lorenzo Bernini
Author: User "Coyau"
Source: Wikimedia Commons
License: CC BY-SA 3.0

Figure 8.15 | Winter Palace, St. Petersburg
Author: User "Florstein"
Source: Wikimedia Commons
License: CC BY-SA 4.0

mainly known for opulent and imposing buildings he designed after Peter
the Great's death in 1725. Continuing
the modernization and transformation
of St. Petersburg, Francesco Rastrelli's
structures are associated with luxurious
exuberance of the Baroque, and Russia's Romanov rulers of the eighteenth
century. One of Francesco Rastrelli's
most famous buildings is the Winter
Palace, also bears a striking stylistic
resemblance to a French palace: Ver-
sailles, built for Louis XIV by architects
Louis Le Vau (1612-1670, France) and
Jules-Hardouin Mansart (1746-1708,
France). (Figures 8.15 and 8.16)

Figure 8.16 | Versailles
Author: Marc Vassal
Source: Wikimedia Commons
License: CC BY-SA 3.0

8.3.3 Sex/Gender Identity

Kehinde Wiley (b. 1977, USA) is a contemporary portrait painter. In his work, he refers back
to poses and other compositional elements used by earlier masters in much the same way that
Trumbull did in his portrait of George Washington. Wiley means for his viewers to recognize the
earlier work he has borrowed from in creating his painting, to make comparisons between the
two, and to layer meaning from the earlier work into his own. Due to the strong contrasts between
the sitters in Wiley's paintings and those who posed for the earlier portraitists, however, this comparison often makes for a complex interweaving of meanings.

Wiley's 2008 painting *Femme piquée par un serpent*, or *Woman bitten by a serpent*, (*Femme Piquée par un Serpent*, Kehinde Wiley: http://hyperallergic.com/wp-content/uploads/2015/03/Wiley-NewRepublic.jpg) is based upon an 1847 marble work of the same name by French sculptor Auguste Clésinger (1814-1883, France). (Figure 8.17) When Clésinger's flagrantly sensual nude was exhibited, the public and critics alike were scandalized, and fascinated. It was not uncommon in European and American art of the nineteenth century to use the subject of the work as justification for depicting the female nude. For example, if the subject was a moral tale or a scene

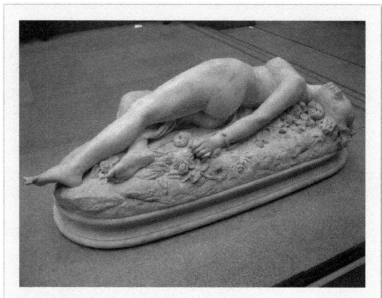

Figure 8.17 | *Femme Piquée par un Serpent*
Artist: Auguste Clésinger
Author: User "Arnaud 25"
Source: Wikimedia Commons
License: Public Domain

from classical mythology, that was an acceptable reason for showing a nude figure. In Clésinger's sculpture, the pretext for the woman's indecent writhing was the snake bite, which, coupled with the roses surrounding the woman, was meant to suggest an allegory of love or beauty lost in its prime rather than simply a salacious depiction of a nude. Unfortunately, the model was easily recognized as a real person, Apollonie Sabatier, a courtesan who was the writer Charles Baudelaire's mistress and well known among artists and writers of the day. Clésinger defended his sculpture as an artful study of the human form but, having used the features and body of a contemporary woman, his sculpture's viewers objected to the image as too real. Wiley's painting is the opposite: it is clearly intended to be a portrait of one individual, but he is clothed and inexplicably lying with his back to the viewer while turning to look over his shoulder. In his painting, Wiley retains the extended arms, and twisted legs and torso of Clésinger's figure, but the sculpted woman's thrown back head and closed eyes are replaced by the man's turned head and mildly quizzical gaze.

Wiley takes that pose and its meanings—indecency, exposure, vulnerability, powerlessness—and uses them in a context that seemingly makes no sense when the subject is a fully clothed black male. Or does it? By using the conventions for depicting the female nude, Wiley asks us to examine the following: what happens when the figure is clothed—with a suggestion of eroticism in the glimpse of brown skin and white briefs above his low-riding jeans; what happens when a young man gazes at the viewer with an unguarded expression of open inquisitiveness; and what happens when a black male presents his body in a posture of weakness, potentially open to attack? The artist uses these juxtapositions of meaning to challenge our notions of identity and masculinity. By expanding his visual vocabulary to include traditions in portraiture going back hundreds of years, Wiley paints a young black man at odds with contemporary conventions of (male) physicality and sexuality.

Ideas about gender identity, that is, the gender one identifies with regardless of biological sex, have developed scientifically and socially, and have in recent years become both more complex and more fluid in numerous cultures. Within other cultures, however, in addition to male or female, there has traditionally been a third gender, and gender fluidity has been part of the fabric of society for thousands of years. Among the ancient Greeks, for example, a hermaphrodite, an individual who has both male and female sex characteristics, was considered "a higher, more powerful form" that created "a third, transcendent gender."[5] In Samoa, there is a strong emphasis on one's role in the extended family, or *aiga*. Traditionally, if there are not enough females within an aiga to properly run the household or if there is a male child who is particularly drawn to domestic life, he is raised as *fa'afafine* or "in the manner of a woman." Thus, *fa'afafine* are male at birth but are raised as a third gender, taking on masculine and feminine behavioral traits.

In India, those of a third gender are known as *hijra*, which includes individuals who are eunuchs (men who have been castrated), hermaphrodites, and transgender (when gender identity does not match assigned sex). The role of *hijras* is traditionally related to spirituality, and they are often devotees of a god or goddess. For example, the *hijras* or devotees of the Hindu goddess Bahuchara Maja are often eunuchs, having had themselves castrated voluntarily to offer their manhood to the deity. Other *hijras* live as part of the mainstream community and dress as women to perform only during religious celebrations, such as a birth or wedding, where they are invited to participate and bestow blessings.

Although *hijras* had been a respected third gender in much of Southeast Asia for thousands of years, their status changed in late nineteenth-century India while under British rule. During the twentieth century, many *hijras* formed their own communities, with the protection of a guru, or mentor, to provide some financial security and safekeeping from the harassment and discrimination under which they lived. In 2014, the supreme court of India ruled that *hijras* should be officially recognized as a third gender, dramatically changing for the better the educational and occupational opportunities for what is estimated to be half a million to two million individuals.[6]

Tejal Shah (b. 1979, India) is a multi-media artist who often works in photography, video, and installation pieces. She began the *Hijra Fantasy Series* in 2006, (*Southern Siren - Maheshwari from Hijra Fantasy Series, Tejal Shah:* http://tejalshah.in/wp-content/themes/ tejalshah/lib/timthumb.php?src=http://tejalshah.in/wp-content/uploads/2011/10/Image-03. jpg&w=0&h=197&zc=1) creating "tableaux in which [three *hijras*] enact their own personal fantasies of themselves."[7] Shah was interested in how each woman—they all had transitioned from male to female—envisions her own sexuality, separate from the perceptions and projections of others. As described by Shah, "In *Southern Siren—Maheshwari*, the protagonist envisions herself as a classic heroine from South Indian cinema in the throes of a passionate romantic encounter with a typical male hero."[8]

---

5   Aileen Ajootian, "The Only Happy Couple: Hermaphrodites and Gender" in *Naked Truth: Women, Sexuality and Gender in Classical Art and Architecture*, ed. Ann Olga Koloski-Ostrow and Claire L. Lyons (New York: Routledge, 1997), 228.

6   http://www.npr.org/sections/parallels/2014/04/18/304548675/a-journey-of-pain-and-beauty-on-becoming-transgender-in-india

7   Tejal Shah, Artist Statement, *Hijra Fantasy Series*, accessed July 7, 2015, http://tejalshah.in/project/what-are-you/hijra-fantasy-series/

8   Ibid.

In the **tableau**, or staged scene, Masheshwari sees herself as resplendently dressed in a blue sari, a traditional Indian draped gown, an object of admiration and desire. In this photograph and the others in the series, Shah found it noteworthy that each *hijra*, participating fully in the creative process, expressed feelings about herself by using visual cues and types from mainstream sources such as, in this example, Indian popular culture. How each hijra represented herself was the stuff of universal human fantasies, Shah found, regardless of sexual or gender identity: "being beautiful, glamourous and powerful, having a family, giving love and being loved in return."[9]

8.3.4 Class

Maria Luisa of Parma was a member of the highest circles of European royalty. Born in 1751, she was the youngest daughter of Phillip, Duke of Parma, Italy, and his wife, Princess Louise-Élisabeth of France, the eldest daughter of King Louis XV. In 1765, she married Charles IV, Prince of Asturias. She was the Queen consort of Spain from 1788, when her husband ascended to the throne, until 1808, when King Charles IV abdicated his throne under pressure from Napoleon.

Royal marriages were intended to foster allegiances and cement alliances. The bride and groom generally did not meet one another until after lengthy negotiations were completed and the wedding date was near. It was not uncommon for portraits of the prospective couple to be exchanged; in addition to the descriptions by the negotiators and others, an artist's representation was the only way to learn what one's possible spouse looked like at a time when journeys were not easily or quickly undertaken. At the time of their engagement, Laurent Pécheux (1729-1821, French) painted this portrait of Maria Luisa (Figure 8.18) in 1765 for Princess Maria Luisa fiancé's family.

Figure 8.18 | *Maria Luisa of Parma*
Artist: Laurent Pécheux
Source: Met Museum
License: OASC

Maria Luisa of Parma depicts the fourteen-year-old bride-to-be holding a snuffbox in her right hand containing a miniature portrait of her future husband inside its lid. This detail was a formula in formal engagement portraits: the sitter holds a gift such as this finely made and costly trinket to express appreciation and budding affection for one's betrothed. Additionally, to demonstrate her wealthy and cultured family background, Maria Luisa is posed within an

---
9   Ibid.

interior setting displayed in a silk brocade gown trimmed with lengths of delicate, handmade lace, a medallion of the Order of the Starry Cross suspended from a diamond-encrusted bow on her breast, and diamond stars in her powdered hair. While this is indeed a likeness of the princess, the portrait is meant to convey far more than the color of her eyes or shape of her nose. This portrait is a statement about the prestige and power she will bring to the marriage, and a congratulatory note to the groom's family on the beauty and worth of the mutually beneficial asset they are gaining.

Figure 8.19 | *Maria Luisa of Parma Wearing Panniers*

Artist: Francisco José de Goya y Lucientes
Author: Prado Museum
Source: Wikimedia Commons
License: Public Domain

Maria Luisa's dress is the exclamation point to that visual statement. She is wearing a style known as a mantua or robe *a la française* (in the French style), a dress for formal court occasions, of silk brocade woven into alternating bands of gold thread and pink flowers on a cream field. This very costly fabric, probably made in France, is stretched over panniers, or fan-shaped hoops made of cane, metal or whalebone extending side-to-side. The panniers create a horizontal but flattened silhouette that allowed the tremendous quantity of magnificent fabric required to be fully displayed. To wear such a gown was a pronouncement of one's wealth and status, a sign of which was one's comportment, that is, one's bearing and behavior. And, it was indeed a challenge to stand or move with the grace expected of a highborn woman in eighteenth-century society while wearing such cumbersome, restrictive, and heavy clothing. Maria Luisa, however, is depicted as poised and charming, the perfect consort for a king.

Twenty-four years after her portrait by Pécheux, Maria Luisa was thirty-eight years old and had borne ten children, five of whom were still alive, when Francisco Goya created this portrait, *Maria Luisa Wearing Panniers*. (Figure 8.19) , Francisco Goya was named painter to the court of Charles IV and Maria Luisa in 1789, and in celebration of Charles IV's ascension to the throne, created a portrait of the King, to go along with the Queen's portrait. Neither the years nor Goya were kind to Maria Luisa. (Between 1771 and 1799, she would have fourteen living children, six of whom grew to adulthood, and ten miscarriages.)

In Goya's depiction, she is even more richly dressed than in her earlier portrait, but her elaborate and sumptuous costume serves only to provide an unflattering contrast with the Queen's demeanor. Goya depicts Maria Luisa with her arms awkwardly held to each side to accommodate her rigid, box-like tontillo (the Spanish variation of panniers); her plain, expressionless face is almost comically topped by a complexly constructed hat of lace, silk, and jewels. The hat represents one extravagant trend in women's fashion of the 1780s, and Goya did paint its proliferation of textures and surfaces with great skill and sensitivity, but the contrast between the Queen's hat and her features makes them appear even more coarse and unrefined, regardless of her wealth and class.

What explanation could there have been for the court painter to create such an unflattering representation of Maria Luisa, Queen consort

Figure 8.20 | *The Third Class Carriage*
Artist: Honoré Daumier
Source: Met Museum
License: OASC

of Spain? In her years of living in her adopted country, she had not endeared herself to members of court or her subjects. Considering that the King preferred to hunt, running the country fell largely on the shoulders of Maria Luisa, who was vain and bad-tempered. Goya's presentation does not, in fact, contradict that assessment. The emphasis on her luxurious and elegant attire and on the robe and crown to Maria Luisa's right—signaling her status as Queen consort—represent that she is the individual who is literally in touch with the robes of state. This work and her engagement portrait of nearly twenty-five years earlier were not so much depictions of her as a person as they were means to communicate the power and prestige of her place and her role.

Figure 8.21 | *The First Class Carriage*
Artist: Honoré Daumier
Author: Walters Art Museum
Source: Wikimedia Commons
License: Public Domain

Honoré Daumier (1808-1879, France) in 1864 painted a different sign of

Figure 8.22 | *The Second Class Carriage*
Artist: Honoré Daumier
Author: Walters Art Museum
Source: Wikimedia Commons
License: Public Domain

prestige, or lack thereof, in *The Third-Class Carriage*; it was one of three paintings in a series commissioned by William Thomas Walters. (Figure 8.20) The other two paintings were *The First-Class Carriage* and *The Second-Class Carriage*, the only one in the series thought to be finished. (Figures 8.21 and 8.22) Walters, an American businessman and art collector, would later found the Walters Art Museum in Baltimore, Maryland, with work from his collection, including these three paintings.

When Daumier created the works, he had been working prolifically as a painter, printmaker, and sculptor for forty years. In his lifetime, he would create approximately 5,000 prints, 500 paintings, and 100 sculptures. From the beginning of his career, he was interested in the impact of industrialization on modern urban life, the plight of the poor, the quest for social equality, and the struggle for justice. He was especially known for his biting satire of politics and political figures, and his less stinging, ironic commentary on current society and events. Because of the subject matter he chose—everyday people, contemporary life—and the straightforward, truthful, and sincere manner in which he depicted them, Daumier is considered to be part of the Realist movement or style in art.

In *The Third-Class Carriage*, the artist presents four figures in the foreground, bathed in light, with numerous, less individualized figures crowded in the background. The young mother nursing her baby, an elderly woman sitting with folded hands, and a boy sleeping with his hands in his pockets encompass four generations, as well as different stages of life. Although the passengers sit near one another, they appear isolated from each other. They, including the boy, are probably traveling to or from work in the city, and both their body postures and facial expressions convey the toll of hard labor and long hours. Daumier shows compassion for these workers whose lives hold nothing but repetitive drudgery.

Forever changing the mainly agricultural society that existed in much of Europe and the United States prior to the second half of the eighteenth century, the Industrial Revolution is the start of the mechanization and manufacturing that would lead to people shifting from country to city life, and from farms to factories. While the shift to an industrial, money-based society improved the lives of many and created the middle class as we know it today, Daumier was well aware that others were being left behind and were essentially trapped in a cycle of little education, unskilled labor, and low wages.

The artist represents different life expectations based on class through the way he paints the windows and through his use of light in each of the three paintings. In *The Third-Class Carriage*, the figures in the foreground have light shining on them from a window to the left, outside the picture plane. There are windows in the background, as well, but nothing can be seen outside of them. Daumier is implying there is nothing to be seen, especially in the case of the literally non-existent window. In *The Second-Class Carriage*, a landscape can be seen through the window, and one of the figures looks out intently. The other three, paying no attention to the world outside, are cocooned in their winter clothes in an attempt to fend off the cold in their unheated train car. But the man who leans forward to observe the passing scenery appears to be younger and is perhaps more eager and capable of adapting to and moving upward in the world of business—suggested by the bowler hat he is wearing, which at the time was associated in city life with civil servants and clerks. In *First-Class Carriage*, the passengers are all alert, each attending to their own business. One young woman looks out at a green landscape; considering her lightweight outerwear, it appears this is a springtime scene, which is suggested, as well, by the colorful ribbons on the two women's fashionable bonnets. With their relaxed postures and placid, composed expressions, these first-class passengers give the impression of confidence. They are more secure in themselves and their places in the world than either the second-class or third-class passengers.

8.3.5 Group Affiliation

History suggests that the quality of human survival is best when humans function as a group, allowing for collective support and interaction. Social psychological research indicates that people who are affiliated with groups are psychologically and physically stronger and better able to cope when faced with stressful situations. Gregory Walton, a social psychologist who studies group interaction, has concluded that one benefit individuals receive is the satisfaction of belonging (to a group, culture, nation or) to a greater community that shares some common interests

Figure 8.23 | *The Syndics of the Amsterdam Drapers' Guild, known as the "Sampling Officials"*
Artist: Rembrandt
Author: Google Cultural Institute
Source: Wikimedia Commons
License: Public Domain

and aspirations. The unity of groups is achieved through members' similarities or their having experiences based on the history that brought them together.

Artists throughout history have been associated with groups, movements, and organizations that protect their interests, forward their cause, or promote them as a group or as individuals. The most visible groups during the Renaissance period in Italy, for example, were people belonging to the Catholic Church and other religious organizations, wealthy merchant families, civic and government groups, and guilds, including artists' guilds. (Figures 8.23 and 8.24)

Figure 8.24 | *Officers of the St. George Civic Guard, Haarlem*
Artist: Frans Hals
Source: Wikimedia Commons
License: Public Domain

8.3.6 Personal Identity

The city of Palmyra, in modern Syria, had long been at the crossroads of Western and Eastern political, religious, and cultural influences, as it was a caravan stop for traders traveling the Silk Road between the Mediterranean and the Far East. In the first century CE, the city came under Roman rule and under the Romans, the city prospered, and the arts flourished. Following a rebellion by Queen Zenobia of Palmyra in 273 CE, Roman Emperor Aurelian destroyed the city, ending the period of Roman control.

The Palmyrenes, or people of Palmyra, built three types of elaborate, large-scale monuments for their dead called houses of eternity. The first was a **tower tomb**, some as high as four stories. The second was a **hypogeum**, or underground tomb, and the third was a tomb built in the shape of a temple or house. All were used by many generations of the same extended family and were located in a necropolis, a city of the dead, what we today call a cemetery. Inside the tombs were **loculi**, or small, separate spaces, each of which formed an individual sarcophagus, or stone coffin. Inside the opening to the tomb, the first sarcophagus held the remains of the clan's founder; it was often faced with a stone relief sculpture depicting him as if attending a banquet and inviting others to join him. Surrounding the founder in the *loculi*, on the face of each family member's sarcophagus would be a relief portrait of each person interred there. (Loculi: http://romeartlover. tripod.com/Palmyra5.html)

This stele, a portrait of a father, his son, and two daughters, dates to between 100 and 300 CE, sometime during the era of Roman rule. (Figure 8.25) The man is reclining on a couch decorated with flower motifs within circles and diamonds. He holds a bunch of grapes in his right hand and, in his left, a wine cup decorated with flowers similar to those on the couch. His two daughters

Figure 8.25 | Funerary Relief
Source: Met Museum
License: OASC

flank his son in the background; the son holding grapes and a bird. The son and daughters all wear necklaces. Additionally, the daughters wear pendant earrings and brooches holding the drapery at their left shoulders. The chiton, or tunic, and himation, or cloak, that each daughter wears has some affinities with Greco-Roman types of clothing, but the style of the ornamented veil covering their heads is a local type of garment, based on Parthian, or Persian, styles. Also wearing local garments, the two males wear a loose fitting tunic and trousers, each with a decorative border. The fine fabrics indicated by the embellished borders of both men and women's clothing indicate goods and wealth amassed from trade, as does the abundant use of precious metals and gems in the variety of jewelry adorned by the Palmyrenes. Thus, the stele is a blend of Greco-Roman and Palmyrene (and larger Parthian) styles and cultural influences.

Coupled upon many Palmyrenes grave steles are inscriptions of text in both Aramaic and Latin that give the person's name and genealogy, markers of distinctive individual and family traits. While many of the depictions of the frontal-facing, wide-eyed figures—a defining feature of Palmyrene art—show little individualization of features, the coupling with such inscriptions are evident signs that each stele was intended to denote the characteristics of the person entombed within. The figures actively engage the viewer, and provide the reminder that personal identity is an amalgamate of individual, socio-cultural, spiritual, and historical influences.

In July 2015, the city of Palmyra, its people, and its art were again in danger. In April of 2015, Islamic State (ISIS) forces overtook the 3,000-year-old Assyrian city of Nimrud and destroyed its buildings and art. On May 21, 2015, ISIS overtook the city of Palmyra, inducing fear that they would destroy buildings and art there as they did in Nimrud. On July 2, 2015, ISIS was reported to have destroyed grave markers similar to the one discussed here. (Grave Marker Reliefs, http://www.timesofisrael.com/is-destroys-iconic-lion-statue-at-syrias-palmyra-museum/) They lined up six bust-length reliefs of people who lived in Palmyra nearly 2,000 years ago, and smashed them, obliterating the visual and written record of each person. So many have had their portraits made for posterity with the hopes of staying alive, against the odds. And, this is why we need art: it gives us memories of ourselves and our deeds, who we identify with, and how we identify others.

8.4 BEFORE YOU MOVE ON

Key Concepts

National and personal identities do not magically happen; they are built on and influenced by immediate and past events, environments, traditions, and cultural legacies. Artists capture and document not only the physical conditions of a society but also the emotional and mental conditions. They construct a sense of who we were and are as a person and as a nation. Society's identity is always fluid. When we see identity as static, we record people with stereotypes and do not see them for who they are. Art is one way to challenge static notions of identity by engaging the viewer in visual narratives that are unfamiliar to them, and that educate and challenge their previously held notions.

Since the 1970s, postmodern theories have challenged historical and traditional notions of ethnic and cultural identity by developing a model that views identity as being multifaceted, fluid, and socially constructed. Some scholars contend that we are in a period of post-identity and post-ethnicity, repudiating the old essentialist view of identity. Globalization of people, the Internet, and travel have all brought about fluid cultures—which may have contributed to people's more fluid sense of identity, and also to their interest in researching their heritage, culture, and ethnic identity. Heritage is the treasure and symbols of pride for an individual, country, and nation. Many works of art are seen as part of national heritage because they help citizens appreciate their past. Art provides life to the past, something that can be visualized, touched, walk through, and identified as being part of a legacy and culture.

Test Yourself

1. On the surface Kim Sooja's art seems simple, but underneath it is an enigma of traditions that make a metaphoric identity statement; for example, her use of fabric as an art form evokes intimacy and honor of her culture and history. Discuss and identify at-least two artists whose work makes a personal and historical statement. Be specific as you reference each image associated with your essay. (minimum of 500 words).

2. A number of circumstances throughout history have compelled artists to confront the context of social issues, select at-least two works of art that best describe an event or issue. Discuss the problems associated with the issue, and how the event and art shaped the legacy or identity of the country or nation. Describe the power the work communicates, discuss the significance of the work and how it convey a message, and identity of the people in that period of time. At the end of your essay make commentary on why you selected the art works what you think about the art. (Attach selected work with captions.) Answer to the question is located throughout the chapter)

3. Throughout history building were constructed in a manner to symbolize power; spirituality; and godlessness. Structures house institutions that guide, influence and shape a society's morals, values, politics, religious and social conditioning. Select 4 structures that best symbolize the

identity or culture of a society. Describe its impact on influencing a nation, significance to the nation and how the structure contributes to national or individual identity. At the end of your essay discuss why you selected the structures and the aesthetics of the building. (Attach selected structures with captions.)

4. Compare and contrast four works of art that best describe a personal or national identity. Discuss with specifics how the artist is able to capture the character of the person or nation. At the end of your essay add a commentary why you selected the works and their significance. (Attach selected works with captions.)

8.5 KEY TERMS

Baroque: a style of architecture and art that originating in Italy in the early seventeenth century

Bottari: Cloth wrapped and tied around clothes , fabric, or/and items into a bundle for carry

Grave stele: is a stone or wooden slab, generally taller than it is wide, erected usually in Greek cemeteries as a monument, for funerary or commemorative purposes.

Hypogeum: an underground prehistoric burial site

Impressionism: is a nineteenth-century art movement that developed in France during the late nineteenth century by a group of artists called the Anonymous Society of Painters, Sculptors

Impressionist: A painter whose painting have characteristics of the impressionism movement, emphasizing accurate depiction of light in its changing qualities, uses small, thin, yet visible brush strokes, open composition,

Individualism: emphasizes potential of man and self development own beliefs. The Individualism during the Renaissance period became a prominent theme in Italy

Industrial Revolution: period during the late eighteenth and nineteenth centuries in western Europe and the United States when industry quickly developed due to the invention of steam-powered engines and the growth of factories. Fundamental changes occurred in agriculture, textile and metal manufacture, transportation, economic and policies, and had a major impact on how people lived

Obas: The title of "oba," or king, is passed on to the firstborn son of each successive king of Benin, Africa at the time of his death

Renaissance Period: a period of time from the fourteenth to the seventeenth century in Europe. The era bridged the time between the Middle Ages and modern

Tableau: is an incidental scene, as of a group of people

Tower tomb: are mausoleums, built in 1067 and 1093

Art and Power

Pamela J. Sachant and Rita Tekippe

9.1 LEARNING OUTCOMES

After completing this chapter, you should be able to:

- Describe why and how art and artists have in some cultures been considered to have exceptional power.

- Distinguish between images of persuasion and propaganda, and specify characteristics of each.

- Recognize how and why images are used for such purposes as to display power, influence society, and effect change.

- Indicate ways that images establish and enhance a ruler's position and authority.

- Identify changes in images of conflict, heroic action, and victims of violent confrontation in various cultures and time periods, including the artist's intentions as well as the public response.

- Distinguish between and describe the prohibition of images enforced within some religions.

- Describe why protestors or conquerors might destroy images and monuments of a past or defeated culture.

9.2 INTRODUCTION

Art has always been associated with power. At times in history, the individuals who made art were seen as having special powers. They could conceptualize shapes and forms and then bring them into being. They could create images and objects from dirt, ashes, and stone that looked like living creatures. These individuals were set apart—they could transform, they could give life. And the images and objects they created held powers, as well. They were a means of communication with an unseen world, of exerting influence over the well-being and actions of humans. So both the artists and their art were considered to be magical in that they were out-of-the-realm of everyday, common, and shared existence: they were super-natural and extra-ordinary.

The ancient Greeks believed the creativity artists possessed came to them from a **muse**, a personification of knowledge and the arts that inspired them to write, sculpt, and compose. The ancient Romans, who strongly believed in the family as the most basic and essential hub of societal organization, called its guiding spirit the *genius*, from the Latin verb meaning *genui* or "to bring into being or create." The

Figure 9.1 | Apadana staircase, Persepholis, Iran
Author: User "Fabienkhan"
Source: Wikimedia Commons
License: Copyright, Special Permissions Granted

word **genius** came to be associated with the arts during the Renaissance, when it took on the meaning of inspiration and ingenuity visited upon the artist, often as a form of possession, setting the artist apart from, and at odds with, non-geniuses.

In addition to the power of the artist, there is the power of the art itself to imitate or mimic life. Again, according to the ancient Greeks, art's power resides in its ability to represent nature; the closer, more real, and more natural the representation, the closer the art work is to truth, beauty—and power. Among other cultures, especially those that avoid representation, art is still a means of aesthetic expression with considerable power, but with abstracted forms. For example, in Islamic cultures the human figure and forms based on direct observation are not used in religious art and architecture as only God has the ability to create living things. Instead, elaborate ornamentation based on the written word and human, animal, and plant forms is used to decorate surfaces with intricate motifs, or patterns.

The visual force of the image or object, whether representational or non-representational, has been used throughout the ages by those in power to give form to and communicate messages about themselves, their wishes or dictates, their accomplishments, and their very right to rule. Literacy has, until the recent past, in human history been a skill few had the means to develop, but leaders in secular and religious roles have fostered among their subjects and followers a visual literacy, the ability to "read" and understand images through a common "language" of subjects, symbols, and styles. Those who wish to use their art as a means of protest against an established power have traditionally used the same "vocabulary" to visually communicate their messages, as well. Especially in times of war and during periods of oppression, art has been used as a tool to protest, document, provide an alternative version, and communicate to others about people and events that become our historical record.

9.3 PROPAGANDA, PERSUASION, POLITICS, AND POWER

The word **propaganda** has gotten a bad reputation. The Latin origin of the word propaganda is *propagare*, meaning "to spread or disseminate." As it is used today, the word mainly refers to promoting information—often biased or misleading, sometimes hidden—in order to influence views, beliefs, or behavior. Originally, the word was not associated with politics, as it is generally today, nor did it imply lies or bad faith; propaganda was simply a means of publicly communicating ideas, instruction, and the like. In such a case, we now are more likely to use the word **persuasion**, which has a more neutral connotation and suggests convincing rather than coercing. For example, advertising tries to persuade—or entice—the consumer to make a choice or purchase. To many, however, there is a fine line between propaganda and persuasion. They are separated more by purpose and intention—good, bad, or neutral—than how they are carried out. Garth Jowett and Victoria O'Donnell describe the fine but crucial differences between the two words:

> Propaganda is the deliberate, systematic attempt to shape perceptions, manipulate cognitions, and direct behavior to achieve a response that furthers the desired intent of the propagandist. Persuasion is interactive and attempts to satisfy the needs of both persuader and persuadee.[1]

King Darius I (r. 522-486 BCE) had both persuasion and propaganda in mind when he built the Apadana at Persepolis, today Iran. (Figure 9.1) Darius I was the first king of the Achaemenid Empire (c. 550-330 BCE) to have royal structures erected on the site, but construction would continue under succeeding Persian kings for approximately one hundred years. The Apadana was begun in 515 BCE and completed thirty years later by Darius I's son, Xerxes I. Apadana means hypostyle hall, a stone building with a roof supported by columns. It originally had seventy-two columns—thirteen still stand—each sixty-two feet tall in a grand hall that was 200 x 200 feet, or 4,000 square feet. Needless to say, a building of such monumental proportions was an overwhelming sight for those who approached it. Brightly painted in many colors and raised on a platform with the Kuh-e Rahmat or Mountain of Mercy rising behind it, the towering structure could be seen for miles from the sparsely vegetated plain to the east.

For King Darius I, the Apadana and Persepolis—the city of Persians—as a whole was a statement of propaganda. The hypostyle hall and the city were awe-inspiring and intimidating; they in no uncertain terms let the viewer know the King had formidable power and tremendous resources. Upon entering the King's hall, the viewer was surrounded by his strength in the form of columns the height of a modern six-story building, holding up a ceiling of incalculable weight. How small and powerless the visitor was in the midst of such force. But Darius I, whose empire stretched from Egypt in the west to the Indus Valley, today Pakistan, to the east, knew that he could not effectively rule through domination and fear. So, he had elements of persuasion included at Persepolis, as well.

In addition to the building's resplendent majesty, it was adorned with sumptuous and masterful frescoes, glazed brickwork, and relief sculpture. Two staircases led up to the platform on

---

1   Garth Jowett and Victoria O'Donnell, *Propaganda and Persuasion,* 6th ed. (California: Sage Publications, 2014), 7

Figure 9.2 | Reliefs at Persepholis
Author: User "Ziegler175"
Source: Wikimedia Commons
License: CC BY-SA 3.0

which the Apadana was built, on the north and east sides, but only the north staircase was completed during Darius's lifetime. That staircase and the platform walls to either side are covered with reliefs: figures in even, orderly rows as they approach the Persian King's hall. (Figure 9.2) They are representatives of the twenty-three countries within the Achaemenid Empire, coming to pay homage to the King during festivals for the New Year, carrying gifts. Accompanying them are Persian dignitaries, followed by soldiers with their weaponry, horses, and chariots. The native Persian and foreign-born delegates are shown together in these **friezes**, or rows, of relief sculpture. (Figure 9.3) They have facial features that correspond with their ethnicity, and hair, clothing, and accessories that indicate what region they are from. Even the gifts are objects and animals from their own countries. Rather than showing the foreigners as subservient to the Persians, they mingle with one another and at times appear to be in conversation.

The staircase reliefs, as opposed to the magnificent building as a whole, can be seen as a form of persuasion. It was in the king's better interests to win over his subjects, to gain their trust, allegiance, and cooperation, than to bend them to his will through force and subjugation. Having already demonstrated from a distance that he had the power to defeat his enemies, Darius I could, as the delegates ascended the stairs to his great hall, literally show them the respect with which he treated his loyal subjects.

In more recent history, Jacques-Louis David (1748-1825, France) painted five versions of *Napoleon Crossing the Alps* between 1801 and 1805. (Figure 9.4) David was born and raised in Paris and entered the École des Beaux-Arts in 1866 at the age of eighteen. After eight years of mixed success in his studies there, David won the Prix de Rome in 1774, a prestigious government scholarship that also included travel to Italy. He lived in Rome from 1775 to 1780, studying the art of great masters from the classical past, through the Renaissance, and

Figure 9.3 | The Apadana Palace, Persepolis, Iran
Author: User "Happolati"
Source: Wikimedia Commons
License: Public Domain

Figure 9.4 | Napoleon Crossing the Alps
Artist: Jacques-Louis David
Author: User "Garoutcha"
Source: Wikimedia Commons
License: Public Domain

to the present. But, he was most impressed with the philosophical and artistic ideals of some of his contemporaries, the Neoclassical thinkers and painters he met in Italy.

When he returned to France, he soon began exhibiting work in this new style; with their somber, moral tones, stories of family loyalty and patriotic duty, fine detail, and sharp focus, works in the Neoclassical style (c. 1765-1830) were in stark contrast to the frivolous, sentimental subjects and delicate, pastel hues of the prevailing Rococo style (c. 1700-1770s). Over the course of the 1780s, as social disconnect and political upheaval were building toward the French Revolution of 1789, the self-sacrificing, stoic heroes from classical and contemporary history David painted increasingly reflected the public desire for *liberté, egalité, fraternité*, or liberty, equality, and fraternity (universal brotherhood).

In the aftermath of the revolution, during the mercurial times of the 1790s, David was first a powerful figure in the short-lived Republic and then a jailed outcast. When Napoleon Bonaparte, named First Consul in 1799, commissioned David to paint his portrait in 1800, however, David's return to official favor was complete.

The commission came about this way: in the spring of 1800, Napoleon led troops south to support French troops already in Genoa, Italy, in an effort to take back land captured by the Austrians. He did so on June 9th at the Battle of Marengo. The victory led to France and Spain re-establishing diplomatic relations eleven years after the French Revolution and, as part of the formal exchange of gifts to mark the occasion, King Charles IV of Spain requested a portrait of Napoleon to hang in the Royal Palace of Madrid. Learning of this, Napoleon requested three more versions from David (and the painter independently created a fifth, which remained in his possession until his death.)

It was to be an equestrian portrait, Napoleon specified, that is, depicting him on horseback, crossing the Great St. Bernard Pass in the Alps, leading the Reserve Army south to Italy. David was to show Napoleon on a spirited, rearing horse as a calm and decisive leader, much like his heroes Hannibal and Charlemagne, who crossed the Alps before Napoleon and whose names are inscribed with his on rocks in the left foreground of the painting. In actuality, however, it did not happen that way at all: Napoleon crossed on the Alps on the back of a mule, in good weather, a few days after the soldiers went through the pass.

What Napoleon was asking David to paint was a piece of propaganda. And, the artist succeeded admirably. With the wind whipping his cloak around him, assuredly holding the reins of his wild-eyed horse in one hand while gesturing the way up and over the peaks with the other, and holding the viewer's gaze with his look of complete composure, David has shown Napoleon as a leader who guides his people to victory and who will be remembered as a hero throughout the ages. That was the story Napoleon wanted told: the timeless ideal of the great man, not the transitory pettiness of his physical likeness. For, as Napoleon is attributed with claiming, "History is the version of past events that people have decided to agree upon."

9.4 IMAGERY OF WAR

Considering the potential for art to give expressive form to ideas and emotions, it is not surprising that art has often been used to present a wide range of messages about war, one of the most dramatic of human events. All forms of art have been used for documenting war, stating reasons for supporting or opposing it, and showing reflections about its meanings, implications, and effects. On a broader scale, all human activities, of course, may be occasions for people to criticize one another, to condemn ideas, ideals, and actions, to promote or oppose causes that express cultural, societal, or individual values. We will examine a number of works that are concerned with these issues in various ways.

9.4.1 Historical/Documentary

From the earliest times, artists have responded to issues of war and conquest and their implications for the cultures in which they took place. Often, the art appears to have been created to mark a moment of triumph and to interpret the conquest as a validation of a leader's right to rule, established through the victory. Such was the case with the Palette of Narmer. (Figure 9.5) On the two-sided palette are relief-carved depictions of the subjugation of the

Figure 9.5 | Narmer Palette
Author: User "Nicolas Perrault III"
Source: Wikimedia Commons
License: Public Domain

enemy by Egyptian King Narmer (also referred to as Menes)—under the watchful protection of the deities—and a procession of the King and his attendants toward the decapitated bodies of ten of the defeated. On the first side, Narmer wears the crown of Upper Egypt and on the reverse he wears the crown of Lower Egypt, symbolizing the union of the two regions under one ruler (c. 3,100-3,050 BCE). He is depicted far larger than both his enemies and his own men, showing the figures' relative importance. Narmer is literally depicted as a powerful, firm, and resolute warrior who will be a strong and worthy leader.

Grand artistic depictions of rulers in battle have always been used to help form their reputations and to bolster the images of their good and wise rulership. Military success has long been equated, correctly or not, with political prowess. The heroic feats of Alexander the Great (r. 336-323 BCE) at the Battle of Issus (333 BCE) with the powerful Persian King Darius III (r. 336-330 BCE) were portrayed in a Greek painting that no longer exists. Like much of Greek art, though, it was copied by the Romans, so we do have a mosaic version of the tumultuous battle that was created for the House of the Faun in Pompeii, Italy. (Figure 9.6) This enormous depiction, although damaged and now incomplete, gives a lively, somewhat riotous account of the dramatic encounter of these two renowned warriors. Alexander can be seen to the left on his chestnut horse, staring with wide-eyed intensity at the fleeing Darius, who turns to look at his opponent with one arm extended as if pleading for mercy while the driver of his chariot whips the King's horses into a frenzy of motion.

Figure 9.6 | Alexander Mosaic
Author: User "Berthold Werner"
Source: Wikimedia Commons
License: CC BY-SA 3.0

We should consider to what extent these accounts are **documentary**, based on factual records, and what we can discern that is propagandistic in purpose. In many eras, the glorification of heroes and heroic deeds in war was perhaps paramount, not only from a political and patriotic standpoint, but also because these were the values promoted as part of artistic training in academic settings (values that prevailed for most successful artists at least through the middle of the nineteenth century, when anti-academic rebellions began in art circles).

Figure 9.7 | *The Death of General Warren at the Battle of Bunker's Hill, June 17, 1775*
Artist: John Trumbull
Author: Boston Museum of Fine Arts
Source: Wikimedia Commons
License: Public Domain

American heroism in war was certainly envisioned in these terms, as evidenced in *Death of General Warren at the Battle of Bunker Hill* by John Trumbull. (Figure 9.7) As discussed in Chapter 8 Art and Identity, Trumbull was an aide-de-camp to General George Washington. After witnessing Warren's death in Boston, Trumbull was commissioned by Warren's family to immortalize the event. The Battle of Bunker Hill took place in 1775, the first year of the American Revolutionary War. Although the colonialists were defeated, the British were stunned by their far greater number of casualties, boosting the morale of the young army. In his painting, Trumbull focused on the General's tragic death as the colonial forces retreated, as well as the compassion of British major John Small, who held back one of his men as the soldier was about to bayonet Warren. Doing so, Trumbull could celebrate the heroism of the Americans while also acknowledging the honor-

Figure 9.8 | *Washington Crossing the Delaware*
Artist: Emanuel Leutze
Author: Google Cultural Institute
Source: Wikimedia Commons
License: Public Domain

able behavior of the enemy, an expectation in eighteenth-century codes of conduct during pitched battles.

Trumbull's depiction of the battle scene is greatly romanticized: an historically accurate rendering of General Warren's death was neither expected nor desired by viewers of the day. Many questions have been asked, as well, about the accuracy of the grand tableau by Emanuel Leutze (1816-1868, Germany, lived USA) of *Washington Crossing the Delaware*, a painting that is an iconic

Figure 9.9 | *Charge of the Rough Riders at San Juan Hill*
Artist: Frederic Remington
Author: User "Julius Morton"
Source: Wikimedia Commons
License: Public Domain

symbol of the American Revolutionary War and the first president of the United States. (Figure 9.8) Leutze created the work in 1851, seventy-five years after the Battle of Trenton occurred in 1776. Far from attempting to reconstruct the scene as it took place, Leutze intended his work to be an evocation of a grand and inspirational event, dramatically pictured.

By the time Frederic Remington (1861-1909, USA) painted *Charge of the Rough Riders* in 1898, warfare and depictions of it were much different. Remington gives us the spirit of the fray—more down to earth, momentary, and rough and tumble. (Figure 9.9) The implications are much less aggrandized and heroic, the viewer's sense of the event much more intimate. And by the time of the World War I appearance of *Gassed* by John Singer Sargent (1858-1925, USA, lived England), we see a different tenor altogether. (Figure 9.10) Here, we are privy to Sargent's personal response to the deadly aspects of war, to the after-effects for the individuals who were each physically assaulted by poison mustard gas and are showing its ill effects as they were weakened, nauseated, and felled.

The changes in interpretation are due in part to those changes towards realism in art during the nineteenth century that we have explored. Also, they were heightened by the advent and evolution of photography, which had enhanced potential for documentation of actual conditions. But

Figure 9.10 | *Gassed*
Artist: John Singer Sargent
Author: User "DcoetzeeBot"
Source: Wikimedia Commons
License: Public Domain

Figure 9.11 | Photograph of bodies on the battlefield of Antietam during the American Civil War
Photographer: Alexander Gardner
Author: User "Shauni"
Source: Wikimedia Commons
License: Public Domain

Figure 9.12 | Photograph of Allan Pinkerton, President Abraham Lincoln, and Major General John A. McClernand
Photographer: Alexander Gardner
Author: User "Bobanny"
Source: Wikimedia Commons
License: Public Domain

photography did not, by any means, always present the viewer with unvarnished truth, since it could, like painting, be manipulated in its effects. Nonetheless, the potential for a different view of war and its effects was ushered in with the advent of photography.

The American Civil War provided a venue for photographers to use the new medium in recording exactly what they were seeing, through the lens. But the processes were still not up to the task of capturing the actions, because equipment was cumbersome, and exposed photographic plates had to be developed on the spot in specially outfitted wagons. The result was that most of the photographs were of groups of dead bodies and battlefields laid waste, after the actual event. (Figure 9.11) The sights were nonetheless sobering to the viewers who had never before been privy to views of the result of war on such a scale. Alexander Gardner (1821-1882, Scotland, lived USA) was one of a number of photographers who captured many battlefield scenes, as well as views of campsites and many other details of the deployments, including visits from such dignitaries as President Lincoln. (Figure 9.12)

The potential for a more critical interpretation afforded by photography had in the past been taken at times, even though not as the norm. Notable examples come from several periods when artists responded to the horrors and agonies of war and injustice in various ways and created memorable interpretations that reveal their protests of conditions. In 1633, Jacques Callot (1592-1635, France) created a suite of panoramic etchings that dramatize *The Miseries of War*. (Figure 9.13) Francisco Goya's monumental *Third of May, 1808*, painted in 1814, showed the fear and horror of an encounter between Napoleon's troops and citizens of the town

Figure 9.13 | *The miseries of war; No. 11, "The Hanging"*
Artist: Jacques Callot
Author: artgallery.nsw.gov.au
Source: Wikimedia Commons
License: Public Domain

of Medina del Rio Seco, where 3,500 Spaniards lost their lives. (Figure 9.14) Goya's sympathies are clear in his presentation of a terrified white-shirted martyr-like figure facing a firing squad while in the midst of his equally horrified compatriots.

Similarly, Honoré Daumier dramatized the injustice of a night raid in the home of a working-class family in Paris during protests in 1834. Following a shot having been fired from a window in the building where twelve members of the Breffort family lived, soldiers stormed their apartment and killed them all. Six months later, Daumier created, a stark lithograph depicting helpless family members as they fell. (Figure 9.15) Daumier had been jailed two years earlier, in 1832, for **caricatures** (portraits containing features or characteristics exaggerated for comic effect) he made ridiculing King Louis Phillipe I (r. 1830-1848). Immediately after the artist created *Rue Transnonain*, the street on which the Breffort family lived, the lithographic stones he used were confiscated by government officials and all copies of the print were destroyed. The following year, political caricatures were banned entirely. This indicates the power Daumier's work was perceived as having and the danger it could hold for those in power. As noted, the potential for a different view of war and its effects was ushered in with the advent of photography. The American Civil War in the 1860s provided a venue for photographers to use the new medium in recording exactly what they were seeing, through the lens. But the processes were still not up to the task of capturing the actions, because equipment was cumbersome and exposure

Figure 9.14 | *The Third of May*
Artist: Francisco de Goya y Lucientes
Author: Prado in Google Earth
Source: Wikimedia Commons
License: Public Domain

times were still relatively long and slow. Alexander Gardner's photographic corps created many after battle scenes as well as portraits of generals, the president, campsites, and many other details of the deployments. (Figures 5.18 and 5.19) The potential for capturing action and momentary pathos only increased from then on, and the capacity for documenting graphic events has been used widely ever since. (Figures 5.20, 5.21, 5.22, 5.23) Compare the image of corpses being bulldozed and buried wholesale to the photos of Gardner and the previous painted glorifications of the battlefield.

Figure 9.15 | *Rue Transnonain, le 15 Avril, 1834, Plate 24 of l'Association mensuelle*
Artist: Honoré Daumier
Source: Met Museum
License: OASC

9.4.2 Reflective/Reactionary and Anti-war

One of the most powerful anti-war statements ever painted was by Pablo Picasso, created in 1937 following the bombing of the town of Guernica during the Spanish Civil War. He was commissioned by the Spanish Republican Government to create a mural for that country's pavilion at the 1937 World's Fair in Paris and, after learning of the attack, designed this poignant abstraction of symbolic and iconic motifs to express the horror of the event. (Pavilion of the Spanish Republic at the Paris International Exposition, 1937: https://thespacearchitecture.files.wordpress.com/2013/05/int2.jpg) His knowledge of the details had been gleaned from newspaper reporting, so he elected to create the imagery in the graphic black, gray, and white of the photographs through which he learned of the bombing and its impact. His dramatic distortions of form convey the deep anguish and disgust that had been engendered in him, his fellow Spaniards, and the world.

Figure 9.16 | Aerial Photography Before the First World War
Artist: Laws F C V (Sgt)
Author: User "Fae"
Source: Wikimedia Commons
License: Public Domain

Over the course of the twentieth century, documentary photography was used not only to capture the brutal events of war, but also to broadcast moments of utter horror in such graphic ways that they have influenced public sentiment, sometimes turning opinion from support to outrage. By the time of World War I, technology permitted the reproduction of photographs in newspapers, which meant that the average citizen had far greater access to visual news of the war than in earlier conflicts. Some leaders, such as German Kaiser Wilhelm II (r. 1888-1918), were in favor of using photographs as a means of bolstering public support for the war, but others restricted photographers' access and censored photographs, citing security concerns. Shortly before the beginning of World War I, the British Army was the first to realize the potential of photography for aerial reconnaissance, greatly expanding their research capabilities and troop maneuverability. (Figure 9.16)

During World War II, American military and government agencies tremendously expanded the use of photography for purposes ranging from conducting espionage and assisting training, to recording atrocities and providing documentation. (Figures 9.17 and 9.18) During the Vietnam War (USA involvement, 1955-1975), the American military gave unprecedented access to non-military reporters and photographers. As the war extended in the 1960s, far longer than the American people expected, images of conflict and suffering in the war-torn country began having an impact on public opinion. (Women and children crouch in a muddy canal as they take cover from intense Viet Cong fire, Horst Faas: http://media2.s-nbcnews.com/j/streams/2013/october/131016/8c9400532-pb-131016-vietnam-01.nbcnews-ux-2880-1000.jpg) By 1972, when Nick Ut (b. 1951, Vietnam, lives USA) photographed children fleeing their village after it was attacked with napalm, the tide had turned and many Americans no longer supported the Vietnam

Figure 9.17 | Bones of anti-Nazi German women in the crematoriums in the German concentration camp at Weimar (Buchenwald), Germany
Photographer: Pfc. W. Chichersky
Author: User "Petrusbarbygere"
Source: Wikimedia Commons
License: Public Domain

Figure 9.18 | Two enlisted men of the ill-fated U.S. Navy aircraft carrier LISCOME BAY, torpedoed by a Japanese submarine in the Gilbert Islands, are buried at sea from the deck of a Coast Guard-manned assault transport.
Author: User "W.wolny"
Source: Wikimedia Commons
License: Public Domain

War. (Phan Thị Kim Phúc running down a road near Trảng Bàng, Vietnam, after a napalm bomb was dropped on the village of Trảng Bàng by a plane of the Vietnam Air Force, Huynh Cong Ut: https://upload.wikimedia.org/wikipedia/en/d/d4/TrangBang.jpg)

9.4.3 Prohibition or Destruction of Imagery: Iconoclas

Controversy over imagery and its use, especially in sacred contexts, also has a long history. Debates on the topic have, at times, erupted into deep and bitter arguments. It has often been thought that, because of the Old Testament statements forbidding the use of idols, the Jewish religion has never allowed pictorial or figural art as part of its religious expression. More current findings, though, lead to the conclusion that the biblical statements were actually pointedly made at times against the real danger of idolatry, or the

Figure 9.19 | Part of the fresco at the Dura-Europos synagogue
Author: User "Udimu"
Source: Wikimedia Commons
License: Public Domain

worship of idol images, rather than being a broad prohibition of images altogether. Dura-Europos was a military outpost in Syria held by the Romans 114-257 CE where the garrisoned soldiers obviously practiced a wide variety of religions. The site has a great number of different pagan temples, a Christian house church, and a Jewish **synagogue**, or house of worship, that is decorated with a great array of lively figural frescoes that depict Old Testament stories. (Figure 9.19)

Early Buddhist art was, according to some, **aniconic**, or characterized by the avoidance of figural imagery that represented Sakyamuni Buddha, its fifth-century BCE founder. Others disagree. We have no examples of Buddhist art until the second century BCE, well after the death of Sakyamuni, probably because early works were of impermanent materials and have not endured. In the earliest we do have, the figure of the Buddha does not appear; rather, we see the seat where he achieved enlightenment and the Bodhi tree that shaded it (Figures 9.20) Scholars disagree as to whether the absence

Figure 9.20 | Mara's assault on the Buddha
Author: User "Gurubrahma"
Source: Wikimedia Commons
License: CC BY-SA 3.0

of the Buddha confirms a prohibition of showing his figure.

On the contrary, we do know there is a general aversion to the use of figural imagery in sacred uses in Islam, although it is not universally heeded. There is no specific prohibition in the Koran, the central sacred scripture for Islam; however, there are authoritative statements among the writings of the Hadith, the commentaries on the Koran that supplement its teachings. The rationale is that the creation of human and animal form is reserved for God and should not be an act of man. Thus, the decorations of mosques and related structures are usually accomplished with lavish linear scripts, embellished with arabesques and vegetal and floral motifs. (Figure 9.21) The script is usually drawn from the Koran or is simple praise of Allah; this sort of design is often also applied to all sorts of goods and décor for the Muslim household. (Figure 9.22)

Figure 9.21 | Mihrab of Mosque–Cathedral of Córdoba
Author: User "Ingo Mehling"
Source: Wikimedia Commons
License: CC BY-SA 4.0

A dramatic example of the anti-imagery debate took place in the Byzantine Christian Church in the eighth and ninth centuries CE. Based on the perception of the biblical prohibition, an assault was mounted against all religious images, and much of the existing artwork was destroyed in an effort to eradicate what was considered an evil practice. The defenders of the use of imagery argued that the problem was not the images themselves, which could be positive aids to spiritual inspiration and religious devotion, but to their improper usage, which resulted in a sort of idolatry, akin to pagan idol worship. The images, according to proponents of their use, should be seen as tools, associated with understanding God and the saints, and as means of furthering the contemplation of Christian mysteries. Further, they argued, to obliterate existing images, to deface pictures and to destroy statues was to desecrate sacred things and, effectively, to disrespect the holy beings which they represented.

Figure 9.22 | Seventeenth-Century Persian Bowl
Author: User "Udimu"
Source: Wikimedia Commons
License: Public Domain

This notion was expressed in the mid-ninth-century Chludov Psalter with an illustration that equates

Figure 9.23 | Miniature from the 9th-century Chludov Psalter with scene of iconoclasm. Iconoclasts John Grammaticus and Anthony I of Constantinople.
Author: User "Shakko"
Source: Wikimedia Commons
License: Public Domain

Figure 9.24 | Iconoclasts in a church
Artist: Dirck van Delen
Author: User "BoH"
Source: Wikimedia Commons
License: Public Domain

Figure 9.25 | 16th-century iconoclasm in the Protestant Reformation. Relief statues in St. Stevenskerk in Nijmegen, the Netherlands, were attacked and defaced in the Beeldenstorm.
Author: User "Ziko"
Source: Wikimedia Commons
License: CC BY-SA 3.0

the destruction of an icon with insulting Christ on the cross when he was forced to take gall (bile) and vinegar by the mocking Roman soldiers. (Figure 9.23) The controversy was settled in 843 and the use of icons and imagery thrived thereafter. Unfortunately, very little of the religious artwork that was produced prior to this time survived for us to examine.

Other chapters in the debate over imagery open in later centuries. For some Christians, it was one point of disagreement leading to the Protestant Reformation that began in Wittenberg, Germany, in 1517. According to those protesting what they saw as abuses of power in the Roman Catholic Church, the proliferation of images of holy figures and stories from the Bible distracted the faithful from true worship: reading the word of God in the Bible. As new religious practices spread, there

Figure 9.26 | Bronze head of a king, most likely Sargon of Akkad but possibly Naram-Sin.
Author: Iraqi Directorate General of Antiquities
Source: Wikimedia Commons
License: Public Domain

was a widespread removal of religious paintings and sculpture from all churches and public buildings. (Figure 9.24) In the Wars of Religions that raged in many places in Europe (c. 1524-1648), the destruction of images was one of the violent forms of protest by angry crowds that railed against any and all prevailing practices and the powers they held responsible. A great many church portals (doors) were damaged by those who saw lopping off heads of sculptures above the doorways as a fitting expression of their anti-Church sentiment. (Figure 9.25)

Throughout history, such destruction has certainly not been restricted to religious controversies. From very early examples, we know of what is likely purposeful defacement of ruler images that were made either in protest or as a sort of proclamation of defeat and superiority. The gouging out of the jeweled eyes in this bronze head of Assyrian King Sargon II might have been for theft of the precious materials, but it may also indicate conquest over the man himself. (Figure 9.26) In recent times, we have seen the dramatic toppling in 2003 of the statue of Sadam Hussein in a public square in Baghdad, Iraq, as a symbolic overthrow of a despised and despotic ruler. (Figure 9.27) Further humiliation of him was clearly intended by the widespread publication of photos of captors picking lice from his head after his discovery in a spider hole.

Figure 9.27 | Statue of Saddam Hussein being toppled in Firdos Square after the US invasion of Iraq.
Photographer: U.S. military employee
Author: User "Ipankonin"
Source: Wikimedia Commons
License: Public Domain

Figure 9.28 | The taller Buddha of Bamiyan before (left) and after destruction (right).
Author: User "Tsui"
Source: Wikimedia Commons
License: CC BY-SA 3.0

The power of such pointed symbolism in visual terms is employed to fight culture wars, as well. In Afghanistan, in 2001, the Taliban undertook to dynamite two colossal images of the Buddha dating to the sixth century CE that had been carved into the side of a cliff in the Bamyan valley of central Afghanistan. (Figure 9.28) Arguments came from all over the world, pleading with them to preserve monuments that were considered part of the cultural heritage of humankind. Nonetheless, they completed their task, declaring it a duty to eliminate an image that violated their spiritual beliefs.

A similar scenario unfolded more recently, when ISIS militants went on a destructive campaign to destroy historically and culturally valued artwork in the Mosul Museum, Iraq, despite pleas from curators and art lovers around the globe. (Extremists used sledgehammers and power drills to smash ancient artifacts at a museum in the northern city of Mosul: http://i.dailymail.co.uk/i/ pix/2015/02/26/261DB11500000578-2970270- image-a-1_1424957194042.jpg) This sort of protest is often made on a smaller scale, as well, when symbolic or

Figure 9.29 | Desecration of the U.S. Flag by burning
Author: Jennifer Parr
Source: Wikimedia Commons
License: CC BY 2.0

iconic imagery is defaced or destroyed as a means of mocking its value to those who respect it, as with the Nazi symbols made on Jewish gravestones or the burning of the American flag. (Desecrated Jewish gravestones: http://cdn.timesofisrael.com/uploads/2012/10/AP100127022968.jpg) (Figure 9.29) All such incidents reinforce our understanding of the varieties of power that art and visual imagery can have.

9.5 BEFORE YOU MOVE ON

Key Concepts

Due to their ability to create art, throughout history artists have often been considered to have special and mysterious powers. Images can be used to enhance the power of an individual, system of government, or form of religion. Artists can use images to bring attention to and have an impact on social issues. Images of war can be used to validate and strengthen a ruler's authority and power. From the nineteenth century to the present, violent conflicts have been depicted with a greater range of imagery, in part due to technological advances and social attitudes toward the impact of war. Imagery is forbidden within some religions based on interpretations of religious texts. The destruction of images can be the result of religious, social, or political beliefs or protests.

Test Yourself

1. Describe why and how art and artists have in some cultures been considered to have exceptional power.

2. What are propaganda and persuasion, and what are some differences between them?

3. How did King Darius I use images of both persuasion and propaganda at the Apadana in Persepolis?

4. Describe how rulers have used images of them to enhance their authority.

5. How and why did images of war change in the United States from the time of Revolutionary War through World War I?

6. Give an example of an art work that was meant to protest war or social injustice, and describe how it did so.

7. Describe how and why Nick Ut and Pablo Picasso focused on the individual in their depictions of war.

8. Why are images forbidden within some religions? Give specific examples.

9. What prompted the destruction and avoidance of religious images during the Protestant Reformation?

10. Explain why images of a defeated or dead ruler or monuments of an occupied culture might be defaced or destroyed.

9.6 KEY TERMS

Aniconic: the avoidance of figural imagery within a religion

Caricature: portrait containing features or characteristics exaggerated for comic effect

Documentary: in artistic or written forms, work that records actual events as they happened

Frieze: a horizontal row of relief sculpture or painting on a building

Genius: (from the Latin *genui*: to bring into being or create) a person of remarkable intelligence or with outstanding creative abilities

Muse: personification of knowledge and the arts, and inspiration to write, sculpt, and compose

Persuasion: the attempt to influence, convince or entice someone to make a choice (often a purchase)

Propaganda: information (written, verbal, artistic) that promotes a particular viewpoint or set of ideas about a person or event. The word indicates information that is biased, misleading, or sometimes hidden that is used in order to influence views, beliefs, or behavior

Synagogue: Jewish house of worship

10 Art and Ritual Life
Symbolism of Space and Ritual Objects, Mortality, and Immortality

Jeffery LeMieux and Rita Tekippe

10.1 LEARNING OUTCOMES

After completing this chapter, you should be able to:

- Identify and describe the different architectural forms that are used for diverse ritual purposes and those associated with specific religious groups

- Recognize a variety of symbolic and functional components of architectural centers for worship, including building parts, auxiliary structures, and furniture, as well as to discuss its significance and uses

- Identify and describe sculpture, paintings, and a variety of religious objects that are used to express beliefs, to teach religious doctrine, and to perform ritual acts

- Recognize and discuss some of the specific forms of art associated with funerary and memorial functions in different belief systems

10.2 INTRODUCTION

Art and architecture have ever been used to express our deepest human interests, including the universal concerns with the meaning of human life itself and whether or not our spirit will continue in an afterlife. Thought and belief about these concerns have led individuals to create art about them; they also have led people to ally with like-minded individuals, forming philosophical and religious groups and institutions that have frequently further formalized their thought and belief concepts and contemplations and used art and architecture to give concrete form and image to these ethereal notions.

10.3 EXTERIOR RITUAL SPACES

The well-known site of Stonehenge, in Wiltshire, England, although not completely understood today, provides us with insight into the early evolution of a ritual location. (Figure 10.1) It

Figure 10.1 | Stonehenge
Author: User "garethwiscombe"
Source: Wikimedia Commons
License: CC BY 2.0

was developed over the course of some 1,500 years (c. 3,000-1,600 BCE). The site's configuration has astronomical implications, with a design of a ritual offering or sacrifice table, and portal placed in relationship to the sunrise at the summer solstice. (Figure 10.2) Its concentric rings were made of wooden posts, earthen ditches, and thirty **megaliths,** or large stones, each of which is approximately thirteen feet high, seven feet wide, and weighing more than twenty-five tons. In places where two megaliths support another horizontal stone, a **dolmen** or **cromlech** is formed. (Figure 10.3) Other parts of stone, wood, and earth were placed in particular spots for which the choice of location and use are now unclear.

How could Stonehenge have been built with prehistoric knowledge and technology? It is believed that the large stones were quarried from twenty-five to 150 miles away, floated, and log rolled to the final site and then placed by creating inclined dirt ramps. (Figure 10.4) Once the upright stones were placed, the spaces were filled with dirt, the capstones rolled into place, and all the dirt removed. As is clear with these construction methods, it is important to recognize that prehistoric people did not lack in either clever mental ability or tireless devotion.

Many sites across England and other parts of Europe show a kinship to it in their use of space and materials and their desire to engage with the cosmos. Stonehenge is the largest of approximately 1,000 stone circles found on the British Isles. Their existence and the fact that these sites were used for such a long time gives us some insight into the ways our earliest known ancestors devised views of the universe and their place in it, as well as how they addressed such issues through artistic expression.

Human societies from widely separated times and locations have constructed strikingly similar forms

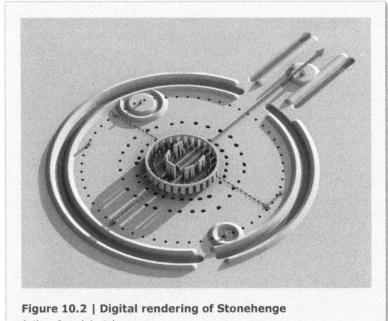

Figure 10.2 | Digital rendering of Stonehenge
Author: Joseph Lertola
Source: Wikimedia Commons
License: Public Domain

Figure 10.3 | Dolmen of Oleiros, Spain
Author: Arturo Nikolai
Source: Wikimedia Commons
License: CC BY-SA 2.0

of symbolic or physical enclosure or elevation of the sacred. The altar is the most simple and expedient means. An altar, found in religious settings and structures to this day, is a piece of **liturgical** (religious ritual) furniture possessing ancient symbolism—primarily as the site of sacrifice, most often in the offering of animals ritually slain for the deity.

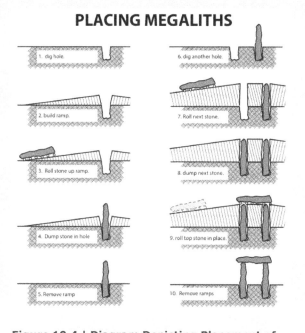

PLACING MEGALITHS

1. dig hole.
2. build ramp.
3. Roll stone up ramp.
4. Dump stone in hole
5. Remove ramp
6. dig another hole.
7. Roll next stone.
8. dump next stone.
9. roll top stone in place.
10. Remove ramps

Figure 10.4 | Diagram Depicting Placement of Megaliths
Author: Jeffrey LeMieux
Source: Original Work
License: CC BY-SA 4.0

It is a short step to placing the altar on a built, raised platform to accentuate its status. For example, a **heiau** is a Hawaiian temple composed of a   Polynesian raised earthen or stone temple platform in an enclosed area that might also contain stone markers and cult images. Heiau were used for a variety of reasons: to treat the sick, offer first fruits, control rain, and achieve success in war (for which human sacrifices were made). Heiau are found throughout the Pacific

Figure 10.5 | Drawing of Heiau at Wimea
Artist: John Webber
Author: User "KAVEBEAR"
Source: Wikimedia Commons
License: Public Domain

island. This print depicts the heiau at Waimea, on Kauai, one of the Hawaiian islands, as it existed prior to European occupation. (Figure 10.5) The print was created by artist John Webber (1751-1793, England), who accompanied British explorer Captain James Cook on this third Pacific expedition (1776-1779). Although many Hawaiian Heiau were deliberately destroyed at the official end of the Hawaiian religion in the nineteenth century, some have since been fully rebuilt and are now public attractions.

Olmec, Maya, and Aztec, built large temple complexes dedicated to religious worship, which included animal and human sacrifice. One such fine example of these large complexes is the Mayan temple at Chichen Itza. It is a four-sided pyramid with staircases of ninety-one steps on each side all leading to a temple at the top. The number ninety-one is no accident: four times ninety-one equals 364, which, paired with one final step at the top, represents the number of days in the solar year. Quetzalcoatl appears in succeeding Central American religions.

In the Aztec culture, Quetzalcoatl was related to gods of the wind, of the planet Venus, of the dawn, of merchants, and of arts, crafts, and knowledge. He was also the patron god of the Aztec priesthood, of learning and knowledge.

The gateway is another architectural method for creating or recognizing a ritual or sacred space. Ritual gateways are found more often in Asian religious settings, though with a broad view any entrance could be construed to be a marker for a physical and spiritual transition.

Shinto is an ancient religion native to Japan. The main focus of Shinto is the veneration of the deeds and images of ancestors in home shrines. In public places, **torii**, or Shinto gateways, are often found marking the sites of important ancient events or framing beautiful views. The "floating gate," so named because when the tide is high, it is surrounded by water and appears to float, of the Itsukushima Shrine near Hiroshima is a good example. (Figures 10.6 and 10.7) The entrance gate was erected in 1168; it has been destroyed, redesigned, and rebuilt several times.

Figure 10.6 | The torii gate at Itsukushima Shrine on the island of Itsukushima at low tide
Author: Dariusz Jemielniak
Source: Wikimedia Commons
License: CC BY-SA 3.0

Figure 10.7 | The torii gate at Itsukushima Shrine on the island of Itsukushima
Author: Jordy Meow
Source: Wikimedia Commons
License: CC BY-SA 3.0

10.4 THE SACRED INTERIOR

Sacred interior spaces offer several advantages over exterior sites such as platforms and gateways. In particular, they offer controlled access to the ritual space, for example, as we saw with complexes such as the Temple of Horus at Edfu (see Figure 7.42) and the Temple of Hephaestus in Athens, Greece, (see Figure 7.44) and they permit a new level of control over who is admitted. The nature of an interior space may also act as a metaphor for a personal encounter with the sacred within oneself.

We have noted that architectural forms have often been adopted and adapted according to the ways they serve group or congregational needs. Many religious centers meet a variety of purposes and needs, so they might include spaces or separate buildings for schools, meeting rooms, and any type of subsidiary accommodations. We will look, however, primarily at the basic distinctions among architectural forms that articulate and address the ritual and practical needs of the group.

Figure 10.8 | Nanzen-ji garden, Kyoto
Artist: Musō Soseki
Author: User "PlusMinus"
Source: Wikimedia Commons
License: CC BY-SA 3.0

It should be added that many practices are personal and individual and so may not require any sort of separate building; some may use a space within another sort of building or a room or corner within the home. Also, many rituals have been conceived as addressing a natural setting, such as an open field, a sacred grove of trees, a grotto or cave, or a specific spring, lake, or seaside spot. (Figure 10.8)

Some of the basic features within many churches and temples reflect these notions. Although there are many exceptions, the layout of a structure most often relates to the four directions of the compass and the sites of most sacred precincts address the rising and setting of the sun. Altars are usually placed in the east. Over time, some adaptations have been made to accommodate other considerations; for example, a church or temple might be situated near a sacred mountain or a place where a miraculous occurrence took place. With these ideas in mind, we will briefly survey a few important types and features.

10.4.1 Features and Forms

Innumerable symbolic features are associated with worship; a few stand out as basic to identification of a building or site associated with a specific belief system. We quickly recognize and identify the distinctive implications of a **steeple** (church tower and spire) or a minaret, or the form of a stupa or pagoda, and we can sometimes discern how these and other such expressions came into use and accrued significance. (Figures 10.9 and 10.10) As discussed in Chapter Seven: Form in Architecture, the Islamic minaret was developed as a tower associated with a mosque that was used primarily to issue the call to prayer (and also to help ventilate the building). (see Figure 7.50) In the

Figure 10.9 | Church of the Covenant
Author: User "Fcb981"
Source: Wikimedia Commons
License: CC BY-SA 3.0

past, the **imam**, or prayer leader, charged with the ritual task would climb to its summit and intone the *adhan* five times each day, making the call in all directions so that the surrounding community would be notified; now, electronic speaker systems achieve this function. But the minaret has other implications and uses, as well. (Figure 10.11) It has become a striking visual symbol of the very presence of the mosque and of Islam's presence in the community; over time, many mosque complex designs have incorporated multiple minarets—most often four, with one at each corner of the main structure. The visual significance may have been further accentuated to rival the Christian presence of a nearby steeple or bell tower.

The bell tower has been used similarly to announce the onset of Christian services by ringing at specific times. Public clocks are sometimes added, with the function of noting the time, ringing or chiming a tune on the hour, the half hour, or the quarter hour. Because churches were often community centers, the bells could also give public notice of celebration, mourning, or warnings of emergency like fire. In the Middle Ages, the control of the bell ringing was sometimes a political issue, especially as urban communities developed governments and sought independence from local churches

Figure 10.10 | Phoenix Hall
Artist: Musō Soseki
Author: User "うぃき野郎"
Source: Wikimedia Commons
License: CC BY-SA 3.0

Figure 10.11 | Minaret of the Great Mosque of Kairouan, Tunisia
Author: Keith Roper
Source: Wikimedia Commons
License: CC BY 2.0

Figure 10.12 | Tournai, Belgium
Author: Jean-Pol GRANDMONT
Source: Wikimedia Commons
License: CC BY-SA 3.0

Figure 10.13 | Washington National Cathedral
Author: Carol M. Highsmith
Source: Wikimedia Commons
License: Public Domain

in certain ways. At Tournai, Belgium, such struggles notably led to a sort of visual combat of towers on the town skyline. The city's civic leaders there were granted the right to control the bell ringing for community notices and built a separate tower away from the church located on the town square. The Church countered by renovating the church building to include four bell towers, seeking thereby to assert its own rights to identify itself with the task. (Figure 10.12)

The steeple or bell tower visually implies a Christian presence and is generally part of the church building, usually on the façade. Over time, builders have added multiple towers, as they did at Tournai and elsewhere. Doing so emphasized the width of the façade, or other parts of the building, such as the transept, the "arms" in a Latin cross plan church, or the **crossing**, where the "arms" meet. For example, at Lincoln Cathedral in England, towers are placed at either side of the façade and another marks the crossing. (Figure 10.13) Some steeples and towers associated with Christian use, however, have been erected independently of other buildings. For example, the Campanile, or bell-tower, by Giotto in Florence follows the Italian tradition of erecting the tower adjacent to the church. (Figure 10.14)

More specific features of church and stupa structures, among others, include space within or outside for circumambulating, walking around a sacred object. In medieval churches that

Figure 10.14 | Giotto's Campanile
Author: Julie Anne Workman
Source: Wikimedia Commons
License: CC BY-SA 3.0

featured display of relics and accommodated pilgrim visitation, the **ambulatory** might be altered to allow visitors to walk around a ring or succession of chapels at the end of the church where the apse was located. (Figure 10.15) As referred to in Chapter 7 Form in Architecture, at the Sanchi Stupa, provisions were made for the devotee to walk around the fence surrounding the stupa, then enter one of the gateways and circumambulate the mound on the ground level, then climb the stairs and circumambulate again on a walkway attached to its exterior surface. (see Figures 7.52) (Great Stupa at Sanchi: https://s-media-cache-ak0.pinimg.com/564x/e2/14/ b2/e214b2c65c63f16198bf64b1dbc63d67.jpg) Since the stupa is an earthen mound faced with masonry, it has no

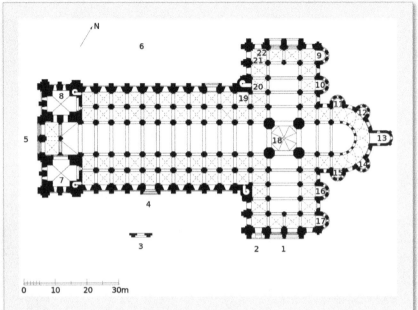

Figure 10.15 | Floorplan of St. Sernin
Author: User "JMaxR"
Source: Wikimedia Commons
License: CC BY-SA 2.0

Figure 10.16 | Relief of a sacraficial alter
Author: Wolfgang Sauber
Source: Wikimedia Commons
License: CC BY-SA 3.0

Figure 10.17 | A Romanesque baptismal font from Grötlingbo Church, Sweden
Artist: Master Sigraf
Author: User "Bilsenbatten"
Source: Wikimedia Commons
License: CC BY-SA 3.0

interior space accessible to the practitioner and all of the rituals are accomplished outside.

The provisions for making an offering of animals ritually slain for the deity can be seen in the ruins of the Anu or White Temple in Uruk (c. 3,000 BCE), today Iraq, which stood atop the ziggurat there. (The White Temple floorplan: https://classics.unc.edu/files/2014/02/UkWhTpl.gif; Temple and Ziggurat: https://classics.unc.edu/files/2014/02/UkWhTRecon.gif) The sanctuary chamber included a large altar table with channels along a sloped ditch to carry away the blood and other fluids resulting from the ritual sacrifice. Other types of sacrificial altars were provided for fire rituals that involved making offerings to a deity of an animal, grain, oil, or other substances, as can be seen in this Roman relief depiction of the sacrifice of a bull. (Figure 10.16) Some of these altars were part of temple complexes, while others were found in homes and used for private devotions. Larger ritual fires are also part of the practices among some sects and are still in use; bonfires are a related practice.

Ritual ablutions, or cleansings, also have artistic accommodations in the forms of fountains and pools, which were once a standard part of Christian atrium courtyards that marked the entryways to churches and are frequently provided in courtyards for mosques. (Islamic Pre-Prayer Ablution Fountain in Kairaouine Mosque Courtyard in Fes, Morocco: http://encircleworldphotos.photoshelter.com/image/I0000EvE9geT8XFA) Vestiges are found in holy water fonts that still stand at portals to Catholic churches, where the practitioner dips the fingers and makes the sign of the cross. Also related are baptismal fonts or tanks used for the ritual cleansing, which, along with other ceremonial rites, signifies the entry into some faiths (Figure. 10.17) Another type of symbolic liturgical furniture that appears in many worship contexts and is given considerable artistic attention is the **pulpit**, or **minbar**, as is it called in Islamic centers. It is the site of preaching, reading scriptures, and other addresses to congregations, and is, sometimes, very elaborately adorned. (Figures 10.18 and 10.19)

Figure 10.18 | Baroque pulpit in the Amiens Cathedral, France
Author: User "Vassil"
Source: Wikimedia Commons
License: Public Domain

Figure 10.19 | Amr Ibn al-Aas Mosque (Cairo)
Author: User "Protious"
Source: Wikimedia Commons
License: CC0 Public Domain

10.4.2 Sculptural and Painted Expressions of Belief

Beyond the types of symbolic features and forms we have explored, there exists a tremendous variety of objects expressing common or personal belief and devotions. In many instances, they adorn temples, synagogues, and churches; at other times, they were designed to be used in private or family settings. Even the sects with the most austere attitudes about the use of art, such as the Shakers, have a design aesthetic that is related to the belief system of finding creative solutions in the functionality of the form. (Figure 10.20). A lot of artistic efforts have been applied to religious expression, often entailing the notion that the most lavish and sumptuous goods should be provided for these purposes.

Figure 10.20 | Rocker in the Shaker Village at Pleasant Hill
Author: User "Carl Wycoff"
Source: Wikimedia Commons
License: CC BY 2.0

Figure 10.21 | Bodhisattva Avalokitesvara (Guanshiyin), Shanxi Province, China
Author: Rebessa Arnett
Source: Wikimedia Commons
License: CC BY-SA 2.0

Sculptures, paintings, drawing, prints, film, video, performance art, visual demonstrations, all have been brought into service in this regard. They might vary as to whether they embody a point of doctrine or a shared tenet, or express a personal veneration for a deity or holy personage, or offer a viewpoint about exuberance or restraint; regardless, they have abounded. Often, they also epitomize the sentiment of a cultural moment in a particular place or the development of a particular line of thought in theology, philosophy, or devotional practice.

Figure 10.22 | Virgin and Child of Jeanne d'Evreux
Author: Ludwig Schneider
Source: Wikimedia Commons
License: CC BY-SA 3.0

Figure 10.23 | The nave of Vézelay Abbey
Author: Francis Vérillon
Source: Wikimedia Commons
License: CC BY-SA 3.0

Figure 10.24 | The central portal of Vézelay Abbey
Author: User "Vassil"
Source: Wikimedia Commons
License: Public Domain

An example is the elegant and graceful Bodhisattva Guanyin, a spiritual figure of compassion and mercy, created in China in the eleventh or twelfth centuries during the Liao Dynasty (907-1125). (Figure 10.21) The sculpture acts as a compassionate guide for the Buddhist devotee who would look to such an elevated being for loving guidance on the spiritual journey. The ideas of patron saints or dedicated intercessors like the Virgin Mary were popular in the West, as well, especially during the Middle Ages, an era when great riches were often lavished on images of veneration for these spiritually accomplished models of sanctity. The graceful Virgin of Jeanne d'Evreux was a gift in the early twelfth century from the French queen to the Abbey of Saint-Denis, the site for royal burial at the time. (see Figure 7.64 and Figure 10.22) The young mother, playfully engaged with her divine infant son, was rendered with striking and inspiring emotional effect.

In Christian churches of the Middle Ages, and for some denominations today, the sculptural embellish-

Figure 10.25 | Lower Compartments Detail, Vézelay Abbey
Author: User "Vassil"
Source: Wikimedia Commons
License: Public Domain

ment of the interior not only showed the respect of believers but also provided considerable food for devotional thought, often in the form of Bible stories, tales of the saints, and theological ruminations. Such was the case at the French Romanesque Vézelay Abbey (1096-1150). (Figure 10.23) The tympanum above the portal contains a relief sculpture by Gislebertus depicting the Last Judgment, with Christ sitting in the center (Figures 10.24 and 10.25) The capitals on the piers in the interior have lively depictions of Old Testament tales such as Jacob and the Angel, and other scenes such as the Conversion of St. Eustace, a Roman general who while hunting saw a vision of a crucifix between a stag's antlers and adopted Christianity. (Figures 10.26 and 10.27) These are all told through delightful, puppet-like Romanesque figural forms. Visual stories such as these were meant to reinforce the importance of remaining true to God despite challenges to their faith in this lifetime.

Figure 10.26 | Reliefs in Vézelay Abbey
Author: User "Vassil"
Source: Wikimedia Commons
License: Public Domain

Figure 10.27 | Reliefs in Vézelay Abbey
Author: User "Vassil"
Source: Wikimedia Commons
License: Public Domain

10.4.3 Ritual and Devotional Objects

In devotional centers where the philosophical or religious beliefs allow the use of figural imagery, the use of cult statues and other images of deities or persons associated with the ideology are important focal points for worshippers. Some, like the cross, are essential statements; others play subsidiary roles, designed for amplifying or enhancing the spiritual experience and providing additional opportunities for contemplation or stimulus of devotional response. As we have noted, Buddhist and Hindu temple complexes often have a great array of portrayals of deities and/or spiritual leaders, as befits polytheistic religions. Part of the complaint of the Protestant revolt was that Christian churches had become too similar in spirit to polytheistic cults, with the wide selection of saints comprising a system that seemed no longer sufficiently focused on the central singular God. Part of the effect, in artistic terms, was that the decoration of many Protestant churches changed character—as well as liturgical focus—eliminating many of the lavish accouterments that had accrued around Catholic ritual.

While few general rules exist for Christian decoration, the Catholic churches usually have a large and prominent crucifix above the main altar where the **Mass/Eucharist, t**he primary religious ritual for Catholics, is celebrated; Protestant sites are more likely to have a plainer cross or none at all, and are unlikely to have an altar. Throughout the ages, the character of the crucifix has seen tremendous variation, from an expression of the extreme suffering of Christ to a much more iconic expression of the belief behind the symbol. Between the time of Christianity's legitimization in 313 CE and the tenth century, for example, representations of Christ on the cross generally showed him as alive, hav-

Figure 10.28 | The Gero Crucifix
Author: User "Elya"
Source: Wikimedia Commons
License: CC BY-SA 3.0

ing gloriously defied death. Crosses also varied considerably in scale. The Gero Crucifix (c. 965-970), now placed over a side altar in Cologne Cathedral, Germany, compared to others of its era was very large at six feet, two inches, and was considered to be provocative in eliciting contemplation of the suffering of Christ. (Figure 10.28) Over the next several centuries, depictions of Christ on the cross in northern Europe would increasingly emphasize the agony of the human being in the throes of death, as opposed to his everlasting triumph, in ever more graphic portrayals of the event central to Catholic worship and to the liturgy of the Mass. (Figure 10.29) The range of

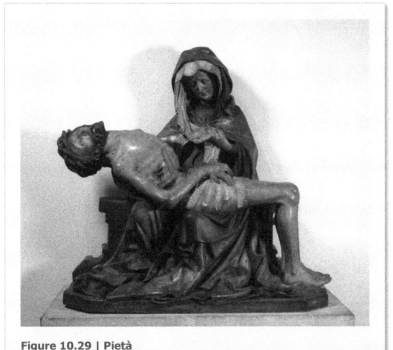

Figure 10.29 | Pietà
Source: Met Museum
License: OASC

Figure 10.30 | Replica of the Chalice of Doña Urraca
Artist: User "Locutus Borg"
Source: Wikimedia Commons
License: CC BY-SA 3.0

emotional content in Christian imagery is vast and ever changing. This diversity is a typical characteristic for objects that are related to devotional use, as the nature of active faith is to grow and change, ever producing fresh new expression.

The variety of liturgical equipment that was conceived for Christian ritual over the centuries provided great outlet for inventiveness. While some versions of ritual objects were simple and utilitarian in design, others clearly spurred flights of great fancy and flair. An important symbolic and functional object in all worship centers is the candlestick and a tremendous variety of these were created. One of the most elaborate was the enormous seven branched candelabra cast of gem studded bronze and covered with a mass of imagery of saints, plants, animals, and angels, with the whole immense and tangled array supported on four large dragon-form feet. (Duomo Milano - Candelabro Trivulzio: https://it.wikipedia.org/wiki/Candelabro_ Trivulzio#/media/File:IMG_6849_-_Duomo_-_Menorah_ Trivulzio_-_Foto_Giovanni_Dall%27Orto_3-Mar-2007. jpg; Candelabro Trivulzio base detail: http://neuteboom.it/ wp-content/uploads/2012/10/20121029-063521.jpg) The complexity of the iconography, as well the intricacy of the work, is befuddling. Candleholders were not simply basic pieces of equipment, but also carriers of implications for the spiritual quest and the nature of religious inspiration, at least in part based on the symbolism of light as a representation of the Holy Spirit, purity, and peace.

Service objects for the altar table also received a great deal of attention, respect, and their fair share of artistic ingenuity. The chalice of Doña Urraca, from Spain, exemplifies spolia, the re-use of precious objects and materials from the past.(Figure 10.30) As daughter and sister to kings, Doña Urraca oversaw monasteries and made provisions for their liturgies with lavish equipment. Made up of two antique onyx vessels for the base and cup, the chalice was fashioned with gem-studded bands and inscribed as a gift from Doña Urraca to the palace chapel in Léon, Spain. An ivory situla, or small bucket, is another liturgical object, used for sprinkling holy water in blessing at the Mass and other rituals, accomplished by dipping a sprinkler or a spray of leaves or straw into the vessel and flicking the water across the crowd. (Figure 10.31) This example is finely carved out of ivory with scenes from the

Figure 10.31 | Situla (Bucket for Holy Water)
Source: Met Museum
License: OASC

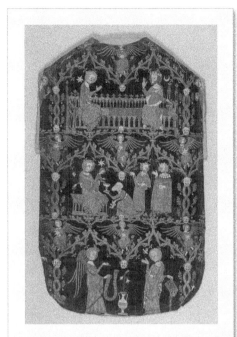

Figure 10.32 | Chasuble (Opus Anglicanum)
Source: Met Museum
License: OASC

life of Christ and supplied with bands and inlay of gilt copper. Additional liturgical equipment includes vestments; these often have received great attention, as well. (Figure 10.32) This fourteenth century example from England is of velvet embroidered with silk, metal thread, and seed pearls that ornament scenes from the life of the Virgin Mary.

Special attention was also paid to books of Scriptures, as well as those that were used for the Mass and other ceremonies. In the Middle Ages, the pages of books had to be created as manuscripts on parchment or vellum, as we have observed before; they were frequently supplied with lavish and showy covers, particularly those that might be used by important people or for important occasions. The commissioning of such was another deep and significant expression of faith due to the sacred writings they contained, the value of all liturgical equipment, and the merit accrued by donating riches for spiritual purposes.

The front and back covers of the Lindau Book Gospels were created at two different times and places with somewhat different design ideas. (Front Cover of the Lindau Gospels: http://www.themorgan.org/sites/default/files/images/collection/download/m1-front-cover.jpg; Back Cover of the Lindau Gospels: https://en.wikipedia.org/wiki/File:Rear_cover_of_Lindau_Gospels.jpg) The front cover (c. 880 CE), which features a crucifix motif of the victorious Christ in gold repoussé, is further embellished with fluttering angels and an extraordinary encrustation of gems set with high prongs. The back cover dates to a century earlier and is thought to have been made for another (lost) manuscript. It is flatter, with engraved and enameled designs in the **Hiberno-Saxon** or **insular style**, which originated in the British Isles around 600 CE. The intricate serpentine and geometric patterns are similar to those found on the delicately crafted gold and cloisonné objects at the Sutton Hoo royal burial site in England. (see Figures 5.18 and 5.19)

The contents of such books also often warranted rich illumination, or illustration, as we see in the prayer book or book of hours called the *Trés Riches Heures du Duc de Berry*. (Figure 10.33) It was created by the Limbourg Brothers (Herman, Paul, and Johan, active 1402-1416, Netherlands) for John, Duke of Berry, a French prince. Throughout its heavily illustrated pages or leaves, it is brightly colored, carefully inscribed,

Figure 10.33 | *The Nativity*
Artist: Limbourg Brothers
Author: User "Petrusbarbygere"
Source: Wikimedia Commons
License: Public Domain

and replete with depictions of the Duke and of his many architectural and land holdings. It is well known for its calendar pages that depict activities associated with the changing seasons of the year, such as this scene of January showing the Duke seated in resplendent blue to the right at a sumptuous feast. (Figure 10.34)

A significant visual spiritual event is the ritual creation of a sand mandala, often performed for a specific occasion by a group of Tibetan Buddhist monks, although there are other spiritual and cultural groups that create related works. (Figure 10.35) To systematically build a complex mandala involves a carefully planned and meticulously executed approach and one that has very specific pictorial implications. Basically a diagram of the Buddhist conception of the universe, mandalas might vary in expression of particular beliefs, teachings, or purposes. The process takes up to several weeks; surprisingly, at its completion, it is destroyed and ritually discarded, perhaps in a fire or a lake, to symbolize the fleeting nature of the material world. An impressive and colorful spectacle to witness, it is accompanied by additional sensual stimulation from the sounds of chanting and the scraping of the colors for the design, as well as the fragrance of flowers and incense.

Figure 10.34 | *January*
Artist: Limbourg Brothers
Author: User "Petrusbarbygere"
Source: Wikimedia Commons
License: Public Domain

Figure 10.35 | Mandala
Author: User "GgvlaD"
Source: Wikimedia Commons
License: CC0 Public Domain

10.5 MASKS AND RITUAL BEHAVIOR

Masks are found in all cultures throughout history. Early human cultures were primarily nomadic, so the portability of masks and other ritual objects may have been an important feature of their design and partly why they are so prevalent. Masks and the rituals in which they function may have been among the earliest ways in which humans acknowledged the objects and forces of nature as spirits or conscious beings.

The design of a mask is determined by its functions, and these functions are determined by the religious worldview of the culture in which they are made. In **animist** cultures, the forces of nature, objects, and animals are all thought to have spirits or essences. Rituals are performed that are aimed to please or guide these spirits in the hope that they will bring good fortune or that will help the culture avoid calamity.

Contemporary African tribal rituals generally center on a number of life issues: birth, puberty, courtship and marriage, the harvest, the hunt, illness, royalty, death, and ancestors. In Burkina Faso, animal masks enter the community to purify its members and protect them from harm. (Figure 10.36) In Nigeria, Yoruba **Egungun**, or

Figure 10.36 | Mask of Burkina Faso
Author: Andrea Praefcake
Source: Wikimedia Commons
License: Public Domain

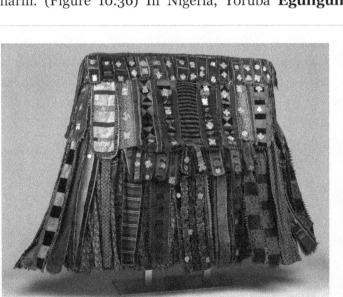

Figure 10.37 | Yoruba Egungun Dance Costume
Author: User "Ngc15"
Source: Wikimedia Commons
License: Public Domain

masquerades, involve both masks and costumes. (Figure 10.37) Costumes are made from layers of cloth chosen not only to demonstrate the family's wealth and status, but also to connect the wearer to the spirits of ancestors who return to the community to advise and to punish wrongdoing. Once completely concealed, the wearer is possessed by and assumes the power of the ancestor through dance: as the pieces of cloth lift, they bestow blessings.

Due to a generally harsh climate not conducive to agriculture, Inuit cultures located in the Arctic regions of North

Figure 10.38 | Eskimo Medicine Man
Photographer: Frank G. Carpenter
Author: User "Yksin"
Source: Wikimedia Commons
License: Public Domain

Figure 10.39 | Havré (Belgium), chaussée du Roeulx - The Gilles
Author: Jean-Pol GRANDMONT
Source: Wikimedia Commons
License: CC BY-SA 3.0

America subsisted mainly on fish and other sea dwelling animals, including whales. Early twentieth-century explorer and anthropologist Knud Rasmussen asked his guide, an Inuit shaman, about Inuit religious belief. His response was that "we don't believe, we fear."

While it is a myth that Inuit elders were sent off into the wild to die (elders were and still are highly valued members of the tribe), many of the totemic and mask images of this culture are warnings against the dangers of making bad choices in a cold, harsh, and unforgiving environment. In this circa 1890 image, a Yupik (Eskimo) shaman exorcises evil spirits from a young boy; note the complex mask and large claws. (Figure 10.38)

Mardi Gras, which is French for "Fat Tuesday," is the day of Christian celebrations immediately before Ash Wednesday. Today, it is commonly considered the season of festivals, or carnivals, extending from Epiphany (Three Kings' Day, when the Magi attested to the infant Christ's divinity) on January 6 each year to the actual day of Mardi Gras, that is, the day before Lent begins. Originally associated with pagan rites of spring—the renewal of life and fertility—Mardi Gras dates back as a Christian rite to the Middle Ages in Europe when people ate as plentifully as they were able before the fasting and lean eating that took place during Lent. The associated festivities were a time to

Figure 10.40 | Mardi Gras in Binche, Belgium
Author: User "Marie-Claire"
Source: Wikimedia Commons
License: CC BY-SA 3.0

ignore normal standards of behavior and celebrate the excesses of life. Often dressed in masks and costumes as a means of casting aside one's identity and social restrictions, the carnivals of Mardi Gras allowed a sense of freedom rarely known in societies that upheld a strict social hierarchy. (Figures 10.39 and 10.40) We could discuss many more such visual experiences in the context of spiritual and philosophical ideas about the artistic expressions we devise to reflect our beliefs about mortality and immortality and how we connect these notions for ourselves. Suffice it to say that we can stay aware of the pervasive nature of art and visual experience in reflecting them.

10.6 FUNERARY SPACES AND GRAVE GOODS

Figure 10.41 | Banditaccia (Cerveteri)
Author: User "Johnbod"
Source: Wikimedia Commons
License: CC BY-SA 3.0

Archaeologists have dated the earliest burial sites found worldwide to around 100,000 BCE, though some argue that certain ones are as old as 300,000 BCE. A considerable body of art related to funerary customs and beliefs has been found at such sites, and in many instances it is much more extensive than other types of evidence of how people lived. This disparity is likely due to the general respect given to sites of tombs and burial grounds. Usually considered sacred places, they have often been left intact when other parts of a settlement have been destroyed and rebuilt. These places, the ways they are marked, decorated, and furnished, supply us with a good deal of data to explore for insights into beliefs and practices related to burial practices and the afterlife, including how

the people prepared for both during their lifetimes. Burial sites often include **grave goods**, such as personal possessions of the buried individual, as well as food, tools, objects of adornment, and even a variety of household goods.

The Etruscans and their culture, predecessors to the Romans on the Italian peninsula, existed from c. 800 BCE until conquered by the Romans in 264 BCE, They are well known for their highly developed burial practices and the elaborate provisions they made for the afterlife. They created a type of mound tomb known as a **tumulus**, made from **tufa**, a relatively soft mineral/rock

Figure 10.42 | Tomb of the Reliefs at Banditaccia necropolis
Author: Roberto Ferrari
Source: Wikimedia Commons
License: CC BY-SA 2.0

substance that is easy to cut and carve, but hardens to become very strong. (Figure 10.41) Like the Egyptians, the Etruscans grouped their tombs into a necropolis, but they were not reserved for the highly born.

Within each tomb, the Etruscans created and decorated chambers in ways that showed what they expected would happen in a "next lifetime." (Figure 10.42) They expected to rejoin their family and friends and to continue many of their ordinary activities and their celebrations. (Figure 10.43) Some tombs were supplied with a complete stock of household furnishings, while others showed scenes of athletic or leisure activities, and still

Figure 10.43 | 5th century BC fresco of dancers and musicians, Tomb of the Leopards, Monterozzi necropolis, Tarquinia, Italy
Author: Yann Forget
Source: Wikimedia Commons
License: Public Domain

others, ritual banquets. Their terra cotta sarcophagi included portraits of individuals and couples who expected to reunite and continue their married life in the afterlife. (Figure 10.44)

In other cultures, as we have seen, the wealthy and powerful were provided with exquisitely detailed tombs and mausolea. The Samanid Mausoleum (892-943) was created in what is today Bukhara, Uzbekistan, for a Muslim amir, or prince, of the Persian Samanid dynasty (819-999). (Figure 10.45) Islamic religious traditions forbid the construction of a mausoleum over a burial site; this is the earliest existing departure from the tradition. The carved brickwork shows remarkably refined design and craftsmanship.

In ancient China, tombs for the important and the wealthy were very richly appointed and it is clear that the expectations for the afterlife included a need for food and other sustenance, as

Figure 10.44 | Sarcophagus of the Spouses, Cerveteri, 520 BCE
Author: User "sailko"
Source: Wikimedia Commons
License: CC BY-SA 3.0

Figure 10.45 | Samanid Mausoleum in Bukhara, Uzbekistan
Author: User "Apfel51"
Source: Wikimedia Commons
License: CC0 Public Domain

Figure 10.46 | Altar Set
Source: Met Museum
License: OASC

well as ongoing ritual appeasement of deities and evil spirits. Artisans' remarkable skills at casting bronze were put to use for a variety of fine vessels for food and wine, altars for ritual, and various other objects. (Figure 10.46) Also included were jade amulets, tools, and daggers. Some tombs were laid out like a household of the living, and nested coffins were decorated with mythological and philosophical motifs similar to those on the bronzes and jades. In the tomb of a woman known as Lady Dai (Xin Zhui, c. 213-163 BCE), a fine silk funerary banner carried mythological symbolism of her life and death as well as a depiction of her and her coffin. (Figure 10.47) The expectation for musical enjoyment was exemplified in tombs that enclosed elaborate sets of tuned bells along with a carving showing how they would be arranged and played.

The Terracotta Army of Qin Shi Huang (r. 247-210 BCE), who unified China and ruled as the first Emperor of the Qin Dynasty (221-206 BCE), is another dramatic example of craft, devotion, and ritual meant

Figure 10.47 | Western Han painting on silk was found draped over the coffin in the grave of Lady Dai
Author: User "Cold Season"
Source: Wikimedia Commons
License: Public Domain

Figure 10.48 | Terracotta Army
Author: Gveret Tered
Source: Wikimedia Commons
License: CC BY-SA 2.0

to honor the dead. The figures were first uncovered in 1974 by local farmers in the Shaanxi Province. The Terracotta Army is a now famous collection of more than 8,000 life-sized, fired clay sculptures of warriors in battle dress standing at attention, along with numerous other figures, pieces of equipment, and animals such as horses, around the mausoleum of Emperor Qin Shi Huang, from whom China's name originates. (Figures 10.48 and 10.49) It is believed the figures were intended to protect the emperor in the afterlife.

Research has shown that the figures were created in local workshops in an assembly line fashion. Heads, arms, torsos, and legs were created separately, modified to give individual character, and assembled. The figures were then placed in rows according to rank. They were originally brightly colored and held weapons. It is believed that most of these weapons were looted shortly after the creation of the Terracotta Army.

Finally, we will take a brief glimpse at a remarkable tomb complex that was developed over time near Beijing, China, for the emperors of the Ming Dynasty (1369-1644). (Figure 10.50)

Figure 10.49 | Terracotta Soldier with his horse
Author: User "Robin Chen"
Source: Wikimedia Commons
License: Public Domain

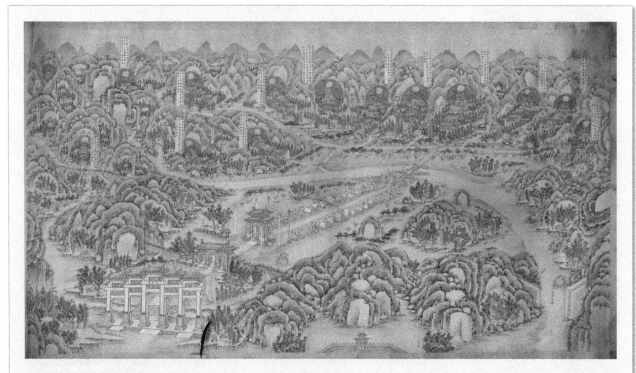

Figure 10.50 | Watercolor overview of the Ming Tombs
Author: User "Rosemania"
Source: Wikimedia Commons
License: Public Domain

A series of thirteen tomb complexes cover more than twenty-five square miles of land on a site nestled on the north side of a mountain, where, according to Feng Shui principles of harmonizing humans with their environment, it would be best situated to ward off evil spirits. The layout includes a number of ceremonial gateways leading to "spirit paths." (Figures 10.51 and 10.52). The walkways are lined with various large sculptures of guardian animals that would also foster protection for the emperors, each of whom had a large and separate tomb complex within the precincts. Mostly unexcavated as yet, the findings so far reveal burial sites that resembled the imperial palaces in form with throne rooms, furnishings, and thousands of artifacts, including fine silks and porcelains. Again the expectation of continued power, prestige, and enjoyment of life's pleasures is clear.

Figure 10.51 | Pavilion with "ways of souls" a turtle-borne stele at the tombs of the Emperors of the Ming Dynasty
Author: User "ofol"
Source: Wikimedia Commons
License: CC BY-SA 3.0

Figure 10.52 | The spirit way at the Ming Tombs
Author: User "Richardelainechambers"
Source: Wikimedia Commons
License: CC BY-SA 3.0

10.7 BEFORE YOU MOVE ON

Key Concepts

As for the design of a building for sacred purposes, its many features will be determined by the requirements of specific rituals and cult usage. Meeting individual or community needs determines the most defining elements of design and plan. If a space is needed for a large gathering, it might be accomplished either out-of-doors or within a building. If an outdoor arrangement serves the purposes, it may or may not require a building, as well. For instance, as we noted with Greek temples, the cult rituals were performed in the open area outside the structure that housed the deity. Similarly, Buddhist stupas were set into a complex where devotees could approach the stupa itself, as well as visit any of the subsidiary shrines or other buildings around it. Some of them might house cult statues for deities or include libraries for scriptures, treasuries, dining halls, or other features of use or interest. Often the grounds of a sacred complex will emphasize natural features of the settings used for contemplation, such as gardens or wooded pathways, fountains, pools, and lakes. These might include careful and meaningful arrangements of statues, iconic imagery, or rocks, trees, and plants. Monastery complexes often provide for all the activities needed to sustain the community, providing for their sacred and social activities in community and individually, while also making accommodation for visitors.

Art and architecture, from the earliest times, have been used to express human beliefs about life and death, as well as to provide for worship, burial, and memorial needs. Basic differences in worship centers are related to ritual purposes and the forms provide for rites that are performed by individuals or congregations. The settings and décor will express the distinctive doctrine and beliefs of the sect that worships there. Burial sites and centers reflect both the customs for treatment of human remains and the beliefs about what will happen to the individuals after death.

Objects created for worship centers and for individual contemplation and devotion are also designed to refer to specific beliefs and to inspire believers in religious practices. Both the religious architecture and the artworks also serve to emphasize and glorify the central beings and concepts of the belief system, often with elaborate or lavish artistic expression.

Test Yourself

1. Discuss some of the implications we can draw from the use of grave goods by citing three specific examples and their meanings.

2. Name several ways in which customs and practice for burial and commemoration affect the creation of art and architecture.

3. Describe the ritual use of tribal masks in different cultures.

4. Describe the specific features of artworks in two different cultures that show their belief that gods reside in the heavens.

5. Describe the uses and meanings of effigy mounds.

6. Discuss specific ways in which religious complexes address astronomical features at two or three different sites.

7. Discuss at least three art or architectural works that are specifically related to ritual use and describe the ways that they work in this regard.

8. Describe the ways and the reasons that some religious groups use or reject artwork that includes figural imagery for sacred context and its results for the artwork they use.

9. Consider the use of precious and luxurious materials for ritual art objects and cite examples, discussing their specific meanings.

10.8 KEY TERMS

Altar: a sacrificial or offertory table.

Animist: the belief that spirits are associated with objects in the natural world.

Burial Mounds: early cultural collections of skeletal remains and grave goods.

Cromlech: a circular arrangement of megaliths.

Dolmen: a large upright stone or marker.

Effigy Mounds: earth mounds formed in the shape of animals or symbols.

Egungun: a general term for Yoruba masquerade rituals.

Elevated Platform: a raised area intended to confer status.

Gateway: a structure intended to mark a passage from one state, world, or phase to another.

Grave Goods: artifacts interred with deceased members of family or tribes.

Imam: Islamic prayer leader, the one charged with the duty to issue the call to prayer at appointed times.

Mandala: a ritual diagram with cosmic significance. Used by many different religions, and either circular or containing circular components, often designed for contemplation of specific teachings or tenets related to the particular belief system. varieties are used in diverse sects of Hinduism, Buddhism, Native American tribal worship, and others.

Mausolea: plural of mausoleum. An above-ground structure designed for entombment of the deceased.

Megalith: literally, "large stone."

Minaret: a tower, usually tall and slender, associated with a mosque and signifying Islamic presence in a location.

Pagoda: a Buddhist structure in China, Japan, elsewhere that signifies the practice of Buddhism in that place. The form evolved from the burial mound conception of the Stupa that appeared in India as the primary structural symbol of the belief system, as it spread to China and took on the native architectural form of the watchtower.

Portal: an exceptionally grand entrance, most often referring to cathedral or other church architecture.

Ritual Mask: masks designed to be used in religious or secular ceremonial events.

Sacred Interior: interior spaces devoted to ritual or ceremony invoking a highest good.

Sacred: held as a highest good.

Sarcophagi: plural of sarcophagus – a burial container, usually of stone or other masonry material, often embellished with sculptural decoration.

Stonehenge: a famous arrangement of vertical stones from prehistoric Britain.

Stupa: a Buddhist monument signifying the presence of relics of Sakyamuni Buddha or sacred objects associated with the beliefs. Formed of an earthen mound, faced with brick, stone, or stucco. Worshippers circumambulate outside the stupa, rather than enter it.

Temple Mound: earthen mounds formed to elevate a ceremony, ritual, or elite.

Terra Cotta: porous low fired ceramic.

Terracotta Army: famous arrangement of 6,000 clay soldiers meant to guard the grave of the first emperor of China.

Toranas: stone structures placed at the Buddhist Stupa at Sanchi and at other stupa sites which form gateways to the circular path around the stupa.

11 Art and Ethics

Peggy Blood and Pamela J. Sachant

11.1 LEARNING OUTCOMES

After completing this chapter, you should be able to:

- Understand why art and ethics are associated

- Identify works of art that were censored due to their failure to meet societal ethics

- Indicate why ethical values change over time by society

- Articulate why some societal groups may consider some works of art controversial

- Identify ethical considerations in the artist's use of others' art work in their own, the materials used in making art, manipulation of an image to alter its meaning or intent, and the artist's moral obligations as an observer

- Identify roles that museums play in the preservation, interpretation, and display of culturally significant objects

11.2 INTRODUCTION

This chapter is concerned with the perception, susceptibility, and ethics of art. It will explore and analyze the moral responsibility of artists and their rights to represent and create without censorship.

Morality and art are connected usually in art that provokes and disturbs. Such art stirs up the artist's or viewer's personal beliefs, values, and morals due to what is depicted. Works that seem to purposely pursue or strongly communicate a message may cause controversies to flair up: controversies over the rights of artistic freedom or over how society evaluates art. That judgment of works created by artists has to do with society's value judgment in a given time in history.

The relationship between the artist and society is intertwined and sometimes at odds as it relates to art and ethics. Neither has to be sacrificed for the other, however, and neither needs to bend to the other in order to create or convey the work's message.

Art is subjective: it will be received or interpreted by different people in various ways. What may be unethical to one may be ethical to another. Because art is subjective, it is vulnerable to ethical judgment. It is most vulnerable when society does not have a historical context or understanding of art in order to appreciate a work's content or aesthetics. This lack does not make ethical judgment wrong or irrational; it shows that appreciation of art or styles changes over time and that new or different art or styles can come to be appreciated. The general negative taste of society usually changes with more exposure. Still, taste remains subjective.

Ethics has been a major consideration of the public and those in religious or political power throughout history. For many artists today, the first and major consideration is not ethics, but the platform from which to create and deliver the message through formal qualities and the medium. Consideration of ethics may be established by the artist but without hindrance of free expression. It is expected that in a work of art an artist's own beliefs, values, and ideology may contrast with societal values. It is the art that speaks and adds quality value to what is communicated. This is what makes the power of free artistic expression so important. The art is judged not by who created the work or the artist's character, but based on the merits of the work itself.

However, through this visual dialogue existing between artist and society, there must be some mutual understanding. Society needs to understand that freedom of expression in the arts encourages greatness while artists need to be mindful of and open to society's disposition. When the public values art as being a positive spiritual and physical addition to society, and the artist creates with ethical intentions, there is a connection between viewer and creator. An artist's depiction of a subject does not mean that the creator approves or disapproves of the subject being presented. The artist's purpose is to express, regardless of how the subject matter may be interpreted. Nevertheless, this freedom in interpretation does not mean that neither the artist nor society holds responsibility for their actions.

Art and ethics, in this respect, demands that artists use their intellectual faculties to create a true expressive representation or convey psychological meaning. This type of art demands a capability on the viewer's part to be moved by many sentiments from the artist. It demands the power of art to penetrate outward appearances, and seize and capture hidden thoughts and interpretations of the momentary or permanent emotions of a situation. While artists are creating, capturing visual images, and interpreting for their viewers, they are also giving them an unerring measure of the artists' own moral or ethical sensibilities.

Ethical dilemmas are not uncommon in the art world and often arise from the perception or interpretation of the artwork's content or message. Provocative themes of spirituality, sexuality, and politics can and may be interpreted in many ways and provoke debates as to their being unethical or without morality. For example, when Dada artist Marcel Duchamp (1887-1968, France) created *Fountain* in 1917, it was censored and rejected by contemporary connoisseurs of the arts and the public. (*Fountain*, Marcel Duchamp: http://www.sfmoma.org/explore/collection/artwork/25853#ixzz3mwCWDOxZ) A men's urinal turned on its side, Duchamp considered this work to be one of his *Readymade*, manufactured objects that were turned into or designated by him as art. Today, *Fountain* is one of Duchamp's most famous works and is widely considered an icon of twentieth-century art.

More recently, *The Holy Virgin Mary* by Chris Ofili (b. 1968, England) shocked viewers when it was included in the 1997-2000 *Sensation* exhibition in London, Berlin, and New York. (*The Holy Virgin Mary*, Chris Ofili: https://www.khanacademy.org/humanities/global-culture/identity-body/identity-body-europe/a/chris-ofili-the-holy-virgin-mary) The image caused considerable outrage from some members of the public across the country, including then-mayor of New York City Rudolph Giuliani. With its collaged images of women's buttocks, glitter-mixed paint, and applied balls of elephant dung, many considered the painting blasphemous. Ofili stated that was not his intention; he wanted to acknowledge both the sacred and secular, even sensual, beauty of the Virgin Mary, and that the dung, in his parents' native country of Nigeria, symbolized fertility and the power of the elephant. Nevertheless, and probably unaware of the artist's meaning, people were outraged.

Traditionally, aesthetics in art has been associated with beauty, enjoyment, and the viewer's visual, intellectual, and emotional captivation. Scandalous art may not be beautiful, but it very well could be enjoyable and hold one captive. The viewer is taken in and is attracted to something that is neither routine nor ordinary. All are considered to be meaningful experiences that are distinctive to Fine Arts. Aesthetic judgment goes hand in hand with ethics. It is part of the decision-making process people use when they view a work of art and decide if it is "good" or "bad." The process of aesthetic judgment is a conceptual model that describes how people decide on the quality of artworks created and, for them individually or societally, makes an ethical decision about a certain work of art.

As we can see, art indubitably has had the power to shock and, as a source of social provocation, art will continue to shock unsuspecting viewers. Audiences will continue to feel scandalized, disturbed, or offended by art that is socially, politically, and religiously challenging. Being considered scandalous or radical, as already observed, does not take away from experiencing or appreciation of the art, nor do such responses speak to the artist's ethics or morality. Art may, however, fail in some eyes to offer an aesthetic experience. Such a failure also depends on the complex relationship between art and the viewer, living in a given moment of time.

11.3 ETHICAL CONSIDERATIONS IN MAKING AND USING ART

11.3.1 Appropriation

Artists have always been inspired by the work of other artists; they have borrowed compositional devices, adopted stylistic elements, and taken up narrative details. In such cases, the artist incorporates these aspects of another's work into their own distinct creative endeavor. **Appropriation**, on the other hand, means taking existing objects or images and, with little or no change to them, using them in or as one's own artwork. Throughout the twentieth century and to the present day, appropriation of an object or image has come to be considered a legitimate role for art and artists to play. In the new context, the object or image is re-contextualized. This allows the artist to comment on the work's original meaning and bring new meaning to it. The viewer, recognizing the original work, layers additional meanings and associations. Thus, the work becomes different, in large part based on the artist's intent.

Sherrie Levine (b. 1947, USA) has spent her career prompting viewers to ask questions about what changes take place when she reproduces or makes slight alterations to a well-known work of art. For example, in 1981 Levine photographed images created by Walker Evans (1903-1975, USA) that had been reproduced in an exhibition catalogue. (*After Walker Evans: 4*, Sherrie Levine: http://www.metmuseum.org/collection/the-collection-online/search/267214) She titled her series *After Walker Evans*, freely acknowledging Evans as the creator of the "original" photographic works. And, she openly stated, the catalogue—containing reproductions of Evans's photographs— was the source for her own "reproductions." Levine created her photographs by photographing the reproduced photographs in the exhibition catalogue; the photographs in the catalogue were reproductions of the photographs in the exhibition.

Visitors to the exhibition who were familiar with Evans's depictions of Alabama sharecropper families struggling to make a living during the Great Depression were being challenged to view Levine's photographs, such as this one of Allie Mae Burroughs titled *After Walker Evans: 4*, independent of their historical, intellectual, and emotional significance. Without those connections, what story did the photograph tell? Did the photograph itself having meaning, or is its message the sum of what meanings the viewer ascribes to it? Levine's work in the 1980s was part of the postmodern art movement that questioned cultural meaning over individual significance: was it possible to consider art in such broad categories any longer, or is there such a thing as one, agreed-upon, universal meaning? She was also questioning notions of "originality," "creativity," and "reproduction." What product can truly be attributed to one individual's thought processes and efforts, with no contribution from a collective of influences? If none exists, then we cannot state something is an original work of art, springing from a single source of creativity, after which all subsequent works are reproductions. One is not more authentic or valuable than the other.

In 1993, Levine was invited by the Philadelphia Museum of Art to be the first artist to participate in *Museum Studies*, a series of contemporary projects: "new works and installations created by artists specifically for the museum." Levine created six translucent white glass "reproductions" of a 1915 marble sculpture by Constantine Brancusi (1876-1957, Romania), titled *Newborn I*. (*Crystal Newborn*, Sherrie Levine: https://s3.amazonaws.com/classconnection/93/flashcards/7114093/ jpg/thenewborn1334629599199-14C4CC989054F51F15F.jpg) She titled her 1993 work *Crystal Newborn*; it is shown here along with *Black Newborn* of 1994. (*Crystal Newborn and Black Newborn*, Sherrie Levine: http://api.whitney.org/uploads/image/file/337061/xlarge_8._crystal_ newborn_1993_black_newborn_1994.jpg) Both works are cast glass, which in the case of *Black Newborn*, has been sandblasted. (*Black Newborn*, Sherrie Levine: http://www.moma.org/ collection/works/89955?locale=en)

Similar to her 1981 photograph *After Walker Evans: 4*, these works are meant to examine notions about something being an original or, instead, being a reproduction. Just as her earlier photographic reproductions of Evans's work themselves could be reproduced, so also were these glass works part of a series; Levine cast a total of twelve versions from one (original?) mold. In addition, although sculpture such as Brancusi's *Newborn I*, is generally displayed on a pedestal or stand that elevates the work to a comfortable viewing height and separates it from its surroundings, Levine had her work displayed on a grand piano. Doing so changed the setting from a more conventional, expected, but consciously neutral mode of display, the pedestal, to the more nuanced, domesticated, yet sophisticated tone of a polished piano top. She wanted the difference to register in the viewer's mind and influence the viewer's response to the work, including thinking of the contrast: the typical museum display is masculine, that is, part of the male world of wealthy collectors and museum board members. The piano, on the other hand, brings to mind the feminine world of the comforting and comfortable home—it is a sculpture of a newborn, after all. But the cool, smooth, hard surface of Levine's glass, as was the case of Brancusi's marble, does not allow the infant head to descend to the level of maternal sentimentality.

Levine maintains tremendous similarities to the works preceding hers that she appropriates from, but she opens up their accumulated meanings to even more, new ones.

11.3.2 Use of Materials

The materials artists use to create their art throughout history have generally contributed to the value of the work. Using silver or ivory or gems or paint made from a rare mineral or numerous other materials that are costly and difficult to obtain literally raised the monetary value of the work produced. If the artwork was made for a political or religious leader, the cultural value of the work increased because it was associated with and owned by those of high status in society. On the other hand, using materials at odds with social values raises questions in the viewer's mind. For example, ivory was—and still is—a desirable material for carving, but it is illegal to trade in elephant ivory within the United States as African elephants are now an endangered species. Viewers' awareness of and sensitivity to the plant and animal life impacted in the production of art is increasing, and may actually be a factor in the materials an artist chooses to use.

Damien Hirst (b. 1965, England) began his career in the late 1980s associated with the Young British Artists (YBA). Hirst, along with others in the group, was known for his controversial subjects and approaches in his art. Much of his art from that time to the present has been concerned with spirituality—Hirst was raised Catholic—and with death as an end and a beginning, a boundary and a portal. One of the motifs he has returned to throughout his career is the butterfly. With its transformative life cycle, from egg to caterpillar to chrysalis to adult, the butterfly serves for Hirst as a "universal trigger." That is, the symbolism associated with the butterfly's life cycle, linked by the ancient Greeks to the psyche, or soul, by early Christians to resurrection, and by many to this day to innocence and freedom, is so deeply imbedded in human consciousness that it springs to the viewer's mind automatically. In his art, those associations are the foundation upon which Hirst builds.

Hirst began his experimentations with butterflies in 1991 when he created a dual installation and exhibition, *In and Out of Love (White Paintings and Live Butterflies)* and *In and Out of Love (Butterfly Paintings and Ashtrays)*. Both contained living butterflies that were intended to and did die over the course of the five-week display. (http://www.damienhirst.com/exhibitions/solo/1991/in-out-love) His first solo show, *In and Out of Love*, set the stage for Hirst's career and reputation as an artist who confronts definitions of art and provokes the viewer to explain how art helps us to grapple with boundaries between and intersections of life and death, reason and faith, hope and despair.

Touching upon his interests in religion and science, including lepidoptery, the study of butterflies, Hirst often makes biblical references in the titles of his artwork, and he mimics aspects of how butterflies have traditionally been displayed in his compositions. He began the *Kaleidoscope* series in 2001, not using entire living or dead butterflies, but using only their wings, symbolizing for him a separation from the unavoidable ugliness and unpleasantness of life—the butterfly's hairy body—to preserve only the fleeting beauty of the wings and their associations with the swift passing of time. *The Kingdom of the Father* is a later work in the series, dating to 2007. (*Kingdom of the Father*, Damien Hirst: http://broadmuseum.msu.edu/sites/default/files/Hirst-Kingdom%20 of%20the%20Father_72.jpg?width=90%25&height=90%25) The title, compositional elements, and overall shape of the mixed-media work are directly linked to the artist's absorption with religion: here, as with a number of works in the *Kaleidoscope* series, the work looks like a stained glass window found in the Gothic cathedrals that fascinated Hirst as a child.

Despite the splendid effect of their vivid colors, energized compositions, and iridescent glow, some viewers object to the materials Hirst uses: the beauty and luminosity is derived from thousands of butterflies killed so that their wings could be used in his work. In 2012, the Tate Modern in London mounted a retrospective of Hirst's art, the first major exhibition in England to review work from his entire career. His 1991 installation, *In and Out of Love,* was recreated as part of the show. (http://www.damienhirst.com/exhibitions/solo/2012/tate) Some critics and animal rights activists lodged complaints about the estimated 9,000 butterflies that died over the course of the twenty-three week event. For example, a spokesperson for the Royal Society for the Prevention of Cruelty to Animals (RSPCA) stated, "There would be national outcry if the exhibition involved any other animal, such as a dog. Just because it is butterflies, that does not mean they do not deserve to be treated with kindness." The Tate Modern issued a statement that the butterflies were "sourced from reputable UK butterfly houses." They also defended their use as integral to Hirst's art, stating, "the themes of life and death as well as beauty and horror are highlighted, dualities that are prevalent in much of the artist's work."

In essence, the museum, along with many other individuals and institutions over the course of Hirst's career, acknowledged the complaints, but accepted the artist's actions as an acceptable part of his creative process, and determined his artistic intentions were of greater importance than any issues of morality raised. Simply, the butterflies were the means to a higher end, his artwork.

11.3.3 Digital Manipulation

Digital manipulation of photographs through the use of Adobe Photoshop and other computer software is so commonplace today it generally goes unnoticed or without comment. Digital manipulation is used by amateur and professional photographers alike, and can be a helpful, constructive tool. When photographs are manipulated with the aim of altering factual information, however, an ethical line has been crossed.

In 2006, freelance photographer Adnan Hajj made changes to a photograph, carried by Reuters Group, a news agency, of smoke rising in the midst of buildings in Beirut following an Israeli attack during the Israel-Lebanon conflict. (The Adnan Hajj photographs controversy revolving around digitally manipulated photographs: https://upload.wikimedia.org/wikipedia/en/0/0f/ Adnan_Hajj_Beirut_photo_comparison.jpg) A blogger commented that the photograph showed signs of manipulation. Comparing the unaltered photograph on the left to the published image on the right reveals that the smoke is obviously darker; in addition, the spreading smoke at the top of the photograph shows the telltale patterning, known as **cloning**, which indicates a digital effect that has been repeatedly duplicated. Reuters immediately retracted the photograph and issued the statement, "Reuters takes such matters extremely seriously as it is strictly against company editorial policy to alter pictures."

The ethical premise is that photojournalists are expected to conform to accepted professional standards of conduct. In fact, the National Press Photographers Association has established a Code of Ethics that addresses the issue: "Editing should maintain the integrity of the photographic images' content and context. Do not manipulate images or add or alter sound in any way that can mislead viewers or misrepresent subjects." Of importance here is that, as news, these images must remain factual, and must represent the events and people truthfully and faithfully. When a photograph is manipulated with the intent to deceive the viewer, as was the case with Hajj's enhancement of the damage done by an Israeli strike against the Lebanese, it changes the historical record; it is unethical.

11.3.4 As an Observer

Photojournalists are expected to follow the National Press Photographers Association (NPPA) Code of Ethics not only when it comes to the manipulation of news images, but also in the acquisition of those images. In times of war, political unrest, or natural disasters, for example, they may be in the midst of events that unfold in unexpected and disturbing ways. The photojournalist is an observer whose role is to make a record of the events, but as a fellow human being, should the photographer become involved or offer aid?

In 1993, photojournalist Kevin Carter (1960-1994, South Africa) photographed a starving young girl being watched by a vulture during a time of famine in Sudan. (*Vulture*, Kevin Carter: http://theunsolicitedopinion.com/wp-content/uploads/2012/10/kevin-carter-vulture.jpg) The photograph was sold to *The New York Times* and was featured in that newspaper and numerous others worldwide, generating tremendous concern about the fate of the child and commentary on the ethics of taking the photograph, especially as the scene was described as a toddler having collapsed on her way to a relief station for food. But, guidelines in the NPPA Code of Ethics state: "While photographing subjects do not intentionally contribute to, alter, or seek to alter or influence events." Many felt, however, that in light of the child's condition and helplessness, the photographer had the responsibility to take action.

According to Carter and Joao Silva, a friend and fellow photographer, the situation and Carter's responses were more nuanced than it may appear in the photograph. Carter and Silva arrived by airplane in the village of Ayod with United Nations personnel bringing provisions to the local feeding center. As women and children began gathering at the center, Carter photographed them. The child was a short distance away in the bush, approaching the center with difficulty on her own; as Carter watched, the vulture landed. As recounted later in *Time* magazine:

Careful not to disturb the bird, he positioned himself for the best possible image. He would later say he waited about 20 minutes, hoping the vulture would spread its wings. It did not, and after he took his photographs, he chased the bird away and watched as the little girl resumed her struggle. Afterward he sat under a tree, lit a cigarette, talked to God and cried. "He was depressed afterward," Silva recalls. "He kept saying he wanted to hug his daughter."[1]

So while Carter did not otherwise aid the child, he did remove a source of immediate danger to her by waving away the vulture. He expressed regret he did not, and felt he could not, further help the girl and the many other victims he saw while on assignments. The unrelenting suffering he witnessed contributed to the depression he was subject to for years. A little more than a year after the photograph of the starving child was published, in April 1994, Carter received the Pulitzer Prize for the controversial image. A week later, Ken Oosterbroek, another friend and fellow photojournalist, was killed during a violent conflict they were photographing in their native South Africa. Haunted by sorrow, regret, atrocities he had witnessed, and the pain he felt, Carter committed suicide three months later.

11.4 CENSORSHIP

The word **censorship** brings up ideas of suppressing explicit, offensive images and written material, perhaps of a sexual or political nature, or accounts of violence. What is considered prurient or sacrilegious or barbarity is not universal, however, so what was acceptable during one era may be banned in the next.

Michelangelo was a sculptor, painter, and architect. He considered his sculptural and architectural works to be of far greater importance than his relatively few painted works. But many know him today as much for the two frescoes, or wall paintings, he completed in the Sistine Chapel in Rome as for the far greater number of marble figures and buildings he created. The chapel is within the Pope's residence in Vatican City, the seat of the Roman

Figure 11.1 | *The Last Judgement*
Artist: Michelangelo
Author: User "Wallpapper"
Source: Wikimedia Commons
License: Public Domain

---

1   Scott Macleod, "The Life and Death of Kevin Carter," *Time*, 24 June 2001, http://content.time.com/time/magazine/article/0,9171,165071,00.html.

Catholic Church, in Rome. The first fresco Michelangelo painted on the 134-foot-long ceiling of the Sistine Chapel, from 1508 to 1512, is a complex series of nine scenes from the Book of Genesis, architectural elements, and figures. It was the first large-scale painting of his career. He returned to paint *The Last Judgment* on the wall behind the altar from 1535 to1541. (Figure 11.1)

The Catholic Church had changed tremendously in the twenty-four years between when the first work was completed and the second one begun. In 1517, the singular authority of the Catholic Church was called into question when Martin Luther, a German monk, issued a series of complaints against Church practices, especially the selling of indulgences, or pardoning of sins. As opposed to the complex hierarchy of the Church, and an emphasis on its teachings as the only means to salvation, Luther championed personal faith and adherence to the word of the Bible. Although his beliefs were denounced, and Luther was excommunicated from the Church in 1521, the new Protestant faith swept through northern Europe. The Protestant Reformation, as Luther's attempts to revise the doctrines of the Roman Catholic Church were known, was not just a serious threat to the Church's authority, it prompted the wholesale examination and revision of the Church's structure, activities, and methods.

Michelangelo began to paint *The Last Judgment* in 1535. In that time of upheaval and uncertainty, the subject of the faithful rising to their reward at Christ's side in eternity while those who doubt or turn away fall to their eternal damnation could have been intended to reassure those remaining true to the Church. Rather than sticking to a clearly structured and hierarchical organization of figures, however, Michelangelo broke from tradition to show dynamic groups of moving, gesturing, and emotion-filled angels, saints, blessed, and damned. Although Christ is in the center with His right arm raised, it is not clear if He is caught up in the erratic and chaotic swirl of the figures surrounding Him or confidently directing them according to their fates. The lack of distinction was originally heightened by the uniformity of clothing, or lack thereof, as Michelangelo painted the majority of figures nude, removing signs of earthly status and riches.

When completed, the fresco was hailed as a masterpiece, but in the following decades, it came under sharp criticism. As the Protestant Reformation by Martin Luther and his followers continued to revolutionize religious doctrine and practices throughout Europe, the Catholic Church formed The Council of Trent (1545-1563) in response. The Counter-Reformation remained adamant in condemning the new Protestant faith but did away with many excesses and leniencies that had grown within the Church, including art that served as a distraction from its proper use as a tool of worship. In its findings, The Council of Trent stated that used properly, art instructed the faithful to "order their own lives and manners in imitation of the saints; and may be excited to adore and love God; and to cultivate piety." Michelangelo's *Last Judgment* lacked the clarity of message and propriety now demanded in religious art so that, at odds with the Council's decree, "there be nothing seen that is disorderly, or that is unbecomingly or confusedly arranged, nothing that is profane, nothing indecorous, seeing that holiness becometh the house of God."

In 1565, two years after the Council's decree and the year after Michelangelo's death, Daniele da Volterra (1509-1566, Italy) was commissioned to paint drapery on the nude figures and alter the positions of some that were deemed too indelicate. Some of his modifications, and others carried out in the eighteenth century, were removed when the fresco was cleaned and restored between 1980 and 1994.

11.5 ETHICAL CONSIDERATIONS IN THE COLLECTING AND DISPLAY OF ART

11.5.1 Collecting/Holding

Art is part of the cultural heritage and identity of the society in which it is made. It shares characteristics with work made by other artists such as how figures of authority are depicted or what is considered appropriate subject matter in art. Because art is closely aligned with the history and values of the people in the society it comes from, individuals and governments alike take care to preserve and protect the cultural treasures in their possession. For the same reasons, invaders often loot and confiscate or destroy the works of art and architecture most cherished by those they have conquered to demoralize and subjugate them.

Representatives of the Nazi Party in Germany took art from its rightful owners, both museums and individuals, from 1933 until the end of World War II in 1945. When Adolf Hitler assumed the role of Chancellor of Germany in 1933, he began a campaign to sell or destroy art he did not approve of in the collections of German museums. Much of that art had been produced by artists who were part of twentieth-century art movements such as German Expressionism, Dadaism, Cubism, and Surrealism. Hitler objected to *avant garde*—experimental and innovative—art and to the artists who were part of those groups. By 1937, his agents had amassed nearly 16,000 works, 650 of which were included in the Degenerate Art Exhibition (*Die Ausstellung Entartete Kunst*) held in Munich that year and viewed by more than 2,000,000 people. Hitler condemned the degenerate art as contributing to, if not the cause of, the decay of German culture, and the art-

ists as racially impure, mentally deficient, and morally bereft. Thousands of the works were then destroyed by fire, and thousands more were sold to collectors and museums worldwide.

The funds generated by works sold were earmarked for the purchase of more traditionally acclaimed artists and subjects that were to go into the *Führermuseum*, or Leader's Museum, in Linz, which Hitler intended to be the greatest collection of European art in the world but which was never built. Art for the Leader's Museum was purchased from museums, private owners, and art dealers, often under pressure to sell the work at a steep discount to Hitler's agents or risk arrest. And, the Nazis acquired

Figure 11.2 | German loot stored at Schlosskirche Ellingen
Author: Department of Defense
Source: Wikimedia Commons
License: Public Domain

art by confiscating it from institutions and private owners, many of whom were Jewish. The Nazis purchased and looted work in every country they occupied during World War II. They had amassed 8,500 works intended for the *Führermuseum* by the time Hitler committed suicide in 1945.

They plundered tens of thousands more for the private collections of Hitler and a few of his top commanders, including Hermann Göring, who held approximately 2,000 works of art by the end of the war. Art and other cultural spoils of war (such as books) were stored in numerous locations throughout Germany and Austria, including air raid shelters, estates that had been seized by the Nazis, and salt mines. In the photograph shown here, hundreds of crates holding sculptures and cloth-wrapped paintings are stacked in the Palace Chapel (*Schlosskirche*) in the town of Ellingen, in Bavaria. (Figure 11.2) Standing guard is a United States soldier.

In 1943, Allied forces created an organization known as Monuments, Fine Arts and Archives (MFAA). At first, the approximately 350 men and women from thirteen countries who were part of the "Monuments Men," as they became known, worked to prevent damage to historically and culturally significant monuments. As the war was ending, they began locating and documenting art held by the Nazis and then led the effort to return art to the country from which it had been taken. By the time they completed their work in 1951, the Monuments Men had located and returned to their owners 5,000,000 works of art and other culturally significant items, as well as domestic objects of value such as silver, china, and jewelry. As of 1997, approximately 100,000 objects were still missing.

11.5.2 Display

Museums of all types play many roles. In the collections they hold, museums act as keepers of the public trust. The objects or artifacts have value to all, from the casual viewer to the avid scholar, in one or more realm: scientific, educational, cultural, social, historical, political. The objects help preserve our memories and carry them into the future; they also help us to understand the lives, thinking, and actions of others. Through the exhibitions they hold and objects they display, museums promote debate, encourage new ideas, and stimulate our imaginations. The objects in museums communicate with us by appealing to our senses, emotions, intellect, and creativity. That is why we continue to wonder about and ponder on what we see and experience in museum settings.

When objects are placed within a context in a museum display, it stimulates our ability to make connections and broaden our understanding. For example, if a historical museum presents information about the geography and history of an area as part of a display on canoes and river trading, we have a context in which to appreciate the objects and interpret the practices of the people in that place and time. That was the approach artist Fred Wilson (b. 1954, USA) took when asked to create an exhibition for the Maryland Historical Society (MHS) in 1992. He titled his show "Mining the Museum." (Metalwork: http://africanah.org/wp-content/uploads/2014/06/FredWilsonMiningTheMuseum2.jpg)

The mission of the MHS is to collect, preserve, and study objects related to Maryland history. This is often accomplished through the display of objects in its collection. As the organizer of the exhibition, or guest curator, Wilson was allowed to explore the thousands of artifacts in storage, many of which are seldom if ever displayed. He was seeking to bring to light, so to speak, objects rarely seen, and to present groupings of objects in unexpected ways, sometimes humorous and at other times disturbing. For example, with the label identifying the objects as "Metalwork 1793-1880," Wilson placed iron slave shackles in the midst of ornately decorated silver tableware. No explanatory text accompanied these things; Wilson wanted viewers to contemplate what they saw and make connections without directions:

> By displaying these artifacts side by side, Wilson created an atmosphere of unease and made apparent the link between the two kinds of metal works: The production of the one was made possible by the subjugation enforced by the other. When the audience made this connection, Wilson succeeded in creating awareness of the biases that often underlie historical exhibitions and, further, the way these biases shape the meaning we attach to what we are viewing.

So, in addition to asking viewers to question the meaning of the objects through his mode of display, he also wanted them to think about how history is made or constructed by what we include and omit; what we value, and why; and how we highlight objects and information of value in exhibitions within museum settings.

11.5.3 Property Rights, Copyright, and the First Amendment

Artist Shepard Fairey (b. 1970, USA) designed a poster with a portrait of President Barack Obama above the word "hope" in red, beige, and two tones of blue in 2008. (Barack Obama "HOPE" poster, Shepard Fairey: https://en.wikipedia.org/wiki/Shepard_Fairey#/media/File:Barack_Obama_Hope_poster.jpg) Sometimes printed instead with the words "progress" or "change," the poster and image quickly became associated with Obama's campaign for presidency and was soon officially adopted as its symbol. After the election, the Smithsonian Institution acquired for the National Portrait Gallery a mixed-media version of the portrait.

It soon came to light, however, that the poster was based on a photograph taken by freelance photographer Mannie Garcia in 2006. The Associated Press (AP) stated they owned rights to the photograph and that Fairey had not obtained permission from AP for its use. The Associated Press claimed they owned the copyright on the photograph, having contracted ownership of the image from its creator, Mannie Garcia. Garcia, on the other hand, stated that according to his contract with AP, he still possessed the copyright. The exclusive legal right to print, publish, or otherwise reproduce a work of art or to authorize others to do so belongs to the artist who created it according to the U.S. Constitution, Article 1 Section 8: "The Congress shall have Power: To promote the Progress of Science and useful Arts, by securing for limited Times to Authors and Inventors the exclusive Right to their respective Writings and Discoveries." That right, or copyright, remains in place for the artist's lifetime plus seventy years, granting the artist the power to control their work, its use, and its reproduction.

Fairey, through his attorney Anthony Falzone, countered with the statement, "We believe fair use protects Shepard's right to do what he did here." Fair use allows for brief excerpts of copyright material to be used without permission of payment from the copyright holder under certain conditions: commentary and criticism, or parody. The idea behind allowing quotes and summaries of copyright material to be used freely is that what is written will add to public knowledge. Parody is referencing a well-known work clearly, but in a comic way; by its very nature, the original work is recognizable in a parody of it. Unfortunately, Fairey's case was settled out of court, so the question of how his use of Garcia's photograph in his poster was an example of fair use was not answered.

11.6 BEFORE YOU MOVE ON

Key Concepts

Traditionally, art has a history of being judged and censored and more than likely in the future artists will continue to blur many boundaries, sometimes even offending the audience's sensitivities. Offenses may address politics, social injustices, sexuality or nudity, among numerous other subjects and concerns. Contemporary societies, on the other hand, generally do not want to endorse any form of censorship; but, at times due to the sensitive nature of art, it happens. Some contemporary art is expected to make some groups in society uncomfortable. Artists over time have pushed many boundaries in society and have brought to the surface questions about a society's moral beliefs. Just the questions alone have perhaps expanded the freedom of artistic manifestation. So, works such as Duchamp's *Urinal*, or Ofili's *The Holy Virgin Mary* challenge society's moral beliefs and values by the nature of the art itself. They also shock segments of society by exploring the notion of aesthetic taste. Such works that challenge traditional notion of ethics and aesthetics, in fact, have led some to believe that contemporary art practices are based more on the idea than the object of art.

Nevertheless, artists do make ethical decisions in such areas as the appropriation of others' work, what materials they use in their work and how they use them, the digital manipulation of their work, and what role they play as observers of the events they capture in their art. And, as we have seen, museums and other places in which art is exhibited play distinct roles and have responsibilities in how art is preserved, interpreted, and displayed.

Test Yourself

1. Is there a relationship between art and ethics? Defend your answer explaining why you agree or disagree. Select works not used in this text to clarify your stance. Attach selected works with captions. Add a commentary at the end of your response explaining why you selected the art works and their significance to the topic.

2. Select two ethically controversial works of art from different periods in history. Explain how each work was received at the time it was made, and how changes in societal values have impacted acceptance of the works today.

3. Should certain types of art be censored? Explain your answer and select at least two examples to assist in clarifying your statement. Give an opposing response with justifications and select works to describe and clarify your opinion.

4. Describe one way appropriation has become acceptable in contemporary art.

5. What does it mean when some contemporary artists question what is an "original" work of art, and what is a "reproduction?"

6. What concepts was Damien Hirst exploring in using butterflies in his artwork? What did the butterflies symbolize for Hirst?

7. Why is it important that news photographs not be altered?

8. What was the ethical dilemma photojournalist Kevin Carter faced when he photographed a child during the 1993 famine in Sudan?

9. What acts of censorship did Adolf Hitler and his associates engage in prior to and during World War II?

10. As guardians of culturally significant objects, what obligations do museums have?

11. Describe how claims of "copyright" and "fair use" came into play in relation to Shepard Fairey's portrait of Barack Obama.

11.7 KEY TERMS

Appropriation: the use of pre-existing objects or images with little or no transformation applied to them.

Censorship: the suppression of art and other forms of communication considered to be objectionable or harmful for moral, political, or religious reasons.

Cloning: the repeated duplication of a digital effect.

Ethical Judgment: an alternative decision between being morally right or morally wrong.

Ethical Values: principles that determine one proper behavior in society.

Formal qualities: the elements and principles of design that make up a work of art.